# Strategic Planning That Makes Things Happen

### Getting From Where You Are
### To Where You Want To Be

## by
## William C. Bean

**with a chapter by Ellen Domb, Ph.D.,
on the linkage between real strategic planning and
Total Quality Management (TQM)**

Human Resource Development Press, Inc.
Amherst, Massachusetts

Published by HRD Press, Inc.
22 Amherst Road
Amherst, Massachusetts 01002
1-800-822-2801

First printing, March, 1993

ISBN 0-87425-212-1



Graphics Design by Carolyn Laughlin

Production Services by Susan Kotzin

Editorial Services by Mary George

Cover Design by Old Mill Graphics

# Dedication

**To:**      *George Martin Bean and*
*Betty Lee Cleveland Bean*

**For their:**    *total commitment*
*unrelenting encouragement*
*vitalizing curiosity*
*generosity of heart*
*sacrificial service*
*spiritual pursuit*
*depth of compassion*
*and unconditional love...*
*not only to their son, family, and friends*
*but to hundreds and thousands of others.*

*Thank you.*

# Table of Contents

**PART THREE**     **ADDENDUM**

**ABOUT THE AUTHOR**

# Foreword

So most of us agree that we live in times of spiraling complexity, acceleration, and change. Now what do we do? Intuition tells us we must drop the restrictive, outmoded templates that guided us in the past. But the sages of industry are filling our eyes and ears with the "why's" and the "whats," but far fewer of the "how's."

It is politically incorrect to stress the "how's" much anymore. We are told to be flexible, decentralized, "customerized," smaller, leaner, experimental, symbiotic, networked, and empowered. Okay, say we buy into most of this based on personal observation and experience. Now what?

Old strategic and business planning systems, programs, processes, and formats mainly didn't work. Why? Two reasons: 1) *They were conceptually incomplete,* focusing on one important piece among 10 or 15 others, like market portfolios, or organization structure, or culture, or vision, or functional support strategies, etc.; 2) They got "credenza'd"—hitting the bookshelf, *never getting implemented.*

It is easy to understand the business mega-voices and the frustration that we as practitioners experience: *past* planning approaches failed in simpler, gentler times. They could never work today! But, I must again ask you, what then are tens of thousands of companies and organizations of all types, shapes, and sizes, and their leadership teams to do in this swarming, churning, wind- and wave-tossed business sea of variables?

*Strategic Planning That Makes Things Happen* is not one of the dozens of failed, old, partial, token fixes, nor is it some academic, cumbersome, esoteric, rationalized system. This planning and implementing process assumes total chaos, unpredictability, and a real-time, fire-fighting daily business life as the background, based on my and my clients' extensive experience running companies or parts of organizations, and the need to form and do plans quickly and effectively.

Not only is what you are about to read not rocket science, but it is intuitively logical, simple material, stress-tested with people like yourself in all kinds of environments and business challenges. The process is not only complete, but it is biased for implementation, for action. Moreover, the more turbulence, the more volatility, the better, because the plan is an organism that is updated on the fly and re-documented in a few minutes each month!

The results: Obviously, if an enterprise shifts from "operational, individualistic reactivity" to "strategic, team-boosted proactivity" to focus on and pull the disproportionately important success levers, adjusting all the time, that enterprise will enjoy a faster rate (sooner in time) and higher degree (more in amount) of business results than before, and better results than the competition!

What is great about this approach is that it is based upon dozens of actual clients' *results* in these difficult times, not on private postulations! What you are getting is a tool kit crammed with great tools you can use as they fit your situation, all within the context of a coherent structure and process not only complete and practical, but flexible because it is driven by you, on your terms, according to your needs!

My intent in writing this book is only secondarily to cover the "why" and "what" of planning and doing, but primarily is to provide you with the "how": helpful materials as "100-100-100" grade fertilizer to turbo-charge your entire business, to the delight of all parties concerned with your enterprise's optimization. I wish you and your business complete success in this culminating decade.

William C. Bean
February, 1993

# PART ONE

# INTRODUCTION TO STRATEGIC PLANNING

**Chapter One**

# Why Business Needs a New Strategic Planning Paradigm

What businesses need is focused planning that is coupled with disciplined action. The kind of strategic planning toyed with over the past quarter-century as an autumnal rite-of-passage or occasional resort event *has not* and *will not* work. Why? It has been treated as an executive adventure, not as an applied technology. Strategic planning has been picked up as something the intuitive generalist knows he or she must do, but without a system, it becomes a weekend experience, aided by the third-party consultant-artist's rendering. Today's company—stretched, pressured, threatened on all sides—does not have the time, money, or priority for planning diversions.

Strategic planning as it has been understood and practiced over recent decades needs a complete overhaul. Why? Because as a discipline, it has failed in implementation. And that has been the basic problem with traditional strategic planning: It and implementation are oxymoric. My direct observation has led me to conclude that the overwhelming bulk of what is discussed and, more disconcertingly, agreed upon in strategic planning never sees the light of day in actuality!

It is not that strategic thinking and planning are not critical to success in business and in life—quite the contrary. But the implementational discipline has not matched the planning effort. Worse, many corporate teams do not even have a good planning process. We would not settle for 0% to 10% efficiency or effectiveness in any other aspect of the business. We should not settle for it in the strategic arena either.

## True Strategic Effectiveness

Strategic effectiveness is achieved by setting the right long-term priorities and implementing them. Many of the business outcomes of the 1980s—the great successes and failures, gains and losses, growths and declines—hinged in large part upon the degree of strategic efficiency and effectiveness an enterprise achieved or did not achieve. Those executive teams who had, for example, much higher strategic effectiveness may have dramatically accelerated the rate and timing of their business objectives and results compared to a competitor's team who had less strategic effectiveness. For strategic effectiveness is achieved when the big-picture prioritized goals are implemented directly and forcefully in the operating arena.

## The Grave Affliction

This discussion is certainly not in the realm of whimsical, academic debate. When one sees companies that essentially are living day-to-day without practical strategic guidance, the observed degree of unfulfilled potential is staggering. Several dozen of my clients, including service and manufacturing companies of all shapes and sizes, did not in most cases have particularly gifted or ungifted people, and were not in particularly attractive or unattractive markets or industries. In other words, the vast majority of my corporate clients were not extraordinarily different in capability or opportunity than all others. The executive teams, corporate cultures, and overall organizational realities reflected a surprisingly common affliction, which I diagnosed as "operational, reactive individualism."

This dreadful and, if undiagnosed and untreated, potentially fatal company disease is not something only "poor," "mediocre," or "industry-follower" companies contract. Rather, any person, executive team, or company—particularly those inspired by rugged individualism and a hale and hearty work ethic—are vulnerable to this ailment.

What is *"operational, reactive individualism"?* It is the gradual deterioration of organizational performance into the day-to-day, repetitive grind of fire-fighting! To be *"operational"* is to be stuck in the realm of "low cloud-cover and poor visibility," slogging business out in poor playing conditions on the muddy playing field of today's business terrain. To be *"reactive"* is to be in the mode of operation where the agenda principally is dictated by the business environment. What is wrong with that? Isn't it mandatory to be responsive to our external and internal clients? Of course. But the problem is that indiscriminate reactivity causes a person, team, or organization to get lost in the blur of "911" calls and lose sight of the "big picture," the larger context of what is more and less important to the *ultimate,* long-term success of the business. Even with my expertise as a strategic consultant, I found that I could not escape the whirlwind of daily events when I became CEO of an international training company. *No matter how strategically minded one is, no matter how much one knows about what should be done, it is so easy to fall into the same "good" traps that everyone falls into: answering the phone, responding to letters, attending meetings, putting out fires, and becoming involved in a variety of distractions.* Even if prioritization is performed, it is "in the triage/emergency-care mode" of what will die, what is salvageable, and what can wait. Companies in that mode have been pervaded by an emergency-room culture. At the end of a business day/week/month/year/career, the business smock, blood-smeared and torn, is hung on a hook appropriately labelled "Survivor." The third descriptive term for the dis-ease—to be in an *"individual"* mode—sounds innocuous and innocent enough, doesn't it? But when even unintentional "individualism" or "ships-passing-in-the-night" syndrome chronically occurs, the loss of potential synergy, the lost economies of poor communication, teamwork, linkage, and interfunctional coordination are enormous, all becoming leaks draining away strategic opportunities and eventually contributing to lost business success. This is the unnoticed tragedy of a company, which is like a gifted composer who goes to his grave with his greatest tunes still in him!

## The Healing Elixir

Then what is the remedy for a malady that has reached epidemic propor-tions in the United States in the 1960s through 1980s? A strong dose of *"strategic, proactive, teamwork."* Indeed, there is no inoculation or corrective power in its "slogan" form. Its power is contained in its realization, achieved first through strategic planning and then through strategic implementation of the plan in a disciplined, systematic manner.

To be *"strategic"* is to conduct one's self, mission, and enterprise in such a way as to slice through the operational cloud cover of day-to-day business life, gaining continuous access to the mountaintop from which to view and evaluate the terrain, the business climate, the entire situation, and even to visualize the future, all in order to direct day-to-day operations through the prism of clear and holistic strategic thinking. Such strategic thinking drives the operational doing of day-to-day business, a way of conducting business far from the confusion, survivalism, and protectionism described earlier.

To be *"proactive"* is more than the opposite of being reactive. It is literally to be for doing the right things in the ultimate sense. Why be efficient in certain activities (doing things right) if the things done right aren't the right things? To be *effective* ultimately means to gather all available pertinent knowledge and options and to select the optimal, preferred course. How very different this kind of proactivity is from the aforementioned "mud foot-ball"—the game of "logical incrementalism"—of not-to-fumble tactics, of not making a mistake, of not being too aggressive. This way of thinking and acting is all too institutionalized in many survivalistic corporate cultures of companies that have become anesthetized by doses of token "quality," "excellence" campaigns, or "teamwork" talk.

Lastly, in this day and age, to promote the *"team"* is nearly to espouse the virtues of motherhood, of love of country. But given the acceptance of teamwork as a virtue, the kind of teamwork I mean here is more than that: It is the kind that is consciously, repetitively, systematically achieved and measured, not merely saluted.

## What Strategic Leverage Is

Now, let us put these words back together into phrases, squaring off the phrases against each other. In one corner stands "operational, reactive individualism"; in the other corner, "strategic, proactive teamwork." Over a long, multi-bout campaign, "strategic" beats "operational," "proactive" overcomes "reactive," and "team" defeats "individualism." The challenge is how to attain the perferred mode.

Beyond theoretical terms, I have personally seen clients move from one corner to the other, establishing dramatic "before's" and "after's." Those leadership teams that are willing to make the transition from one mode to the other have become motivated by a new energy and vision, an *esprit de corps* that has routinely resulted in emergent market presence and enhanced business success.

The ultimate result of strategic, proactive teamwork compared to operational, reactive individualism is greater leverage, as illustrated by Figure 1.1 below:

### Figure 1.1—The Impact of Strategic Planning

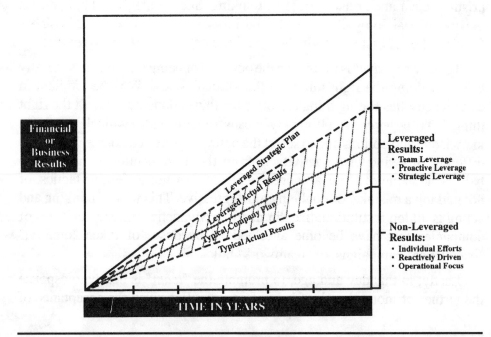

Executives of companies that live from yearly operating plan to yearly operating plan (or, worse, without clear and practical yearly plans at all) usually extrapolate from the previous year's performance to form their expectations of a "respectable" increment of growth over the previous year. With regularity, companies usually do not quite hit their annual plans, but do increase sales over last year's actuals. Sound familiar? That's what you get with the institutionalization of "operational, reactive, individualized" thinking year-in and year-out.

Contrast the above situation with the leverage gained by the holistically effective enterprise. The strategically leveraged plan is unusual in its tenacity, creativity, aggressiveness, initiative, and overall synergy, yet is focused, attainable, and even realistic from a higher strategic vantage point. Call this the "Leveraged Strategic Plan," or more simply, an aggressively focused plan that a company actually intends to carry out. Similar to its inferior counterpart, the "Typical Company Plan," enterprise actuals may not hit the intended target. But there is a huge difference: *These actuals are leveraged actuals.* Look at the dramatic difference between "Leveraged Results" and "Non-Leveraged Results"! And this kind of leverage is not debt leverage. This leverage essentially is free, by means of the entire outfit functioning as a "strategic, proactive team" in thought and deed. Hence, these kinds of teams and enterprises are more likely to be overachievers; if anything, they do "more with less" than their underachieving counterparts, who at times, either unwittingly or stubbornly, somehow manage to perpetuate "less with more" by clinging to the same old traditional way of doing business.

## Distinct, Even Exclusive, Differentiation

To conclude, *those enterprises that achieve extensive, sustained strategic leverage will be far more likely to accelerate the rate (the upward extent) and timing (the quickness it happens) of their business success than those enterprises which do not tap this latent leverage in their organizations.* This strategic leverage converts to actual competitive differentiation and performance advantage in the marketplace. One extra note: This kind of practical strategic planning directly ties into a good total quality management (TQM) or change management process, providing the "Phase 0," front-end vision for what you are trying to improve or change. Chapter Nineteen by Dr. Ellen Domb addresses this linkage more fully.

Of course, talking about strategic leverage is easier than achieving it. Not accomplished casually, strategic leverage needs and is achieved by a clear, practical methodology, system, or process. This book introduces my *Strategic Planning Technology,* including its benefits, its contents, and its use, as the way to harness that great, largely untapped, and free organizational resource: *Strategic leverage.*

# Chapter Two

# The Definition and Benefits of Leveraged Strategic Planning

## A Succinct Definition of Strategic Planning

I have read many definitions of strategic planning. Most are rather esoteric and long-winded. Mine is simple, but packed with important concepts and meanings:

> *"Strategic Planning is the process of determining the long-term vision and goals of an enterprise and how to fulfill them."*

### A Process

Each concept is worthy of brief explanation. First, strategic planning is a *process,* a continuous, closed-looped life cycle perpetuating a healthy, growing entity. This process is not an end in itself, but continuously sustains the goals and actions that are vital to the success of the enterprise.

### A Vision

It is difficult, risky, and ill-advised to establish specific goals without first establishing the organizational context in which those goals will exist and determining the long-term *vision* of the enterprise. By a long-term vision, I mean the overarching, all-encompassing sense of collective identity and direction the entity has. In the Old Testament, a proverb aptly states that "without a vision, the people perish" or "run wild." Therefore, the more lucid the vision, the more clear the context in which the company can set major strategic goals—those preeminently important objectives of the enterprise.

### The Goals

With the process in place and the vision identified, the *goals* that are identified will be major, significant, and specific. These are the actual strategic levers to be pulled synchronously to achieve the desired strategic leverage. These goals are the big opportunities that usually go unaddressed when a company's leadership is overly focused on day-to-day operations.

### The Implementation

The last, and to my mind the most practical, element of strategic planning is the "how to fulfill" part, which is often forgotten about or overlooked. Better than average companies set and articulate visions. Yet stronger companies set and elucidate clear goals. The best companies fulfill their goals by disciplined *implementation.*

What companies have you ever seen that tie specific actions to their visions and goals to fulfill them in operational real-time? Usually, it is the market and industry leaders, pioneers, and long-term successes that do the implementational job the best. *This then is strategic planning: the process of determining the long-term vision and goals of an enterprise and how to fulfill them,* a process that is thoroughly set forth in the heart of this book.

## The "Needs Hierarchy" of the Enterprise

Somewhere along the line, in a college course, in a business book, at business school, or in a management development program, you likely were introduced to the wonderful world of Abraham Maslow's "Needs Hierarchy." Its essential tenet is that the individual has a hierarchy of needs, from the most basic need of physical survival to the eventual, ephemeral heights of self-actualization.

I believe that the business enterprise also has a needs hierarchy, and that it cannot "pass go" to a higher level of attainment until it has achieved the prior level of need-fulfillment. I have developed the following enterprise needs hierarchy, shown pictorially below, to describe the basic phases of organizational life. By observation of many companies, I absolutely believe that strategic planning can and should slot into and lead companies in whatever stage of development they may be at any particular point in time. My organization needs hierarchy in the context of the strategic planning for each stage is shown in Figure 2.1 below:

### Figure 2.1—Enterprise Needs Hierarchy

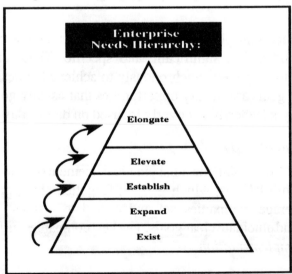

## Exist

First, and most obviously, the enterprise must maintain its *existence*. This is more easily said than done, as the majority of new business ventures fail in the early years. Moreover, if you compare the Fortune 500 lists for every ten years, you may be surprised how many additions and deletions occur at the very top of the business-size pyramid. Therefore, to *exist* is more than a philosophical preference; it takes hard and, more importantly, smart work from the very point of the inception of the new enterprise.

A proper strategic planning system addresses the specific vision, mission, business definition, environmental assessment, markets, products and services selection, the targeted customer, and the competition. Each of these factors must be addressed to ensure an enterprise's basic existence. *To exist, to survive on the business battlefield, requires careful preparation and surgical execution of basic plans.*

## Expand

Once the question of "Will we make it through this week's/month's/ year's/economic cycle?" has been answered in the affirmative, the momentum of success in this first stage vaults the enterprise to the next level: *expansion.* Many of the hundreds of strategic goals that I have seen enterprises develop have addressed the need for expansion. Typically, the "existence" focus is external, concentrated on new products, services, or markets. Past the hurdle of existence, attention logically turns to "*Where* else can we sell [geographic expansion], and *what* else can we sell [product/ service expansion]?" To accommodate expansion, the focus at this second state is internal, concentrated on how better to *support* the sales, the customer, and the business. *This step ensures the enterprise has the sufficient capacity—the sufficiently broad shoulders of infrastructure—to support the business.* Accounting, purchasing, inventory, manufacturing, information systems, development—all internal processes and functions—must grow with sales, or the entire welfare of the company is placed in jeopardy. Effective strategic planning systems will provide the systematic review and addressing of *all* vital aspects of the business, and will generate a coordinated, prioritized, interlocking set of strategic goals for controlled growth.

## Establish

You may ask: "Shouldn't a company first be established before it expands?" In that commonly understood sense, yes, of course. That aspect should have been addressed in the latter part of the Existence Phase, when the basic vision, focus, and support systems were addressed and nailed down, and (metaphorically speaking) the entire beachhead of internal and external presence was "established."

Developing the invasion analogy suggested above may help clarify the matter. What I mean by *"establish"* here is that after the beachhead is secured ("Exist") and the invading force fights its way inland several more miles ("Expand"), the enterprise must hunker down for a period of time to *consolidate its gains and deepen its hold on the new territory* ("Establish"). Enterprises that fail to do so lose the precious ground so newly gained as quickly as they gained it. These losses of ground stem from incomplete establishment of operations, usually reflected in a spate of defects, dropped balls, uneven support, and other "growing pains." Although these problems often occur because the company's external efforts (sales growth) outstrip the supporting supply line (organizational support infrastructure), I have seen many cases where a company does not know "when to say when" and slow down to catch up with its higher sales volumes. As a vegetable plant strips its surrounding soil of nutrients through overgrowth in too short a time, thus becoming pallid, sickly, and diseased, so the perpetual-growth-machine business eventually develops stress fractures (e.g., higher defects), then worse problems (e.g., negative cash flow), due to its "sales-growth" myopia.

An athlete cannot run a marathon at sprint-pace and last for very long. The excellent, holistic strategic planning system must serve as the corporate sanity check on long- and short-range objectives. It must not only serve as the organizing cheerleader to stimulate growth, but as the conscience-driven mechanism, the instrument of reason in a potentially overheating management culture and momentum. The system should channel executive thinking that results in a balanced set of wise and insightful, yet aggressive, objectives.

## *Elevate*

How is the elevation different from the earlier expansion stage? Expansion is a basic growth state, much the same as human growth spurts during the adolescent phase. But the *Elevation* of the enterprise is quite different. For example, as the Expansion and Establishment phases grow and solidify the company's ground-level market share, sales, size, and industry presence, the Elevation phase builds multiple stories on top of the large single-story building that was previously constructed. Elevation is equivalent to the partial attainment of Maslow's self-actualization stage. *Elevation of the enterprise rounds out the company, optimizing the capacity, the height, the depth, the length, and the breadth of the entity,* stretching toward the far-reaching fulfillment of its potential. To elevate the company is to properly inflate it to the highest possible degree. In a pure world, when attained in full, this would be the company that wins the "Baldrige of Corporate Life (not just Quality) Award" as the very embodiment of excellence in all regards. The superior strategic planning methodology drives this stage, ensuring the construction of dozens of masterful action plans that enhance and perfect the company's performance to its customers, employees, vendors, shareholders—all stakeholders of the enterprise.

### Elongate

After achieving elevation, the second part of a company's self-actualization is to *elongate,* for its longevity and perpetuation. You may wonder how the Elongate stage is different from the Existence stage. Think of a new expansion baseball team. For that team, the challenge is a matter of existence, of survival. Now think of the well-established champion team that has won five pennants in seven years and is always a contender, always at the top. Their aspiration is not for existence, but for longevity. *Their challenge is to elongate, to perpetuate their superior performance.* The two share the pursuit for extendibility. However, the nature, stage, and type of extension are absolutely different.

A world-class strategic process must forge a noncorrosive conduit (one standing the test of time) directly from the ongoing determination of continual improvement action plans to implementation of those action plans. The system must ensure that real people in real time perform real activities with real outcomes and effects! Disciplined implementation of needed actions will go a long way to perpetuate the great success of the enterprise.

*At each stage of a company's development, from Exist to Expand, to Establish, to Elevate, to Elongate, strategic planning is essential, causing the "strategic, proactive team" identified earlier to mobilize in order to anticipate and meet the needs of its present stage in superior fashion.*

## A Summary of Benefits

We have mentioned several benefits of Leveraged Strategic Planning. I hope you share at least some conviction that the enterprise on today's earth cannot go on in strategic oblivion and operational myopia. With this thought in mind, you might appreciate the following list of strategic planning benefits that define aspects and attributes of what a good strategic planning system is and does.

1. **Good strategic planning is visionary, yet realistic:** Ideas are explored and set out clearly, but they don't drift off into fantasy land.

2. **A living framework supports it, not a weak scaffolding of extrapolated material:** The plan lives and breathes as an organism, not having been built out of dry, historical bricks of old news.

3. **It is thorough, not piecemeal:** What results is not a collection of loose fragments of vision, values, environmental evaluations, goals, or actions, but a complete and coherent plan.

4. **Teamwork is developed, not fiefdoms:** High-performance teams creating an orchestrated plan of attack are far superior to the low-performance, selfishly motivated empire-building of little kingdoms by small-thinking leaders.

5. **Good strategic planning develops direction, not confusion:** It is better to maintain operational sanity than make matters worse with bad planning. If you are going to plan, be crisp, clear, definite, and precise by using the right approach.

6. **It is customer-driven, not self-driven:** It is driven by the ones who pay the bills, not the ones who generate expenses. The customer is built into the fabric of the planning process.

7. **It is cross-environment, not internal-myopic:** External driving forces may be out-of-sight, but cannot be out-of-mind. The strategic enterprise should be, in a certain sense, "without walls" information-wise, not merely oriented to "what goes on within these walls."

8. **It is opportunistically proactive, not late and reactive:** We have covered the importance of shifting the locus of control to drive the enterprise's strategy rather than drifting in operational happenstance. The company does not have to operate as if it were a ping-pong ball in a wind tunnel, vulnerable to the exigencies of an unpredictable external environment.

9. **Cross-time, not merely historical time, is taken into account:** Human nature hides within the zone of its established comfort level. In the case of strategic planning, the tendency is to hide out in the safe annals of historical, actual financial performance. Cross-time thinking balances the lessons of history with the realities of the present and the opportunities of the future.

10. **Good strategic planning is aggressive, not passive:** The individuals who are "nonplanning reactors" appear to be quite active. After all, they run around from fire to fire in ceaseless activity. But that mode, however active, is strategic passivity, in that the individuals or teams are as quiet in long-term initiative as they are busily reactive in the here and now. A good planning system forces strategic thinking that spawns aggressive initiatives.

11. **It is expansionist, not protectionist:** By definition, the commitment to a process of thinking about the future underscores the belief that often it is better to expand one's position offensively than to defensively protect it, unless a company already has the dominant market position.

12. **Acceleration, not deflation, results:** Laissez-faire, status-quo thinking breeds stagnation and deflation of the entrepreneurial spirit. Future thinking stirs the creative juices to access the team's collective energy, to seek and gain synergy, and to generate newfound momentum.

13. **Good strategic planning is priority-driven, not add-on driven:** A tactic of the reactive mentality, which typically generates guilt about the lack of proactivity, is to add in a few key goals and actions, which is like putting band-aids on top of an underlying disease-ridden condition. Proactive strategies on a clean slate and organized through fundamental, thorough prioritization build the best plans.

14. **It is practical, not academic:** The unfortunate impression many business people have about academia is that it is a purveyor and defender of the arcane, impractical, theoretical, and nonsensical. While in many cases this reputation for academia has been well earned, there is evidence that some change, in the form of "reality shock," has recently begun to permeate the ivory-tower complex. Practicality, that desire to get from Point A to Point B with reasonable dispatch, is embodied in a thorough results-oriented planning system.

15. **Good strategic planning is realistic, not political:** This means asking "What can we really do both now and later to realize our vision?"rather than "What can we do despite the way things are around here [the in-fighting, fiefdoms/ empires, egos, politics, bureaucracy]?"

16. **Implemention is the key, and not only in theory:** Break the oxymoron: plans *can* be implemented, no longer frozen in the wasteland reserves of the theoretical. The only effective system is the one that gets the intended results accomplished. Ultimately, "results" are not the nice-looking plan books on the shelf, but are the chosen, completed *actions* that get *done* in time and space.

17. **Good strategic planning is results-bound, not bookshelf-bound:** This one is my personal favorite and hence, influenced the title of this book. What a paradigm-shifting contrast-jolt this pairing induces—from the bookshelf (gathering dust as the record of an annual resort event, the memorial of a fading memory) to a real live result (something that actually got done from a plan!). *For is this not the desperate need of business today? Plan. Initiate. Complete. Reinforce. Get results.* Now you have room on or in your bookshelf for other things. Meanwhile, your strategic document—dog-eared, coffee-stained, torn—is, like time-release fertilizer, broken down and released into the soil of the actual business terrain to sustain and grow (in metaphoric consistency) the strategic crop portfolio in order for you to reap its bountiful rewards.

18. **It is measurable, not ethereal:** Measurement is an activity chiefly performed during implementation of the action plans against pre-committed tangible criteria (dates, budgets, resources, completed actions, etc.). Measurement is vital because, as the adage says, "What gets measured gets done." And again, there has been the sad track-record of strategic planning: The vast majority of strategic plans remain in the ethereal, safe (and unprofitable) heights of the vague unknown. What is never measured usually is never done—a waste and shame indeed. *My direct observation is that those companies that measure specific progress on their prioritized strategic goals on a regular basis will achieve significant advantage and differentiation against their market competitors by such discipline.*

19. **Actually done, good strategic plans are not forgotten:** After having done quite a few strategic plans with companies, I have made the following historical observation about my clients, which I consider one complete business portfolio.

### Bean's Law of Strategic Implementation

*Generally speaking, those companies that consistently set and implement strategic action plans achieve quicker and higher business results than what they achieved before, better in comparison to their competitors' progress over the same period of time.*

20. **Good strategic planning is ongoing, not episodic:** The extension of logic from the above paradigm shift (a paradigm is like a mental lens, a ruling concept that informs perception and through which we view, explain, and judge the world) is that an enterprise exercising leveraged strategic planning and change management does not do "it" occasionally, in sporadic episodes. Rather, these habits are a way of life, a continual process, an inherent and vital part of the company. You can always tell which corporate leaders live by the strategies they set: Externally, their companies are on the move; internally, strategic planning is intrinsically woven into the cultural fabric of the way they conduct business. If you cannot consider yourself or your company in this category, seriously reflect upon what you are missing, especially in terms of the unfulfilled potential of your enterprise.

# Chapter Three

# Reality Check: Understanding the Pitfalls that Prevent Effective Strategic Planning

To balance the high-level view in the previous chapter, this chapter presents a counterpoint discussion of the basic elements that kill or seriously hamper effective strategic planning. After a succinct explanation of how each element is a strategic pitfall, I will present some summarizing comments on how these elements, individually and in lethal combinations, snuff out the greater part of individual and corporate potential. My list is illustrated in Figure 3.1. How many of these have you seen at work? Which ones top your list?

| **Strategic Trap** | **Why It Is One** |
| --- | --- |
| 1. *Blinded by Success* | Executives don't feel the need to do better or other than what they are now doing. |
| 2. *Bigger is Better* | Growth is the opiate of the sales-driven leader, which hides many sins of omission or oversight. |
| 3. *Eloquence and Flash* | Good pitching, dancing, and dog-and-pony shows do not a good visionary/generalist leader make. Rather, the traits may unwittingly be used to evade reality. |
| 4. *Spread Too Thin* | Short-term thinking optimizes the here-and-now; then the thin safety net breaks, and the landing is very rough indeed. |
| 5. *Stuck in the Middle* | The fatal comfort zone of status-quo sameness ensures a legacy of sustained mediocrity. |
| 6. *Ignore Corporate Culture* | Those leaders that dismiss the importance of building a special environment of vision, values, and norms all their own lose their best people and competitive edge to other companies whose leaders have cultivated and provide a special place to work. |
| 7. *Underestimate Competition* | "We know them; they're not a big factor; we've got the features; we've got the benefits." This attitude of ostrich-pride is the kiss of death to market superiority. Humble, aggressive pursuit of customer delight and of learning the best from competitors is a far safer, more enlightened path. |

## Figure 3.1—What a Good Planning System and Enterprise Avoids

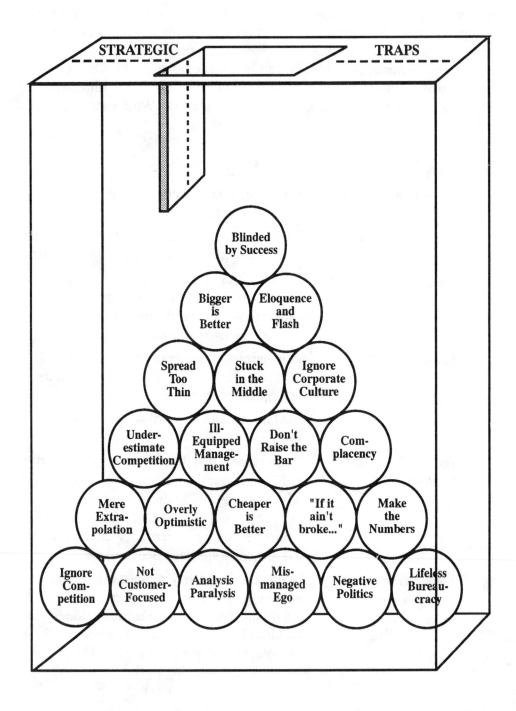

8. *Ignore Competition*    *"What* competition? We're simply the best." See #7! The only difference is that here the level of arrogance is of terminal proportions.

9. *Not Customer-Driven*    "Our company provides great services and products with high-tech manufacturing and world-class technologies." Interpretation: "We are not customer-driven."

10. *Ill-Equipped Management*    "Our guys have fought it out in the trenches. They came up through the business. They've earned the right to do the job." Maybe, but one problem: often, they don't know how to!

11. *Don't Raise the Bar*    "We're quite satisfied with our current levels of performance. Everything about us is great just the way it is." This is sweet music to your fast-responding, lean and hungry competitors.

12. *Complacency*    "Five o'clock yet? What's the latest on the grapevine? Ah, the numbing intoxication of a steady routine." The company: one already dead on the inside—just waiting for everyone else to realize it.

13. *Mere Extrapolation*    "What did we do last year? 5%? Let's go with 6% this year and book it." And leave the "stuff of greatness" unmined, untouched, and deeply buried.

14. *Overly Optimistic*    "30%? No problem! Let me show you our marketing plan—no flaws in *this* strategy." Response: Show me all the other years you hit or exceeded 30%!

15. *Cheaper is Better*    "Business means profits. Today. Now. So, we're no frills. We're a bootstrap operation. The future will take care of itself." And the future will not be kind to you if you refuse to invest anything in it!

16. *"If it ain't broke..."*    It is not a matter of "to break or not to break." Avoid superficial business-fad thinking! Good strategy *is* about big-picture thinking and do- ing. Businesses do not need clever slogans or

| | | |
|---|---|---|
| | | cute concepts. They do need holistic brilliance, or at least strategic thinking. |
| 17. | *Make the Numbers* | The Great American Investor-Myopia. Choice: Make the numbers as an outcome of wise leadership or strip-mine today's soil for a temporary, unsustainable profitability fix. |
| 18. | *Analysis Paralysis* | "What if... what if... what if...?" What about actually *doing* something important? "No, we might fail... we don't have all the facts." Having seen so many cases of this affliction first-hand, particularly in larger companies, it has become evident to me that analysis-paralysis directly reflects a corporate culture of low collective self-esteem and a crippling system-wide fear of failure and rejection. |

The last three elements are given my "special pitfalls" warning label:

## The "Big Three" Enemies

| | | |
|---|---|---|
| 19. | *Mismanaged Ego* | Mismanagement of self—especially afflicts small companies ( e.g., "megalomaniac" entrepreneurs). I liken this condition to enterprise hypertension and high blood pressure due to poor work (eating) habits. |
| 20. | *Internecine Politics* | Mistreatment of others—especially afflicts middle and larger companies (e.g., insecure managers). I liken this to developing a serious corporate heart condition due to poor cultural habits. |
| 21. | *Lifeless Bureaucracy* | Misconduct of the business—especially afflicts multinational and larger national companies (e.g., overgrown policies and procedures). I liken this to the heart attack caused by clogged arteries. Part of the heart muscle has died, and the prognosis is grim for the full attainment of corporate human potential. |

## Some Summarizing Thoughts About Pitfalls

The first eighteen pitfalls likely are intuitively obvious to each of us, and painfully real to those of us who have witnessed or experienced any of them personally. Sometimes just one of these pitfalls is great enough to stumble an entire organization. Take the company for which I once worked for over ten years—IBM. By the mid-1980s, the company's executives knew something was profoundly wrong with our delivery and support strategies, and, hearing increasingly pointed criticism from customers and the computer industry alike, they had the courage to say, essentially: "We took our eyes off of our customers and became fixated on our capabilities; now we need to get back to them." Immediately following was one of the most major redeployments ever of IBM personnel from the plants', labs', and headquarters' locations back to the field in order to reestablish the amount of "face-time" with our clients. As history and today's competitive market realities have shown, customer focus can never be a one-time effort, but must be an ongoing, perpetual, intense daily practice that is part of the automatic, natural "corporate viscera" culture. The IBM of later years, recognizing the difficulty of fundamentally changing culture at a root-level, is still striving to be "customer- and market-driven" and is continuing to reorganize into smaller, more responsive and manageable units. It takes sustained focus, heart, special and inspired leadership to be customer-driven—and that is just one of the eighteen pitfalls if not negotiated well!

*The pitfalls can also act in seemingly synchronized fashion, as if linked in evil conspiracy, yet holistic strategic thinking, planning, and acting is the best antidote to them.*

The saddest part of this strategic pitfall business is that corporate leadership has complete responsibility for and ownership of them. All twenty-one pitfalls are attitudes, opinions, and convictions in the mind(s) of the leader(s), which permeate corporate culture, infecting business operations and affecting business performance. But I believe the greatest and most frightening enemies in the entire history of business are the Big Three: Ego, Politics, and Bureaucracy.

## Ego, Politics, and Bureaucracy

These three elements that were briefly discussed in numbers 19 through 21 are discussed further here.

*Why are these elements so lethal individually or in combination? Because they lurk like unseen germs of illness, less noticeably and more insidiously than other elements, behind the scenes of the day-to-day enterprise.* They infect, cell by cell, all parts of the corporate organism, influencing all organizational activities, then increasing their presence and effect little by little. The point is this: The other eighteen elements (and many other harmful elements like them) are mainly the manifestations of negative business opinions and attitudes that, when identified, can be changed by conscious decision; but ego, politics, and bureaucracy cut deeper and more fundamentally into the individual and corporate psyche. They are harder to deal with. Often, they are directly manifested by the leaders themselves, making the exposure and elimination of their harmful influence nearly impossible to do. These three elements, and the other 18, form grave obstacles to any business struggling to survive and prosper in the 1990s.

Why all of this discussion on strategic pitfalls? Because they must all systematically be looked for, located, and treated, via a battery of organizational "blood-work tests" on a periodic basis. Both kinds of business (the "18") and stylistic (the "Three") pitfalls should be thoroughly assessed in the strategic planning process. Otherwise, introducing any new plans will be like "pouring new wine into old wineskins," which cannot contain but only leak out anything new or different that might enduringly and positively affect the company over the long run.

## Chapter Four

# A Brief Review of Twentieth Century Business Changes and Strategic Responses

In order to have a fuller appreciation of the importance of the dimension of strategic planning in an organization, one must see in brief the evolution of business from 1900 and how executives through time have focused on strategy at each evolutionary step in order to gain market advantage. Then, in the next chapter, a brief overview of the major schools of strategic thinking, planning, and systems will be provided to round out our background discussion of the need for having an inclusive strategic planning system in order to attain maximal competitive advantage.

## Strategic Planning's Historical Responses to Change

Figure 4.1 summarizes both the changes that occurred in the business environment over the past century and the attendant strategic responses that were accordingly initiated.

In the first half of this century, human resources were widely available, markets often were dichotomized as either national or local, technology was simple and stable, basic buyer demands were met, market velocity was slow and steady, and required changes were usually clearly identified well in advance of the need.

Shifting directly to the 1990s, how dramatically different, even opposite, the characteristics of these same business dimensions are! Between then and now, there was a general ramp-up in each dimension in several distinct stages over time. In the quarter-century period from the early fifties to late seventies, across the macro-economic landscape (industries, markets, continents, customers, R&D, technology, and so forth), business started to heat up in bits and spurts, in accumulating fashion, accelerating toward the volatile and turbulent environment of today.

Resources became increasingly constrained, by negative factors in the work force, such as the shortness of engineers in the sixties, of programmers in the seventies, of educators and nurses in the eighties, and of low-end labor in the nineties. Market segmentation became more distinct, with regional enterprises filling the gap between national and local, and multinational companies grew in absolute number, size, and influence. Meanwhile, U.S. domestic markets became increasingly supply-saturated.

The rate of technological advancements quickened, particularly in higher-technology and relatively newer product and service arenas, such as computers and medical technology. The price-tag for research and develop-

## Figure 4.1—Strategic Planning's Historical Responses to Change

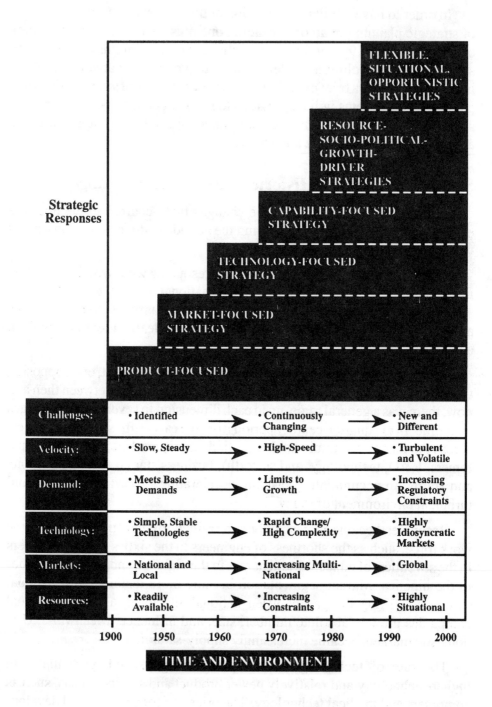

ment grew in tandem with the increasing complexity of technology. Demand was lessening due to the reaching of growth limits in maturing, traditional, and lower-tech markets and in established geographies, such as toasters and coffee percolators in the United States home consumer market.

Business velocity—the overall rate of change and activity generated from the cumulative effects of the aforementioned factors—was moving from medium to high gear. Lastly, challenges, once so readily identifiable across markets and industries, were harder to anticipate and pin down. Nonetheless, the transitional, warm-up years of the mid-fifties to mid-seventies would prove to be preliminary heats for the faster, higher-stakes races set to commence in the millennium's final quarter-century.

From the seventies to the nineties, human resource availability continued to be constrained, although from a segmented, "niche" standpoint. This included spot shortages (e.g., teaching and nursing positions) to major-skill-set deficiencies (trained administrative/office personnel), resulting in specific and nagging resource shortages. The marketplace, once a patchwork quilt of ad hoc activities, has become interwoven and "globalized" due to many factors, such as the attractiveness of new geographies as old ones become saturated and the profound advances in international communications access (fax, phone, modem, satellite, teleconference, television, transportation, etc.). Technology has gone from rapidly changing and increasingly complex to highly detailed and specialized, placing extreme pressures on providers to get it right the first time and quickly satisfy highly sophisticated, discriminating, and tough-minded customers. Demand, while increasing somewhat due to new geographic markets (e.g., cigarettes to the PacRim) has faced a new pressure: increasing regulatory constraints in existing markets (e.g., the increasingly negative exposure and widespread ban of smoking in public places in the United States).

Meanwhile, market velocity has continued to accelerate, from the slightly-above-the-speed-limit pace of the late seventies and early eighties to breakneck speed in the denser traffic of the eighties and the nineties. Thus, the nature of change itself has undergone a major transformation—from being speed-driven to being uncertainty-driven. Whereas at one time the rate-of-speed was the main change-driver, now the degree of unpredictability (turbulent and volatile) is increasingly the major driving force. Accordingly, this latest phase brings challenges that are not only changing continuously, but are often altogether new and different.

For example, major material and design changes in the skateboard market were overshadowed by a brand new roller-blade market that cut into the pre-existing skateboard market, quickly changing the dynamics in that industry. Beyond the larger, eight-theatre movie configurations that have reshaped the cinema market, home videos have substantially influenced the sourcing mix of movie viewing, from public places to the home. Lower-cost business-meeting teleconferencing has become an increasingly attractive new market alternative to the travel-to-meetings/physical-meeting modality of the past thirty years.

The food industry is a particularly volatile area. Food consumption continues to follow macro-societal trends, which run from traditional eating at home to increased traditional restaurant eating out, to fast-food eating out, to micro-waved eating in, to separate single-meal eating, to increased home meal delivery (pizza and much more)—all these and more combinations and permutations, colliding chaotically together and fiercely competing for the same food dollars (or in some cases retracting them), spin in a dizzying blur around us. Seven-Eleven and its convenience-chain competitors took sales from the national/regional chain supermarkets, which had previously over-ridden the little grocery stores. Now Seven-Eleven is double-plagued by imitation chains *and* new marketing channels—the "quick convenient mart" within national gas chains, which gas-card clients can charge on their credit cards. Mobil Oil is in the retail food business! This book could be filled with literally *hundreds* of examples—from nearly every industry, market, country, on both grand and small scales—of myriad change factors spinning concurrently in the whirlwind of today's business environment.

What is the point? Simply this: The more the external market and business forces shift an individual firm's locus of control from one of internal control (by the firm) to external control (by the market or business environment), that enterprise must compensate by taking strong, focused, and concerted actions to regain some control of its own destiny. This can well be done by performing strategic planning in a practical, implementation-oriented manner.

## Strategic Responses to the Changing Environment

Thus far, we have addressed in general terms the change of the macro-business environment over time. During these profound changes, strategic responses have adjusted to address the fundamentally shifting business conditions identified in the previous section.

In the first decades of the 1900s, strategic responses were product-focused because the vast original markets had a seemingly inelastic, insatiable demand for the commodity products being provided, such as cars, early home fixtures, farm equipment, and housewares.

In post-World War II America, a shift began from plain commodity products to product differentiation and segmentation as these basic markets matured. The "Big Three" United States auto manufacturers' extensive acceleration of model/feature diversifications are an obvious and classic example. Basic demographics became increasingly depended upon as key tools in the marketing/selling effort. Early television advertising hints at the beginning of the shift away from pitching the product (e.g., AJAX, "Mule Team" Borax) to marketing differentiation/pricing/niching (e.g., "Lemon-fresh," "With Bleach," "Smaller Portions," "Economy Size," "Environmentally Safe," "Guaranteed to Get Your Clothes Whiter").

The next phase of strategic response was to exploit technology for improved production/process efficiencies inside the company and to develop enhanced products for external consumption. One historic example is IBM's dramatic introduction and expansion of its System 360 mainframe line to revolutionize automated data processing via harnessing the technology advances of the 1960s.

By the 1990s, based on the cumulative foundation of product, market, and technology sophistication, and with general demand in maturing markets in basic commodities tapping out and becoming intensely competitive, shifts were made to be more focused and opportunistically driven by "what our enterprise does best"—hence, the movement toward being "capability-driven." This step is by far the most intense effort yet, differentiating an enterprise not just by a product's "color" or "added feature," but by building strong superiority in a niche market. In the eighties, the strategic response had become yet more sophisticated, driven additionally by the pursuit of cheaper labor costs (e.g., transfer of manufacturing off-shore), sociopolitical influences (e.g., environmentalism, regulations, health focus), and growth strategies (e.g., the Honda plant in Tennessee; MacDonald's in Europe, including Moscow; Great Britain's fighter-jets sold to NATO and Arab nations).

Into the eighties, with growing turbulence, and in some markets outright chaos, the most recent and yet more finely calibrated strategic response has occurred: to develop even more flexible, situational, opportunistic strategies to define, amidst the overall confusion, those few things the enterprise can do in order to take initiatives in clearly defined target markets with crisp plans and performance goals. One of my clients has experienced head-on this extraordinary volatility. This company, one of the largest independent manufacturers of circuit boards in the United States, has a Fortune 50 company as its major client. Due to the sharply changing demand for circuit boards, the company could go from $400,000 to zero in circuit board work within 60 days, causing massive headcount, equipment, space, and cash-flow impacts on a regular basis. Maintaining direction and control in such a volatile environment has been a primary objective of that company. You would probably not be surprised that diversification has been a primary strategy.

In summary, as the overall global business environment has changed over the course of the century, the strategic responses to it have changed, in an effort to maintain some enterprise control. Effective strategic planning and change management is the modern enterprise's means of shaping its business destiny as much as it can in the unforgiving, unchartered, hazardous marketplace that exists at the close of this century.

# Chapter Five

# The Ten Basic Schools of Strategic Thinking and the SPT System

We will briefly inspect the ten major strategic planning schools, using them as a framework for identifying the key aspects which Strategic Planning Technology (SPT) combines into one coherent system. In the extensive reading I undertook before writing my second version of the SPT, I read many of the recent textbooks and business books on strategic planning. Of the many thousands of pages reviewed, I recommend one chapter above all others: the outstanding work of Henry Mintzberg—noted strategic-planning historian, chronicler, and overall subject-matter expert—entitled "Strategy Formulation," found in James Fredrickson's *Perspectives on Strategic Management* (1990).

Mr. Mintzberg provides a fascinating summary of the ten major schools of strategic formulation, presented from field-evolution, major concept, and "strengths and weaknesses" standpoints. The matrix which follows is my summarization of Mr. Mintzberg's analysis, with a column I added regarding how the positive characteristic of a particular school's approach has been included in my SPT system.

The following narrative explains Figure 5.1 and highlights what key requirements from each school should be included in an optimal strategic planning system.

1. **The Design School.** This first school provided a basic structure and simple process for the fledgling field. However, its boilerplate, cookie-cutter template proved to be inflexible, and therefore difficult to use.

   *Emergent "Optimal System" Requirement:* A *clear* yet also *flexible* system.

2. **The Planning School.** Standing on the shoulders of its Design School predecessors, the Planning School added sophistication to the planning system to develop a more *formal system*. However, with its codification of the strategic process came an unattractive degree of bureaucracy.

   *Emergent "Optimal System" Requirement:* A *thorough, complete* system.

3. **The Positioning School.** This school stands upon the shoulders of the process-development work of the prior two schools, yet focuses on the *content* of the plan rather than on *how* the plan should be developed. Hence, it is substance-driven, focusing on an analysis of

## Figure 5.1—The Ten Schools of Strategic Thinking

| Strategic Planning School | Basic Characteristics of School | Distinguishing Strength(s) | Greatest Weakness(es) | Key Element(s) Included in the Strategic Planning Technology |
|---|---|---|---|---|
| Design School | A Basic Structure | A Simple Process | Static/Inflexible | Clear, Flexible System |
| Planning School | A Thorough Process | A Formal System | Highly Bureaucratic | Thoroughness, Completeness |
| Positioning School | Focus on Plan Content | Substance-Driven | Analysis, Not Action | Content- and Action-Intensive |
| Entre-preneurial School | The "Great Men" School | Importance of Leadership & Vision | Lack of System | Focus on Vision Within System |
| Cognitive School | Strategies Are Mentally Formulated | Situational, Individual Assessment | Sketchy, Non-Systematic | Flexibility to Address Individual's Strategic Inputs |
| Learning School | Strategies Evolve & Emerge Over Time | On-Going Learning Based on Reality | Trial & Error, Passive, Visionless | Enable On-Going, Real-Time Calibration |
| Political School | Politics Has an Effect on Strategy | Politics (+ or -) Has Effect on Strategy | Non-Disciplined, Incomplete, Non-System View | Capability to Focus on Company Politics |
| Cultural School | Culture Has a Key Impact on Strategy | Importance of Shared Beliefs and Values | Conceptual, Vague, Unstructured, Undisciplined | Builds in Thorough Cultural Assessment |
| Environmental School | Organizations Must Respond/Fit With Environment | Importance of Environment on Strategy | Passivity and Non-Factor of Management | Builds in Complete Environmental Scan |
| Configuration School | Varying Strategies Flow in Clusters of Time | Form the Right Strategy at the Right Time | Episodic and Ad-Hoc in Nature | Recognize and Allow Situational Fluidity in Planning |

strategic choices. However, the "analysis paralysis" pitfall applies here, as the Positioning School is long on thinking about alternatives and very short on providing a clear action-oriented, implementationally closed loop.

*Emergent "Optimal System" Requirement:* Focus on plan *content* and follow-on *action planning.*

4. **The Entrepreneurial School.** This school is a radical departure from the first three, not focusing on either plan process or content. Rather, it promotes the *"Great Men"* School of Planning, which adheres to the idea that the primary driver of strategic planning is the *leader,* whose vision and leadership is crucial to galvanize the team. As vital as this component may be for achieving strategic effectiveness, its conspicuous lack of focus on process and content—of any kind of system—is its inadequacy.

*Emergent "Optimal System" Requirement:* Focus on *vision* within a specific system.

5. **The Cognitive School.** This school, the most ephemeral and esoteric of them all, is distinguished by its premise that all strategies are mentally formulated (hence "cognitive"). As such, each strategy is to be formed through a *situational,* individual *assessment* of the organization in its actual environment. While such action is necessary for an effective plan, the sketchy, non-systematic, *ad hoc* approach does not lend itself to consistent, high-quality implementable plans.

*Emergent "Optimal System" Requirement:* Focus on the *situational,* environmental, and organizational *factors* of the enterprise for good strategic planning.

6. **The Learning School.** The Learning School logically extends from the Cognitive School's reality-driven approach by propounding that strategies gradually evolve and emerge over time. As such, strategic planning is non-episodic—a good point. Learning is based upon the observation of reality on an ongoing basis. On the downside, this trial-and-error approach is passive and visionless, like a fallen leaf being carried downstream by the flowing waters of ongoing business.

*Emergent "Optimal System" Requirement:* Must enable ongoing, adjustable, *real-time calibration.*

7. **The Political School.** This school's obvious assertion is that organizational politics have an either positive or negative effect on strategy. As with the previous two schools, its shortcoming is a non-disciplined, non-integrated, limited viewpoint that only partially addresses the entire strategic waterfront.

   *Emergent "Optimal System" Requirement:* Provide capability to focus on *company politics.*

8. **The Cultural School.** Much focus has been given to the importance of organization *culture* and its impact, in any number of ways, upon enterprise performance. This school's tenet is that shared *beliefs* and *values* play a critical role in organizational health. Again, the shortcoming of this school is its conceptual nature, and hence, its vague, unstructured, and undisciplined approach.

   *Emergent "Optimal System" Requirement:* Build in a thorough *cultural* assessment.

9. **The Environmental School.** The philosophy of this school is that organizations must respond to and fit in with their environments. The obvious contribution of this school is its underscoring of the importance of *environmental factors* for effective strategies and organizational well-being. However, this orientation by definition precludes an internally initiated and driven strategy. Instead, the attitude is more passive and assumes that management is more an observer than a participating factor.

   *Emergent "Optimal System" Requirement:* Build into the strategic planning process a complete scan of the *external and internal environment* on both a macro- and micro-level.

10. **The Configuration School.** This school has the highest level of integrative complexity and flexibility of the ten. The idea set forth is that varying strategies flow in clusters of time. Therefore, the primary focus is to form the *right strategy* at the *right time.* While the far-seeing executive "generalist" intuitively senses that this hypothesis is close to the mark, experience tells the practitioner that situational optimization of strategic thinking and action is still too episodic, ad hoc, and fluid to get the actual job done. *The challenge is how to allow flexibility within the context of a complete, organized, yet non-bureaucratic process.*

*Emergent "Optimal System" Requirement:* Recognize and allow situational fluidity and *adaptive, well-timed strategies* planned within an efficient and effective process.

*To summarize, I firmly believe that, as much as each school of strategic thinking contributes an important ingredient for holistic, maximally useful strategic planning, none of them comes close to providing a satisfactory level of effectiveness in itself. Moreover, even when the best characteristics of these ten schools are combined into one coherent concept, there remains a conspicuous lack of focus in the arena of implementatio*n. Still, when the best features from these ten schools are summarized and combined into one complete system, they form an outstanding base, and my Strategic Planning Technology has included them all:

| School | Needed Aspect, Included in SPT |
|---|---|
| • Design | A Clear, Flexible System |
| • Planning | Is Thorough |
| • Positioning | Focuses on Content |
| • Entrepreneurial | Sets a Clear Vision |
| • Cognitive | Makes Situational Assessments |
| • Learning | Is Adjustable in Real-Time |
| • Political | Addresses Political Dimension |
| • Cultural | Addresses Cultural Dimension |
| • Environmental | Addresses Internal & External Environment |
| • Configuration | Is Adaptable, Changing to Present Reality |
| – and – | Is Practical, Implementation-Oriented, and Action-Plan Driven for Attainment of Results That Matter. |

# Chapter Six

# Achieving Strategic Leverage

All of the prior five chapters have driven home the same point, although each one has approached the problem from a different angle (leverage, overall enterprise needs, specific traps avoided, historical perspective and conceptual completeness): *The strategic planning system that is needed for successful business in the 1990s and beyond is one that*

- Correctly determines the needs of an enterprise

- Integrates all important elements needed to produce a work plan

- Provides a complete process to implement that plan

- Recognizes that such a strategic plan is an extremely potent resource for an enterprise's preservation, growth, and maximization

Before we launch into the SPT itself, there are several important principles to consider to ensure that the planning process itself is addressed in an appropriate manner.

There are two particularly vital aspects of strategic process leverage that the planning executive should ensure are operative in his or her planning process: *Team/Strategy Leverage* and *Information/Use Leverage*. The first is depicted in Figure 6.1 below:

### Figure 6.1—Team/Strategy Leverage

Level Four (Exclusive Differentiation)

Level Three (Some Realized Potential)

Level Two (Unrealized Potential)

Level One (Greatly Unrealized Potential)

Exceptional / Good / Average / Poor

Degree of Team Quality

None   Some   Considerable   Complete

DEGREE OF STRATEGIC PLANNING/EFFECTIVENESS

**Leverage:** An exceptional team with a complete plan is more likely on these bases to accelerate the time frame and degree of financial results.

## Team/Strategy Leverage

Because most individuals on executive planning teams have a sufficient capacity to think, be creative, and contribute, what is crucial is how these individuals work together and coalesce into a planning and implementing team. *One of the great losses of corporate potential is the gap between each individual's capacity to contribute and the team's lesser actual contributions.* Therefore, from both a cultural and practical standpoint, how productively the team works together is a major ingredient for a company's strategic planning success. In addition, if one or more of the individuals is a weak link in cultural affinity or in capacity, the team's overall effectiveness is further weakened.

The horizontal axis addresses to what degree the enterprise actually does planning and, if planning is done, how effectively it is performed—i.e., to what degree the optimal agenda is developed on a timely basis.

These two factors in combination—the degree of team quality and the degree of strategic planning effectiveness—have a tremendous effect on the degree to which the team reaches its full potential. If both the team and the level of planning are weak, the enterprise likely will have greatly unrealized potential. At the other extreme, *if both the degree of team quality and strategic planning effectiveness are exceptional, that enterprise likely will enjoy considerable, even exclusive, differentiation from its competition.* The second vital aspect that determines strategic effectiveness, Information/Use Leverage, is shown below in Figure 6.2.

### Figure 6.2—Information/Use Leverage

Leverage:
A combination of high quality and high use of strategic information is more likely on these bases to accelerate the time frame and degree of financial results.

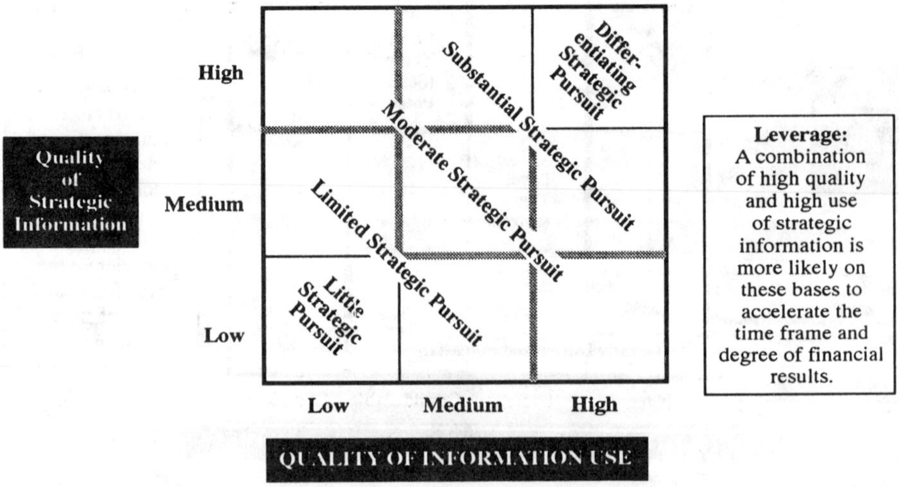

The vertical axis of Figure 6.2 indicates the quality level of the strategic information a company possesses. *What is strategic information? It is the sum total of all knowledge and data a company possesses,* typically of a non-immediate, temporary nature, including all information that the enterprise has about both internal aspects (e.g., technology, financial, process, human resource data) and external arenas (market, competitors, customer, industry, economic, and public sector data). The "quality" of that strategic information is determined by how accurate, thorough, and contextually pertinent that information is to the enterprise. For example, poor-quality strategic information may be inaccurate, incomplete, excessive, or combinations of all three.

On the horizontal axis, "quality of information use" means how efficiently and effectively the enterprise accesses and applies the information that it possesses to achieve the timely fulfillment of its strategic objectives.

In combination, *the degree to which an enterprise achieves both the high quality and high utilization of strategic information is the degree to which that enterprise clicks into and maintains strategic pursuit. I define strategic pursuit as that conscious, proactive, and synergistic focus and action by a team to fulfill the disproportionately important long-term objectives of the enterprise.*

If an organization has both poor quality information and poor use of that information, it most likely has either limited or no strategic pursuit. If, by contrast, an organization has both high-quality information and excellent use of that information, it most likely has an extraordinary degree of strategic pursuit, often to an extent that differentiates it from its competitive comparison group. You may wonder just how pertinent these theoretical concepts of team/strategy leverage and information/use leverage are in the context of the actual working realities of the enterprise. In longitudinal studies with my clients in years two, three, and four of their strategic planning and implementation, their corporate emergence from the competitive pack is clearly evident. Hence, what I have observed is that these levers, when utilized, have palpable, direct effects on an organization's success.

The results for many of my client companies have been as dramatic as they have been varied. By definition, because what was important to each enterprise was different, the outcomes have reflected their priorities. These priorities were far-ranging, focusing on needs such as

- Market share or penetration
- Sales increases for particular products or services

- Cost reductions
- Enhanced cash flow
- Internal process improvement
- Market or industry recognition
- Human resource growth in numbers and expertise

Quite often, clients have had concurrent emphasis and pursuit on several of these.

The one characteristic that all of these enterprises shared was that *each enjoyed attaining its key chosen objective(s) faster and to a higher extent* than it had before pulling the strategic levers of teamwork, planning, information quality, and knowledge application.

There is truly an enormous number of advantages, of both a short- and long-term nature, offered by strategic thinking, planning, and implementing. I hope these first six chapters have successfully conveyed them and that you share my conviction that *one of the greatest opportunities for every enterprise of every kind as it negotiates the 1990s and enters the next millennium is to strategically plan and implement its vital objectives to attain powerful, measurable marketplace advantage.* This opportunity, untapped in its potential, is as profound in importance as it is simple in concept and execution. Moreover, an effective strategic process amplifies your previous or ongoing TQM or change management initiatives.

From my standpoint as an author, *the purpose of this book is to sound a clarion call and to transform strategic planning into a new business practice: implemented strategic planning.* From the standpoint of the enterprise executive, manager, planner, and professional, *this book is a valuable blueprint—* designed with service in mind and replete with accompanying instructions—*which can guide enterprises to plan for the future in a sustainable fashion that may never have been achieved before.*

With these foundational discussions behind us, at last we can begin to explore Strategic Planning Technology itself, viewing it in the context of how to put it immediately to work for you. The final bonus of learning these tools is that they apply to nearly every aspect of life: business, family, and personal. Let's get started!

## Chapter Seven

# An Overview of the Strategic Planning Technology

Strategic Planning Technology offers the most complete and practical strategic planning and implementational system available. It is richly informed by the contributions and lessons of the people, companies, philosophies, and processes that have contributed to the field during the last half-century, and without which my development of this technology would have been impossible. Because Strategic Planning Technology consists of five sections, it is also referred to as a "Five-Venue System."

I define a *venue* in the same way as the word is used in the realm of the international Olympics: *a location, or station, where a specific, unique, and complementary event takes place in the context of the total experience.* The Five Venues in the Strategic Planning Technology, fitting exactly this definition, have an additional characteristic: They are sequentially arranged.

The Five Venues are alliteratively named: *Origination, Opportunities, Objectives, Operations, and Outcomes.* There are several ways of explaining how these Venues work complementarily and sequentially to each other. It is important to see the big "40,000-foot" picture before launching into the dense forest of details. Perhaps the simplest way to grasp each Venue is to know what questions each venue asks the enterprise planning team to answer.

## Venue One—Origination

Venue One, *Origination,* asks the questions: "*Who* are we? *Where* are we? *Why* are we?" To use the analogy of a journey, its purpose is to perform the necessary preparations before launching on the long strategic expedition. There are four distinct sections to Venue One with four specific preparations that must be sequentially performed prior to the trip's onset: *Valuation, Values, Vision,* and *Variables.*

| SECTION | PURPOSE |
|---|---|
| 1. Valuation | Serves to conduct a thorough "strategic inventory" of the enterprise |
| 2. Values | Determines the shared and prioritized values of the enterprise |
| 3. Vision | Identifies the shared view of the destination of the enterprise |
| 4. Variables | Enables the undertaking of a complete environmental scan of all major internal and external factors influencing, or of importance to, the enterprise |

## Venue Two—Opportunities

Venue Two, *Opportunities,* asks the question: *"What* should we do to fulfill our vision and mission?" With the "Who," "Where," and "Why" questions answered in Venue One, the journey now has been clearly and compellingly justified, for the enterprise team knows who it is, where it is and, more fundamentally, why it exists.

Now the focus shifts to the *"What"* in order to identify what opportunities are to be earnestly considered by the enterprise. The entire structure of this section, which is composed of four master goal-categories (the strategic *enterprise, resources, knowledge,* and *response*) and sixteen subcategories, is designed to provide a framework for identifying and prioritizing all important strategic goals in order to identify and synthesize the company's strategic portfolio.

## Venue Three—Objectives

Venue Three, *Objectives,* asks the question: *"When* will we achieve key financial and business results?"

Based upon Venue One, which has charted out all the pertinent matters required at Origination before the launch of the strategic journey can begin, and Venue Two, which has identified what the most important Opportunities for the enterprise are, Venue Three builds a staircase to the strategic future. It is dedicated to the act of quantification of both existing and new strategic product and service deliverables into "units" and "dollars" of opportunity, in order to construct tangible targets or clear, measurable objectives.

The effect that Venue Three has on the strategic team is to calibrate thinking from the realm of soft possibilities to the reality of harder data with assumption-backed plans. This process is done by first identifying the important financial and business variables necessary to quantify the objectives. Next, a simple strategic revenue structure is formulated for each product or service opportunity and then summarized in aggregate. How revenues will change over time can be pegged at a fixed growth rate or customized specifically by year. Lastly, strategic income statements are completed by pegging total expenses, which, when subtracted from total revenues, yield estimated total profits over a five-year period.

## Venue Four—Operations

Venue Four, *Operations,* asks the question: *"How* should we implement the vital year-one actions needed to lay the foundation of our strategic future?"

This Venue builds directly upon Venue Two's opportunities by taking the planning process deeply into the practical realm. *Venue Four focuses the entire plan on very specific, measurable, person-responsible, time-bounded actions that serve as the critical success factors of the entire plan.*

In the early chapters of this book, we discussed the powerful concept of strategic leverage—the kind that occurs when operational, reactive individual functions and departments/divisions become coordinated into a strategic, proactive team that synchronously focuses on identifying and executing the truly important long-term agenda. This leverage cannot, and in actual business life does not, occur without disciplined, conscious action planning and implementation.

**The Definition of an Action Plan.** The definition of an action plan deserves more scrutiny at this early point, as it is the building block of the entire enterprise strategy. A solid and complete action plan has each of the following characteristics:

1. **It is a Specific Activity,** not fuzzy, general, or minor.

2. **It is Measurable,** involving a tangible, clear result. Afterward, you know with stark clarity whether it got done or not!

3. **It is Time-Bounded,** with a specific beginning and end point. It is not hazily begun, open-ended, or uncertainly completed.

4. **It is Person-Responsible,** done by an actual person or group of people, not by the "royal we" or "them," or even worse, by being "delegated to the operating units" as some strategic planning models inexplicably suggest. Responsible parties also must have the authority and capability, as well as the obligation, to get the job done.

5. **It is Followed Up Through Completion and Beyond.** Just as many strategic plans never get to the action-planning stage, so many plans, made with the best of intentions, never see the light of day. The action plans, never systematically followed up, are forgotten, dropped, or at best only partially done. In fact, this aspect of action planning is so important that my entire last Venue, Venue Five, is dedicated to it!

## Venue Five—Outcomes

Venue Five, *Outcomes*, asks the question: "How can we ensure that now that we have *planned our work* we will successfully *work our plan?*" In the prior Venue, I defined success in implementation as a simple, two-step process: First, *set* the action plans; second, *do* them. Through these two simple yet vital steps, actual strategic leverage is realized—and the possibility of having quicker and higher business results or having a better top-, middle-, or bottom-line return on investment. There are two very important aspects to the implementation stage, which follow.

**Chronologically-Ordered Action Plans.** It has been said that the acid test of any theory is practice—how easily the matter can reach fruition in time and space. The entire thrust and effect of the Strategic Planning Technology is to produce a docket or portfolio of action plans. Each action plan, having a specific date and person responsible, can be placed in the chronological order of the date the action plan is due to be completed for implementation or completion. Once done, the enterprise's entire strategic universe of data and considerations has been boiled down to a one- to five-page list of chronologically ordered action plans. An entire strategic plan boils down to an ordered list of actions! Simple. Practical. Implementable. Trackable. Accountable. Combined with the next key aspect of Venue Five, the planning methodology is complete, close-looped, and self-perpetuating.

**The Monthly Executive Review Meeting.** This term is packed with meaning. First, some kind of *monthly* follow-up is needed to ensure that the strategic plan of work is on track for implementation. Second, the same *executives* who formulated the plan are responsible for overseeing its implementation. This does not in any way suggest that strategic planning should not be conducted throughout every level of an organization in coordinated, "waterfall" fashion. Every person in an enterprise needs to develop creative, strategic thinking skills within his or her overall sphere of the business.

Also, whatever plan those at the top of an enterprise develop should be influenced by significant and comprehensive input from all levels of that enterprise. Accordingly, the generated plan should be communicated clearly to all parts of the enterprise and internalized, customized, and applied to each department by each department for complete organizational ownership and plan integration.

The third adjective in the term, after "monthly" and "executive," is *review*. What is being reviewed are the action plans as they come due for completion. That old managerial phrase *"What gets measured gets done"* absolutely pertains to strategic plans. Typically, as we have realized with long-range plans, *"what does not get measured atrophies on the bookshelf."* Of course, more unfortunately and fundamentally, most strategic plans and processes never get to the point of generating practical actions anyway, much less of tracking their implementational status. I have seen many plan reports end up with no more than a list of "functional objectives." I cannot recall even one time in such a situation when these objectives got done quickly or well when left at that point, and sometimes they did not get done at all.

At the base of this descriptive term is a *meeting:* this meeting absolutely and unequivocally is the most important noncustomer, internal meeting for the enterprise. When introducing this stage of strategic implementation and initiating the meeting, I occasionally have heard client executives moan, "Oh, *another* meeting." I like to hear this honest objection, to which I respond: "There are about two hundred work hours per month. If you 'zero-based-plan' your month, prioritizing all of your time usage by the importance of the activity, particularly the length, substance, outcome, and value of your regular meetings, I will eagerly put this monthly executive review meeting up for value against any other meeting you run. *It is the one meeting that systematically and economically reviews key past-month operational performance measurements and the strategic action plans, thereby comprehensively taking the pulse on the past, present, and future of the enterprise.* It is your current down-payment on future returns." I have never heard a single objection that this is not the case *once* these meetings were experienced. Sometimes I cannot help but add: "Eliminate or make more efficient all of your other meetings, and this 1% to 2% of your month (two to four hours at most) is a worthy, even "no-brainer" investment to ensure you are working to optimize the enterprise's strategic potential and to integrate those opportunities into your operating performance."

My clients who have adopted the practice of regularly holding monthly executive review meetings have been very heartened by the experience. When I call to check in on their planning progress, the CEO or executive in charge of planning usually says something like, "We're really on track. People are excited. We're getting *most* of the action plans [reality being what it is] done. Marketing and sales are moving. Internal operations are energized. *The plan is working!*"

In contrast, clients who do not stick with holding monthly executive review meetings or who are inconsistent accordingly reflect a relatively lesser degree of progress, from minor discouragement to outright levels of frustration. Therefore, experience has borne out that this one little monthly meeting makes *all* the difference between wish-list objectives and real strategic progress.

With the overview of the Strategic Planning Technology's Five-Venue System completed, it is time to explore this methodology step by step, Venue by Venue, in enough detail to provide a real understanding of the components of effective planning.

# PART TWO

# THE FIVE VENUES OF STRATEGIC PLANNING TECHNOLOGY

# Chapter Eight

# Venue One: Performing a Valuation of the Enterprise

## Introduction

Venue One is organized to assist the enterprise in answering the following questions: *"Who* are we?" *"Where* are we?" *"Why* are we?" What the people of the enterprise find out helps them make thorough preparations for their strategic journey. The above questions are answered by performing four analyses: (1) performing a *valuation* of the enterprise's current condition; (2) identifying the *values* of the enterprise's leadership; (3) generating the long-range *vision* for the enterprise; and (4) scanning for all of the internal and external environmental *variables* affecting the enterprise.

A thorough valuation of the enterprise is made by performing written or oral, one-to-one Pre-session Interviews of selected key members of the organization and by completing the Strategic Enterprise Assessment (SEA). The Pre-session Interview is the recorded oral or written *qualification* (anecdotal, narrative insights) of the company's strategic condition, and the Strategic Enterprise Assessment is the *quantification* (statistical, measured insights) of the current strategic health of the company. Together, they provide very useful insights (like an initial battery of blood-work tests used to assess the physical condition of the body prior to further treatment) before actual planning process is carried out.

## Pre-Interviews

The objective of the Pre-session Interviews is to afford session participants (and anyone else who has valuable insights about the organization) the opportunity to provide personal insights about the company in a variety of arenas. These "interviews" can be conducted either on a one-to-one basis between the enterprise interviewee and the third party consultant, or in confidential, written fashion. In the latter case, the company member fills out the interview, then seals the envelope for collection and shipment to the consultant or internal plan coordinator for confidential processing and group summarization.

## A Continuity of Strategic Elements

Throughout the Strategic Planning Technology the same sixteen strategic categories are used. The first time they are used is right at the start of Venue One, in this initial Valuation section, where they make up the sixteen segments of the Pre-session Interview form. In this capacity, they serve to initiate an exploration of each of the sixteen strategic elements that are the continuous frame of reference throughout the goal-setting and eventual action-planning stages. In light of this structured approach, please review the questions from the actual Pre-session Interview form, presented in Figure 8.1.

**Figure 8.1—Pre-session Interview Form**

---

### PRE-SESSION INTERVIEW FORM
Page 1 of 4

1. How would you characterize the enterprise's **organizational structure** and effectiveness? (Any particular strengths or weaknesses?)

   _____

   _____

2. How would you characterize the enterprise's **corporate culture**? (Any particular strengths or weaknesses?)

   _____

   _____

3. How would you characterize the quality and effectiveness of the **executive team**? (Any particular strengths or weaknesses?)

   _____

   _____

4. How would you characterize the capabilities and effectiveness of the entire **management team**? (Any particular strengths or weaknesses?)

   _____

   _____

---

**Figure 8.1—Pre-session Interview Form (continued)**

PRE-SESSION INTERVIEW FORM
Page 2 of 4

5. How capable, involved, and effective are all of your enterprise's **employees**? (Any particular strengths or weaknesses?)

   _____

   _____

6. How clear, timely, and effective are **intra-company communications**? How strong is company teamwork? (Any particular strengths or weaknesses?)

   _____

   _____

7. How well is **technology** utilized in the company to its advantage? (Any particular strengths or weaknesses?)

   _____

   _____

8. How well do the various **organizational functions**/divisions/units work together, internally for common enterprise objectives? (Any particular strengths or weaknesses?)

   _____

   _____

**Figure 8.1—Pre-session Interview Form (continued)**

PRE-SESSION INTERVIEW FORM
Page 3 of 4

9. How well does the enterprise know of or address the needs of its **customers**? (Any particular strengths or weaknesses?)

_____

_____

10. How well does the enterprise know of all aspects of its **competitors** and take appropriate competitive actions? (Any particular strengths or weaknesses?)

_____

_____

11. How informed is the enterprise team in all external and internal **business arenas**? This means, how clear an understanding do you have of your overall business processes, and of your market, industry, and the economy in general. (Any particular strengths and weaknesses?)

_____

_____

12. How informed and effective is the enterprise team in all **financial** and cost management areas? (Any particular strengths or weaknesses?)

_____

_____

**Figure 8.1—Pre-session Interview Form (concluded)**

PRE-SESSION INTERVIEW FORM
Page 4 of 4

13. How committed to and effective is the enterprise in the arena of making **strategic and business plans**? (Any particular strengths or weaknesses?)

   _____

   _____

14. How focused upon or effective is the enterprise in the arena of making **market and product /service strategies**? (Any particular strengths or weaknesses?)

   _____

   _____

15. How clear, thorough, and effective is the enterprise's **planning system**? (Any particular strengths or weaknesses?)

   _____

   _____

16. How thorough, timely, consistent, and effective is the enterprise's capability to **implement the plans** that have been set? (Any particular strengths or weaknesses?)

   _____

   _____

The one guideline that must be followed faithfully throughout this process is the interviewer's/processor's keeping of strict and absolute confidentiality of the interviewee's oral/written comments (unless the specific and express permission of the interviewee allows otherwise). The goal is never to reveal individual inputs that are in any way traceable or attributable to an individual, but to use the data to determine the overall strengths and weaknesses of the organization according to the interviewed group when the data is taken as a whole.

## The Strategic Enterprise Assessment (SEA)

Complementing the Pre-Session Interviews is the Strategic Enterprise Assessment, or SEA, an appropriate acronym because its function to reduce a complex sea of strategic issues to a simple summary. It is used to *quantify* the strategic health of the organization in sixteen complementary categories. Remember that the Strategic Planning Technology uses the same sixteen strategic categories throughout its five Venues, and therefore these sixteen categories form the sixteen sections of the SEA. While the categories will be defined and addressed in greater detail in Venue Two, a brief identification of them is helpful here in order to understand the SEA (see Figure 8.2.).

The sixteen titles of the sixteen strategic categories are defined from an assessment standpoint and will be changed slightly when used for goal-setting in Venue Two.

The SEA wheel is divided up into four 90-degree slices. These four major sections are

I. **ENTERPRISE,** including the four categories of
1. Organization
2. Corporate Culture
3. Executive Team
4. Managerial Climate

II. **RESOURCES,** including the four categories of
1. Human Resource Leverage
2. Communications Leverage
3. Technology Leverage
4. Cross-Functional Leverage

III. **KNOWLEDGE,** including the four categories of
1. Customer Knowledge
2. Competitive Knowledge

## Figure 8.2—Strategic Enterprise Assessment Wheel

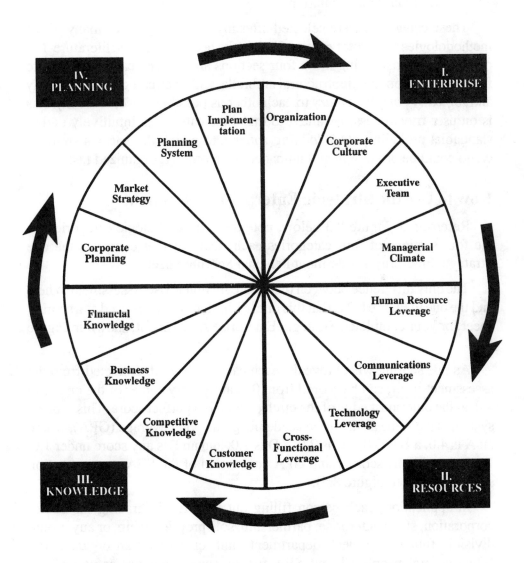

3. Business Knowledge
4. Financial Knowledge

IV. **PLANNING,** including the four categories of
1. Corporate Planning
2. Market Strategy
3. Planning System
4. Plan Implementation

These categories were selected after my close scrutiny of many of the methodologies and prototypes set forth in the body of strategic literature. My objective in constructing these four sections and sixteen categories was to form a complete strategic structural umbrella, with each category as distinctly and *logically complementary* to each other as possible. Also, since my bias is on user-friendliness, I wanted to make the categories intuitively understandable, providing *clear loading zones* into which the various strategic cargo could be brought in and unloaded in an orderly, organized fashion.

## How to Use the Strategic Enterprise Assessment

Referring to Figure 8.3 below, note the sixteen strategic categories (in the four sections of four categories each) that together comprise the one Strategic Enterprise Assessment Personal Scoring Sheet.

The only difference between this Strategic Enterprise Assessment Wheel and the one in Figure 8.2 is that this one has hash marks to be used as a scoring sheet for your completed Strategic Enterprise Assessment, shown in Figure 8.4.

As this scoring wheel reveals, each category's total, collected from the assessment itself, can be scored from 0.0, at the very center of the circle, to 4.0, at the outermost edge of the circle, which is a perfect score. This scoring system is the same as the basic academic grade point average (GPA), where an A is 4.0, a B is 3.0, a C is 2.0, a D is 1.0, and an F is any score under 1.0. For help with the scoring and GPA conversion of the SEA, a computation sheet is used (see Figure 8.5).

In application, each person filling out the SEA is grading his or her corporation, small enterprise, partnership, sole proprietorship, or any group, division, function, project, department, unit, or team of an organization. When several people fill out SEA for the same company or part of the company, these scores can be anonymously combined by an appropriate

*Text continued on page 83*

## Figure 8.3—Strategic Enterprise Assessment Personal Scoring Sheet: Strategic Enterprise Assessment Wheel

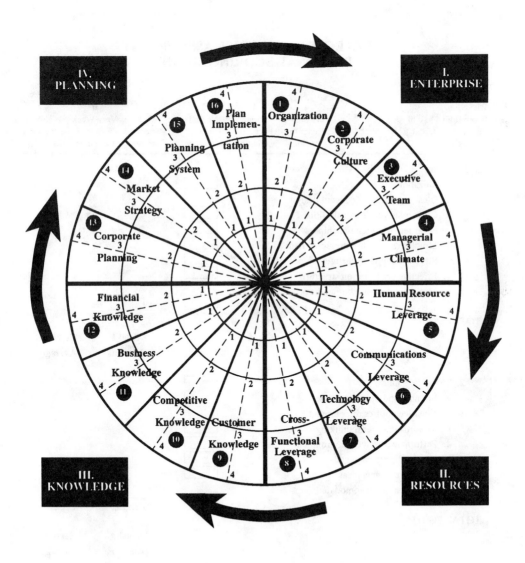

## Figure 8.4—Strategic Enterprise Assessment Personal Scoring Sheet: Strategic Enterprise Assessment

### STRATEGIC ENTERPRISE ASSESSMENT
### PERSONAL SCORING SHEET

| Directions:<br>Score from 4 to 0 in<br>boxes to right. Put "/" if<br>not applicable. | Scoring<br>Options: | **4**<br>Very Strong<br>Factor or<br>Condition | **3**<br>Strong<br>Factor or<br>Condition | **2**<br>Neutral<br>Factor or<br>Condition | **1**<br>Weak<br>Factor or<br>Condition | **0**<br>Very Weak<br>Factor or<br>Condition | **/**<br>Not<br>Factor or<br>Condition |
|---|---|---|---|---|---|---|---|

I. Enterprise

   1. Organization

     a. Clear organization concept/design

     b. Clear roles and responsibilities

     c. Clear reporting relationships

     d. Structure supports entrepreneurism

     e. Structure supports change & innovation

     f. Effective organization structure

     g. Minimal enterprise bureaucracy

TOTAL POINTS

$$\boxed{\phantom{xx}} \div \boxed{\phantom{xx}} = \boxed{\phantom{xx}}$$

Total #     Section
Answers    Average

   2. Corporate Culture

     a. Friendly and open atmosphere

     b. Negative politics discouraged

     c. Rewards long-term thinking

     d. Performance-driven environment

     e. Egos well self-managed

     f. Receptive to new ideas

     g. Various styles accomodated

TOTAL POINTS

$$\boxed{\phantom{xx}} \div \boxed{\phantom{xx}} = \boxed{\phantom{xx}}$$

Total #     Section
Answers    Average

## Figure 8.4—Strategic Enterprise Assessment Personal Scoring Sheet: Strategic Enterprise Assessment (continued)

### STRATEGIC ENTERPRISE ASSESSMENT
### PERSONAL SCORING SHEET (continued)

| Directions:<br>Score from 4 to 0 in boxes to right. Put "/" if not applicable. | Scoring Options: | **4**<br>Very Strong<br>Factor or<br>Condition | **3**<br>Strong<br>Factor or<br>Condition | **2**<br>Neutral<br>Factor or<br>Condition | **1**<br>Weak<br>Factor or<br>Condition | **0**<br>Very Weak<br>Factor or<br>Condition | **/**<br>Not<br>Factor or<br>Condition |
|---|---|---|---|---|---|---|---|

I. Enterprise (continued)

   3. Executive Team   ☐

     a. Solid generalist skills   ☐

     b. Competence in strategic arenas   ☐

     c. Competence in operational arenas   ☐

     d. Sensitive to external constituencies (groups)   ☐

     e. Set clear business priorities   ☐

     f. Successfully implement business priorities   ☐

     g. Active in human resource development

TOTAL POINTS     ☐ ÷ ☐ = ☐

                               Total #     Section
                               Answers     Average

   4. Managerial Climate   ☐

     a. Have appropriate autonomy   ☐

     b. Exhibit considerable creativity   ☐

     c. Appropriate ongoing development   ☐

     d. Individuals make appropriate decisions   ☐

     e. Consensus decisions made as needed   ☐

     f. Demonstrate people management skills   ☐

     g. Various management styles allowed

TOTAL POINTS     ☐ ÷ ☐ = ☐

                                 Total #     Section
                               Answers     Average

### Figure 8.4—Strategic Enterprise Assessment Personal Scoring Sheet: Strategic Enterprise Assessment (continued)

## STRATEGIC ENTERPRISE ASSESSMENT
## PERSONAL SCORING SHEET (continued)

| Directions:<br>Score from 4 to 0 in<br>boxes to right. Put "/" if<br>not applicable. | Scoring<br>Options: | 4<br>Very Strong<br>Factor or<br>Condition | 3<br>Strong<br>Factor or<br>Condition | 2<br>Neutral<br>Factor or<br>Condition | 1<br>Weak<br>Factor or<br>Condition | 0<br>Very Weak<br>Factor or<br>Condition | /<br>Not<br>Factor or<br>Condition |
|---|---|---|---|---|---|---|---|

II. Resources

   5. Human Resource Leverage
- a. Rewards and pay based on performance
- b. Measure employee efficiency and effectiveness
- c. Subordinates usually conferred with
- d. Employees involved in decision
- e. Strong support of management
- f. Strong support for CEO
- g. Strong belief/loyalty to company

         [ ] ÷ [ ] = [ ]

TOTAL POINTS

            Total #      Section
            Answers     Average

   6. Communications Leverage
- a. Information flows top—down
- b. Information flows bottom—up
- c. Information flows quickly, freely
- d. Clear communication systems/methods
- e. People work smoothly with teamwork
- f. High synergy among organizations is achieved
- g. High participatory climate

         [ ] ÷ [ ] = [ ]

TOTAL POINTS

            Total #      Section
            Answers     Average

## Figure 8.4—Strategic Enterprise Assessment Personal Scoring Sheet: Strategic Enterprise Assessment (continued)

### STRATEGIC ENTERPRISE ASSESSMENT
### PERSONAL SCORING SHEET (continued)

| Directions: Score from 4 to 0 in boxes to right. Put "/" if not applicable. | Scoring Options: | 4 Very Strong Factor or Condition | 3 Strong Factor or Condition | 2 Neutral Factor or Condition | 1 Weak Factor or Condition | 0 Very Weak Factor or Condition | / Not Factor or Condition |
|---|---|---|---|---|---|---|---|

II.  Resources (continued)

    7. Technology Leverage

       a. Understand technology changes in industry

       b. Understand today's technology needs

       c. Understand future technology needs

       d. Regularly review technology needs

       e. Have replacement plans for key technologies

       f. Make timely investments in technologies

       g. Use technology as a strategic lever    ☐ ÷ ☐ = ☐

TOTAL POINTS

                                                  Total #       Section

                                                  Answers     Average

    8. Cross-Functional Leverage

       a. Strong inter-functional/departmental teamwork

       b. Sales and marketing is linked to team

       c. Manufacturing is linked to team

       d. R&D/engineering are linked to team

       e. HQ staff is linked to team

       f. Support & indirect staffs linked to team

       g. Functional synergy achieves company results    ☐ ÷ ☐ = ☐

TOTAL POINTS

                                                  Total #       Section

                                                  Answers     Average

## Figure 8.4—Strategic Enterprise Assessment Personal Scoring Sheet: Strategic Enterprise Assessment (continued)

### STRATEGIC ENTERPRISE ASSESSMENT
### PERSONAL SCORING SHEET (continued)

| Directions:<br>Score from 4 to 0 in boxes to right. Put "/" if not applicable. | Scoring Options: | **4**<br>Very Strong<br>Factor or<br>Condition | **3**<br>Strong<br>Factor or<br>Condition | **2**<br>Neutral<br>Factor or<br>Condition | **1**<br>Weak<br>Factor or<br>Condition | **0**<br>Very Weak<br>Factor or<br>Condition | **/**<br>Not<br>Factor or<br>Condition |
|---|---|---|---|---|---|---|---|

III. Knowledge

   9. Customer Knowledge

     a. Focus on strategic needs of customers

     b. Customers principally buy on value

     c. Driven by key customers' strategies

     d. Have some customers who are market leaders

     e. Have complete customer support programs

     f. Accurately predict customers' demands

     g. Have total commitment to please customers    [  ] ÷ [  ] = [  ]

TOTAL POINTS

                                               Total #     Section<br>                                               Answers   Average

  10. Competitive Knowledge

     a. General, current competitors' knowledge

     b. Know competitors' strengths & weaknesses

     c. Know competitors' opportunities & threats

     d. Thorough knowledge of competitors' products

     e. Thorough knowledge of competitors' pricing

     f. Know competitors' major strategies

     g. Know exactly where you stand among competition  [  ] ÷ [  ] = [  ]

TOTAL POINTS

                                               Total #     Section<br>                                             Answers   Average

## Figure 8.4—Strategic Enterprise Assessment Personal Scoring Sheet: Strategic Enterprise Assessment (continued)

### STRATEGIC ENTERPRISE ASSESSMENT
### PERSONAL SCORING SHEET (continued)

| Directions:<br>Score from 4 to 0 in<br>boxes to right. Put "/" if<br>not applicable. | Scoring<br>Options: | 4<br>Very Strong<br>Factor or<br>Condition | 3<br>Strong<br>Factor or<br>Condition | 2<br>Neutral<br>Factor or<br>Condition | 1<br>Weak<br>Factor or<br>Condition | 0<br>Very Weak<br>Factor or<br>Condition | /<br>Not<br>Factor or<br>Condition |
|---|---|---|---|---|---|---|---|

III. Knowledge (continued)

    11. Business Knowledge

        a. Understand economy & markets

        b. Knowledge of government & social arenas

        c. Set and track key business measurements

        d. Know general public's perception of company

        e. Know customer/industry/competitive
           perception of company

        f. Hold regular, effective business reviews

        g. Optimally manage vendors & suppliers    $\boxed{\phantom{xx}} \div \boxed{\phantom{xx}} = \boxed{\phantom{xx}}$

TOTAL POINTS

                                        Total #       Section
                                        Answers   Average

    12. Financial Knowledge

        a. Have sufficient financial resources

        b. Set clear financial operating measurements

        c. Regularly track actuals to targets

        d. Manage product/service costs effectively

        e. Have little wasted expense in organization

        f. Have clearly known key financial targets

        g. Manage cash flow & financing needs well    $\boxed{\phantom{xx}} \div \boxed{\phantom{xx}} = \boxed{\phantom{xx}}$

TOTAL POINTS

                                        Total #       Section
                                        Answers   Average

## Figure 8.4—Strategic Enterprise Assessment Personal Scoring Sheet: Strategic Enterprise Assessment (continued)

### STRATEGIC ENTERPRISE ASSESSMENT
### PERSONAL SCORING SHEET (continued)

| Directions: Score from 4 to 0 in boxes to right. Put "/" if not applicable. | Scoring Options: | 4 Very Strong Factor or Condition | 3 Strong Factor or Condition | 2 Neutral Factor or Condition | 1 Weak Factor or Condition | 0 Very Weak Factor or Condition | / Not Factor or Condition |
|---|---|---|---|---|---|---|---|

IV. Planning ☐

   13. Corporate Planning ☐

      a. Positive commitment to plan strategically ☐

      b. Executives have strong planning capability ☐

      c. Clear focus on major company issues ☐

      d. Clear vision communicated to all ☐

      e. Set clear qualitative & quantitative goals ☐

      f. Set & communicate clear action plans

      g. Enterprise management team plans & organizes well ☐ ÷ ☐ = ☐

TOTAL POINTS

☐    Total #      Section
         Answers     Average

   14. Market Strategy

      a. Successful with existing products/services in existing markets ☐

      b. Deploy existing products/services in new markets ☐

      c. Bring new products successfully to existing markets ☐

      d. Bring new products successfully to new markets ☐

      e. Appropriately address international opportunity ☐

      f. Maximize product & company differentiation

      g. Have strong mix of products and markets

☐ ÷ ☐ = ☐

TOTAL POINTS

            Total #      Section
            Answers     Average

## Figure 8.4—Strategic Enterprise Assessment Personal Scoring Sheet: Strategic Enterprise Assessment (concluded)

### STRATEGIC ENTERPRISE ASSESSMENT PERSONAL SCORING SHEET (concluded)

| Directions:<br>Score from 4 to 0 in<br>boxes to right. Put "/" if<br>not applicable. | Scoring<br>Options: | **4**<br>Very Strong<br>Factor or<br>Condition | **3**<br>Strong<br>Factor or<br>Condition | **2**<br>Neutral<br>Factor or<br>Condition | **1**<br>Weak<br>Factor or<br>Condition | **0**<br>Very Weak<br>Factor or<br>Condition | **/**<br>Not<br>Factor or<br>Condition |
|---|---|---|---|---|---|---|---|

IV. Planning (continued)

   15. Planning System   ☐

     a. Effectively deals with future uncertainty   ☐

     b. Resolves existing conflicts   ☐

     c. Surfaces real agendas & needs   ☐

     d. Improves quality of long-range decisions   ☐

     e. Clear investments in capital, R&D, mkt. devel.   ☐

     f. Scarce resources deployed to high-yield arenas

     g. System accomplishes corporate needs   ☐ ÷ ☐ = ☐

TOTAL POINTS

                                                Total #     Section

                                               Answers   Average

   16. Plan Implementation   ☐

     a. Tracks & meets quantitative goals   ☐

     b. Tracks & meets qualitative goals   ☐

     c. Have disciplined implementation system   ☐

     d. Rigorously track & finish action plans   ☐

     e. Planned items don't slip or get forgotten

     f. Flexibility is demonstrated to address<br>       new priorities   ☐

     g. Overall, people "plan the work & work the plan"   ☐ ÷ ☐ = ☐

TOTAL POINTS

                                               Total #     Section

                                             Answers   Average

## Figure 8.5—Strategic Enterprise Assessment Computation Sheet

**ENTERPRISE ASSESSMENT COMPUTATION SHEET**

| Total Points for Category | ⑦ Answers | ⑥ Answers | ⑤ Answers | ④ Answers |
|:---:|:---:|:---:|:---:|:---:|
| 28 | 4.0 | — | — | — |
| 27 | 3.9 | — | — | — |
| 26 | 3.7 | — | — | — |
| 25 | 3.6 | — | — | — |
| 24 | 3.4 | 4.0 | — | — |
| 23 | 3.3 | 3.8 | — | — |
| 22 | 3.1 | 3.7 | — | — |
| 21 | 3.0 | 3.5 | — | — |
| 20 | 2.9 | 3.3 | 4.0 | — |
| 19 | 2.7 | 3.2 | 3.8 | — |
| 18 | 2.6 | 3.0 | 3.6 | — |
| 17 | 2.4 | 2.8 | 3.4 | — |
| 16 | 2.3 | 2.7 | 3.2 | 4.0 |
| 15 | 2.1 | 2.5 | 3.0 | 3.7 |
| 14 | 2.0 | 2.3 | 2.8 | 3.5 |
| 13 | 1.9 | 2.2 | 2.6 | 3.2 |
| 12 | 1.7 | 2.0 | 2.4 | 3.0 |
| 11 | 1.6 | 1.8 | 2.2 | 2.7 |
| 10 | 1.4 | 1.7 | 2.0 | 2.5 |
| 9 | 1.3 | 1.5 | 1.8 | 2.2 |
| 8 | 1.1 | 1.3 | 1.6 | 2.0 |
| 7 | 1.0 | 1.1 | 1.4 | 1.7 |
| 6 | .9 | 1.0 | 1.2 | 1.5 |
| 5 | .7 | .8 | 1.0 | 1.2 |
| 4 | .6 | .7 | .8 | 1.0 |
| 3 | .4 | .5 | .6 | .7 |
| 2 | .3 | .3 | .4 | .5 |
| 1 | .1 | .1 | .1 | .1 |

*Continued from page 72*

internal coordinator or external consultant, providing a collective scoring of the organization for each of the sixteen "strategic health" categories.

To calculate the score of an individual assessment, simply add up the *scores* at the end of each section, add up the *number* of items answered (from 0 to 7 for each category), and then refer to the SEA Computation Sheet. Survey items "not applicable" should have a slash mark ("/") in the answer box and are not counted.

When you have determined the sixteen GPA scores (one per category) you will be able to see clearly the organization's relative strengths and weaknesses. You will find that the high and low areas usually will correlate closely with your written pre-interviews. In fact, the two instruments are two sides of the same organizational-assessment coin: the interviews provide the "pluses and minuses" in qualitative terms, *in words;* the SEA's provide the "grades" for the company in quantitative terms, *in numbers.* Together, they paint an overall picture.

The 16 GPA's, one per category, can be added up (and divided by 16) to develop a single, overall GPA figure for the organization (each of the four sections of four categories can be subtotalled as well). Why? Every year, this survey can be repeated within an organization to determine, by category, section, and total, how the organization has improved annually in its strategic health. I say "improved" because that has been my clients' experience: Their plans, once implemented, bolster their company's health in all or most categories year by year.

Referring back to the SEA Scoring Sheet, once the Strategic Enterprise Assessment has been completed, the scorer has generated a GPA number (#.#) for each category. (Remember, the computation sheet in Figure 8.5 helps the scorer convert the scores into the GPA grade.) Typically, an organization clusters around a basic number, like 2.5, but when the 16 dots are written in on the SEA Scoring Sheet and then connected, it will form an imperfect circle, complete with spikes and ruts.

A spike is created when one category receives a significantly *higher* score than the others around it. A rut is created when one category receives a significantly *lower* score than the other categories around it. *The quantity and the degree of spikes and ruts reveals the degree of roughness in the organization's strategic journey.* Conversely, the smoother the circle, the smoother the journey. For example, if an organization has 16 scores all ranging from 2.4 to 2.6, two things can be said of that organization's strategic health: (1) Its elements are fairly consistent, since there are no significant spikes or ruts, and therefore, its fairly circular strategic rotation reflects a *synchronicity of strategic movement;* (2) the overall SEA scores are only average in the 2.5 range. We know from an academic standpoint that a 2.5 GPA is in the "high C, low B" range. This means that there is a large swath of strategic opportunity (the gap between the current inner circle and the circumference of the SEA wheel, where 4.0 indicates "perfect smoothness" and "perfect strategic performance") in all areas of the organization.

A simple real-life example may help you. One financial service client of mine received an aggregate grade of 3.9 in Financial Knowledge—"A+"— yet in Corporate Culture received a 2.0—a straight "C." One can easily surmise that "high-high's" and "low-low's" would make the "strategic journey" rocky, as indeed had been the case with that company. Accordingly, a number of strategic goals and requisite actions were developed to get at the root needs and corrective actions required to build a stronger, more healthy corporate culture and working environment. At last visit, the executive team has unanimously reported a marked improvement in its actual day-to-day business culture. Therefore, if an organization scores "all over the board," there likely is serious "trouble in River City," and, of course, all-around low scores obviously indicate an enterprise greatly underfulfilling its potential.

Through all of the cumulative SEA's I have seen from participating enterprises, a couple of trends prevail: First, the vast majority of enterprise overall scores are in the mid-2 range, the "C+" neighborhood, the first time the SEA is used; second, each enterprise usually has a couple of high points and a couple of low points that in combination contribute to a rocky strategic journey. Overall, enterprises typically are much stronger in operational aspects than they are in strategic arenas.

In summary, the SEA pinpoints particular strengths and weaknesses, and typically underscores the pure amount of *strategic potential* an enterprise has, and how much improvement is possible for that enterprise if it chooses to think, plan, and implement strategically. *Hence, the SEA is the organizational "CAT scan" to determine where the enterprise is before the planning process is begun, and it serves as an ongoing frame of reference during the planning and implementing activities, ensuring that all matters are being properly addressed.* This frame of reference is easy to keep and maintain for future/annual comparisons, and provides a consistent form of assessment because the same 16 categories are used throughout the planning process.

**Remember:** *Anyone* can coordinate this process, either internal or external to the company, as long as trust exists and confidentiality of individual inputs is absolutely and strictly maintained. I recommend unsigned responses in sealed envelopes placed in (or mailed to) a destination only accessible by the designated person who will conduct the summary of this pre-work.

## Summarizing All of the Pre-Work

After collecting all of the written pre-interviews and SEA's from the participants, the collector has the task of summarizing the data into a high-level format to get the major messages from the inputs.

## The Written Pre-Interviews' Data Digestion

I have found it very helpful to summarize the written pre-interviews in the following manner. When looking at the aggregate interview comments, you will find a number of "positives," "negatives," and a few "neutrals" for each of the 16 categories. You simply summarize these comments, using one page (or more if necessary) per category, with three columnar headings—POSITIVE, NEUTRAL, and NEGATIVE—dividing the page into thirds. Next, compress observations into simple phrases, removing extraneous words. Positive, negative, and neutral phrases should be split out and placed in their respective categories.

Once you have gone through each one of the participants' written pre-interviews and placed key comments in the appropriate slots, trends will emerge. Categories with a high volume of strongly positive or negative write-in comments will stand out.

Some categories will receive a high volume of comments, positive and negative, while other categories will receive little input at all. I have a theory, based upon actual experience, about why this is so. Quite often you will find that surveys are a "cathartic," "watershed" experience to the participants, whereby the valves of participative input are opened on certain issues they feel very strongly about. Accordingly, participants tend to fill the first two to four categories with a high volume of responses, often with data that more rightfully belongs in other, later categories. After this front-end venting is done, comments tend to trail off, and are more focused and netted out in the later categories. Nonetheless, this method of written pre-interview summarization crystallizes the major messages that the inputs are sending.

## Digesting the Strategic Enterprise Assessment (SEA) Data

The basic way to summarize the SEA inputs is to list each participant's GPA score for each of the 16 categories. Since inputs are anonymous, you can number each participant down the left-hand side of the page, with scores for each category spread across the page, left to right, under sixteen columns. With all scores posted to the summary sheet, each of the categories' scores can be totalled and averaged at the bottom to calculate a GPA for each category. Then, by adding up the 16 categories' GPAs and dividing by 16, you can derive the total strategic grade point average for the entire enterprise.

Then the analysis begins. What are the three highest categories? What are the three lowest? Do the high and low SEA categories match the overall comment trends from the written interview categories? Typically, there is a very close correlation. For example, if the Human Resources category contains a high quantity of positive inputs in the written pre-interviews, it is quite likely the Human Resources SEA grade point average will be one of the highest among the 16 categories' scores.

The great aspect of the SEA instrument is that it can be used on an annual or semi-annual basis to track how the leadership team perceives the enterprise is doing in aggregate and in each of the sixteen strategic arenas over time.

## The Pre-Work Enterprise Review Summary Form

After all of the data crunching and sectional summarization has been completed, an Enterprise Review Summary Form is filled in. Its purpose is to provide participants and all other reviewers with a thumbnail sketch of the pre-work results. Its three sections are very straightforward and easy to complete, and are shown in Figure 8.6.

First, the *Executive Summary* wraps up all of the pre-work on one page, culling the major findings of the summary. Although it is the first section of the *Enterprise Preview Summary Form,* it must be completed last, after sections II and III are filled out. Second, the *Strategic Enterprise Assessment Summary* provides a one-page format to input the three most prominent highlights, the three major strengths, and the three areas most in need of improvement that resulted from the SEA. Third, the *One-to-One Interview Summary* provides the same format for the interview results.

Figure 8.6—Enterprise Preview Summary Form

---

## ENTERPRISE PREVIEW SUMMARY FORM

I. **Executive Summary**

  A. Prominent Highlights Overview

- _____
- _____
- _____

  B. Major Strengths

- _____
- _____
- _____

  C. Areas for Improvement

- _____
- _____
- _____

---

**Figure 8.6—Enterprise Preview Summary Form (continued)**

---

**ENTERPRISE PREVIEW SUMMARY FORM** (continued)


II. **Strategic Enterprise Assessment Summary**
(See SEA Summary Sheet)

   A. Prominent Highlights

- _____

- _____

- _____


   B. Major Strengths

- _____

- _____

- _____


   C. Areas for Improvement

- _____

- _____

- _____

---

Figure 8.6—Enterprise Preview Summary Form (concluded)

**ENTERPRISE PREVIEW SUMMARY FORM** (concluded)

III. **One-to-One Interview Summary**
(General Highlights Only)

    A.  Prominent Highlights

       • _____

       • _____

       • _____

    B.  Major Strengths

       • _____

       • _____

       • _____

    C.  Areas for Improvement

       • _____

       • _____

       • _____

## Pre-Work Conclusion

If you intuitively believe this kind of baseline pre-work is important for preparing the team for strategic planning, I can experientially confirm it to be so. If you are thinking "overkill and overplayed," my response is: When you try it, you likely will feel quite differently! Minimally, this front-end pre-work accesses and opens the hidden veins of the corporate mountain, priming the waters to come to the surface to flow in fresh strategic thinking.

## Bonus Section:  Actual Pre-Work Trends

As I have mentioned at earlier points in this book, the SPT planning and implementation system has been developed through field work with my clients over the years, identifying their needs and assessing how best to help them reach their goals. Pre-work was an evolutionary addition to what was once my core SPT values/vision/driving forces/goals/action-plan template. The following are some interesting findings I have noticed from aggregate clients' pre-work of recent years.

1. **Communications and teamwork** difficulties afflict nearly every organization of every size. It seems that people cannot communicate too much or work together enough to ensure synergy up, down, over, in, and out of their company.

2. **Corporate culture** marks generally are inversely related to the size of the company, meaning that the smaller the company, the better and more healthy the corporate culture is perceived to be. The larger the company, the less healthy the corporate culture. Why? Sheer size dilutes the intense commitment of entrepreneurial or visionary leaders at the top of organizations. The larger the company, the more bureaucratic procedures and political agendas insulate, dampen, or even snuff out esprit de corps, replacing interpersonal high-spiritedness with organization structure and policy.

3. **Larger companies** tend to score better on areas requiring capital investment, such as technology, financial, and information systems, generally because they have the **critical mass** to invest in longer-term, infrastructurally-strengthening programs.

4. The great majority of enterprise leaders rate their **human resources,** their people, higher than themselves—the executive and/or leadership teams—and have a great deal of pride and confidence in their people's ability and performance. This is heartening, and is sample

evidence that businesses committed enough to embark on strategic planning also have at least relatively enlightened and proactive attitudes and intents toward their employee constituencies. Effectiveness in meeting their needs is another matter, borne out by employees' responses on my surveys citing leadership's good and well-meaning intent, but often fumbling, inadequate results.

5. My idea that companies that undergo a strategic planning process generally have **proactive, far-seeing executives** is based upon observation. As the "rich get richer," so do *those enterprises that recognize and invest in a better planning system, because leadership believes they and their company are worthy of the investment.* This has been the case with the companies I have worked with, the great majority of which were already in the upper third of their markets and industries when I began work with them. Through better planning, quite a few went from top ten or top five to the top three or outright leaders in their markets. *Leadership that wants to improve aggressively will make the necessary investments in planning, in its people, and in whatever it takes to win in its industry.* Unfortunately, that intensity of purpose is *not* the same among the leadership teams of all companies in the United States, undoubtedly an underlying factor in America's competitive decline during the 1980s.

6. Very few enterprise leadership teams feel that they have anywhere near a satisfactory **planning system,** current plan of record, or implementation system, regardless of their size or success otherwise. Therefore, to develop these areas well proves to be a *very strong competitive differential* for companies that do so.

7. The **categories** of customer, competitor, business knowledge, and market/product/service planning are extremely **volatile.** Some companies are at the top in one or all of these; others are conspicuously weak in these areas.

8. Participants **grade** their enterprises and themselves **very hard.** Very rarely does a company score itself at a composite 3.0 GPA, or even 2.8, or higher. Most range in the 2.4 to 2.6 range. Participants see a tremendous amount of room for improvement in their organizations. It is not that they cannot score a 4.0 in one dimension, but that *generally they feel there is a pronounced lack of total optimization and total synergy, with too many leaks in the enterprise vessel, leaks that are identifiable and fixable with specific plans and actions.* Since, on average, companies have scored themselves at about an

aggregate of 2.5 on a 4.0 scale, they have scored themselves only 60% efficient and effective in reaching their strategic potential. To boost that GPA to 3.0 and 3.5 over time through real strategic actions has a very noticeable effect on the performance in their markets, industries, and bottom-lines.

# Chapter Nine

# Corporate Values

## The Importance of Values

Every enterprise is driven by its leaders' individual and collective values, whether those values are consciously understood or unconsciously influential, spoken or unspoken, written or unrecorded.

Thomas J. Watson, Jr., the former Chairman of IBM, spoke prophetically of the importance of beliefs for an enterprise in an ever changing world:

> This, then, is my thesis: I firmly believe that any organization, in order to survive and achieve success, must have a *sound set of beliefs* on which it premises all of its policies and actions. Next, I believe that the most important single factor in corporate success is *faithful adherence to their beliefs.* And finally, I believe that if an organization is to meet the challenges of a changing world, it must be *prepared to change everything about itself except those beliefs* as it moves through corporate life.[1] *(emphases my own)*

Because I was employed by IBM from 1978 to 1988 (working in eleven company levels on twelve different job assignments, and in various environments, including a manufacturing plant, a development lab, the field, and corporate headquarters), I was present during the last stage of IBM's greatness when many IBMers believed Watsonian values pervaded its corporate culture from top to bottom. By the late 1980s, in the early stages of continuous retrenchment and "affordability" reductions of staff and expenses, the special quality that had made IBM unique by comparison to the rest of corporate America, and which had earned it recognition as the most admired corporation in the United States in the 1980s, began to dissipate steadily.

Of course, this sense of gradually lost greatness, widely shared by many who both remained in and left IBM during the late 1980s into the 1990s, was hard to gauge and difficult to pinpoint, but clearly discernable nonetheless. Of course, market and economic conditions, IBM's centerpiece excuse in recent years, has hurt the company, but those same conditions absolutely do not explain Microsoft's or Dell's relative success in the same industry over the same time frame. During such times, there is the irreplaceable requirement for *leadership greatness,* which I define as that galvanizing energy and

---

[1] Watson, T.J., Jr. (1963). *A business and its beliefs.* New York, New York: McGraw-Hill, p. 5.

vision to inspire ordinary people struggling in difficult circumstances to do extraordinary things—to rise above the cloud-level of mediocrity and excusitis, to overcome the urge to blame, and to fight the inclination to rely on the deflective defensiveness which results from not having the creative and energetic capacity to meet the challenges of the hour. Concerning the strategic fortunes of the company, you have to place responsibility squarely on the desk of the leadership. Values and vision greatness is that special catalyst that energizes and inspires ordinary people to dream and fulfill great dreams.

*Herein lies a very important lesson about values: Corporate values and the intensity with which they are felt and bought into by all of the employees, are disproportionately influenced by the leader.* As Thomas Watson, Jr., continued the legacy of his father by "walking the talk," so every leader of every venture, in business and in life, sets the tone, the direction, and the velocity of the enterprise, and whether knowingly or not, signals to every constituency what he or she feels are truly the most important values for the perpetuation of the enterprise.

## What Is An Enterprise Value?

If you share with me the conviction that values are more than motherhood and that they form the intrinsic essence of almost any human endeavor, then we need to pinpoint the measures that characterize a sound enterprise value. I see three such measures:

1. **Value is Distinctive**
   A sound enterprise value is *distinctive*. It is specially characteristic of what people deem to be the *intrinsic essence* of the organization. Distinctive does not mean lip-service, motherhood, token correctness, conventional wisdom, or a superficial trend. The values transcend external, day-to-day, surface things and are the *very heart and soul of the enterprise.*

2. **Value is Enduring**
   A sound enterprise value is *enduring*. It passes the test of time. It is not fleeting, cyclical, or temporary. This kind of value is a perceptible undercurrent amidst changing shorter-term ebbs and flows of business, market, economic, and industry tides. It is a *fine, sturdy, brightly-hued thread woven evenly through the overall corporate fabric* that constantly changes with the passage of time.

3. **Value is Influential**

A sound enterprise value is *influential*. It has a significant effect inside and outside of the enterprise. It is not only distinctive, capturing the spirit of the enterprise, and enduring, as a living, extending, distilling tradition. It packs an *impactful* punch, serving as a lighthouse beacon, a lanemarker, and a safety net all at once. It channels and calibrates individual and collective decisions made consciously and even unconsciously. Again, such a value is not necessarily what is on the corporate foyer wall, or even the annual president's report. It has an *actual influence* on the enterprise.

Typically, an organization has one, two, three, or four such transcendent values that pass these three tests of being distinctive, enduring, and influential. IBM has had three such values, which through the decades its employees could recite with genuine conviction: *(1) excellence; (2) service; (3) respect for the individual.* I can remember many times when managers in sensitive employee situations addressed difficult situations in terms of preserving and demonstrating respect for the individual. It drove policies, procedures, practices, and, most importantly, the spontaneous thinking and decisions of people on a day-to-day basis.

## Basic Principles Concerning Values and Strategy

In a very important and enlightening work entitled *Corporate Strategy and the Search for Ethics,*[2] Edward Freeman and Daniel Gilbert set forth several logical principles concerning the relationship between ethics and strategy. What I appreciate about their work is the clarity of logic and the simple yet profound linkage between values and corporate strategy. Their four basic tenets are identified below.

1. **The Values Principle:**

*Individual and organizational actions are caused in part by the values of individuals and organizations.*

In my mind, the operative thought here is *"values drive actions."* Actions are not executed in a values vacuum. Whether knowingly influenced or not, people in organizations do things not only according to their personal values, but also according to what they feel are the enterprise's values as well. Undoubtedly, one of the great, fundamental areas of conflict in professional

---

[2]Freeman, R. E., & Daniel R. G., Jr. (1988). *Corporate strategy and the search for ethics.* Englewood Cliffs, New Jersey; Prentice-Hall.

life is when an individual has that certain conviction that there is a serious disparity between the enterprise's core values and his or her own values.

## 2. The Interdependence Principle:

*Organizational success is due in part to the choices and actions of those groups that have a stake in the organization.*

What seems obvious on the surface, upon further refection has more to it. Organizational success does not just happen because of timely investment, good products, and attractive markets. Those and many other factors in corporate success are driven by *choices and actions* of key groups and individuals. Implicitly, these choices, which result in actions, are influenced by prevailing organizational as well as personal values. You may remember the old logic algorithm: "If A = B, and B = C, then A = C." Here, if *values* precede *actions,* and *actions* drive *success,* then *values* affect *success!*

## 3. The First Axiom of Corporate Strategy:

*Corporate strategy must reflect an understanding of the values of organizational members and stakeholders.*

As I noted earlier in the book, one of the great limitations of traditional strategic planning has been its generally non-holistic orientation, with a staid, classical focus on markets, portfolios, organizations, and other partial aspects of the enterprise whole. This first axiom establishes a very important base-line assumption that the corporate strategy must include, reflect an understanding of, and be molded by the values of its strategic team and other key constituencies.

## 4. The Second Axiom of Corporate Strategy:

*Corporate strategy must reflect an understanding of the ethical nature of strategic choice.*

This axiom, resting on the shoulders of the prior one, goes further to state that strategic choices are not mere calculations based on careful analysis of all known facts. Strategic choices have ethical ramifications because they are moored in beliefs, preferences, and values that have a personal and collective pecking order of influence whether people consciously recognize it or not. We have seen gross examples when an individual's values-sets are expressed in strategic choices that occasionally jolt the mainstream's values sensibilities.

I don't believe it is tiresome reiteration to consider the Wall Street of the 1980s as a study on personal and collective values-sets that drove individual and group strategic choices. A unique market opportunity tempted certain well-placed individuals to act out a certain set of values rooted in a consuming drive to maximize personal wealth quickly, which led, in certain cases, to significant, and even flagrantly illegal, actions.

But I had a personal experience with one company's leadership team that was an extraordinary example of "the ethical (and powerful) nature of strategic choice." This client, a mid-tech manufacturer who had vaulted from zero to 1.5 million dollars a month in sales in about four years, had developed a complete strategic plan one year earlier and was meeting with me to perform an annual strategic plan update. In the initial session, we developed a clearly defined set of values for the organization. One foundational value was integrity. I asked a simple question: "Does every aspect of your company reflect demonstrated integrity?"

In the discussion that ensued, an issue was raised. The company has measurable technical product superiority in all of the lines it manufactures. The problem was that certain low-volume parts were sourced from other manufacturers. The quality of those parts was not better than the rest of the industry. Yet in its marketing presentations, company representatives would speak boldly of its outstanding product superiority. The problem was that it was only 85% true, as about 15% of the parts were out-sourced. This posed a real integrity problem regarding the accuracy of the marketing claims. The only acceptable solution to both passing the integrity test and accurately claiming product-quality superiority was to build a second plant and manufacture these out-sourced parts internally—to bring them in-house to make them at the higher quality standard. In that very session, the executive team agreed that it must commit to the new manufacturing facility, which has since been outfitted, brought on-line within a year of that decision. Now the company can make the marketing claim without any compromise of integrity. This company indeed demonstrated "the ethical nature of strategic choice."

In this case, the value of integrity lived and breathed, and governed the strategic choice. The integrity gap was closed. Collectively, the corporate conscience operated to live up to its felt value. For me, this has been a beautiful and inspiring example of values governing strategic decisions.

## Values Identification

Companies that are in business for the long run are not propelled merely by short-term objectives, but by a governing set of values constantly aspired to and pursued. The key question is this: *For any kind of organization, or for yourself as an individual, what values do you most feel should be manifested consistently in every personal attribute and business aspect of this enterprise?* These are the values or beliefs that you want to govern your business, right down to the way of thinking and the manner in which you execute every action.

## A Personal Values Exercise

In Figure 9.1, you will find a list of values. Circle the ones that particularly appeal to you, that you can relate to the most. Of these, narrow your selections to *five* values. Spaces are provided in case you have your own word or phrase other than those noted. After selecting those five values, rank them from *5* (for your *first* choice) to *1* (for your *last* choice), recording your ranking in the boxes alongside them.

## Group Values Prioritization

Now that you have done this Values Identification exercise for yourself on an individual basis, you will find that it is a very profitable, teambuilding, clarifying exercise to develop the prioritized values of the team with whom you work. The CEO can do this with his or her direct reports, the first-line manager can do this with his or her direct reports, any member of the team can do this—and any group that works together will profit in a number of ways from this exercise. It is nonthreatening, because there are no right or wrong answers; it is just an expression of how people really feel. And it is generated via a "constructive democracy," not via haphazard discussions. Each person selects his or her own five values and then contributes these selections in a group setting; the facilitator documents the selected values and adds up the votes. This process is explained in detail below.

## How to Generate Prioritized Group Values

The group values exercise can only be done after each group member has privately performed the Values Identification exercise. The facilitator (as well as anyone else who wants to take notes) uses the group worksheet shown in Figure 9.2 to record the results of each member's Values Identification work. Small boxes are included on the worksheet so that the vote-points for the values can be noted. To conduct the exercise, the facilitator directs each group member to verbally provide, in turn, his or her top five values, from the first choice (5 points) down to the fifth choice (1 point), in order from high to low. The values and their vote-points are entered into the worksheet

**Figure 9.1—Personal Values Identification Worksheet**

# PERSONAL VALUES IDENTIFICATION WORKSHEET
### (First circle your elected values, then score them per directions.)

| | | |
|---|---|---|
| Accuracy | Financial | Recognition |
| Achievement-Oriented | Growth-Oriented | Reliability |
| Best Investment | High Energy | Respect for Individual |
| Best Products | High Market Perception | Respectability |
| Cohesive | High-Spirited | Responsiveness |
| Commitment | Highest Value | Results-Oriented |
| Compassion | Highly Specialized | Rewarding |
| Consistency | Industry Pioneer | Safe-Choice Provider |
| Cooperation | Industry Standard | Social Responsibility |
| Cost-Effective | Innovation | Solution-Oriented |
| Creativity | Integrity/Honesty | Special Expertise |
| Credibility | Leadership | State-of-the-Art |
| Customer-Oriented | Loyalty | Success-Oriented |
| Customer Service | Market Leader | Supportive |
| Decisive | Most Competitive | Teamwork |
| Dependability | Most Efficient & Effective | Technology-Driven |
| Discipline | Performance-Driven | Trustworthy |
| Empowerment | Proactive | Unique |
| Enthusiasm | Profitability | Visionary |
| Entrepreneurial | Progressive | _____(Your Own) |
| Excellence | Quality | _____(Your Own) |

## Figure 9.2—Group Worksheet for Values Prioritization

| Final* Order | Selected Value | Page 1 of 2 Individual Points Received | Total Points | % of Total Points | # Voters | # First- Place Votes |
|---|---|---|---|---|---|---|
| | | | | | | |
| | | | | | | |
| | | | | | | |
| | | | | | | |
| | | | | | | |
| | | | | | | |
| | | | | | | |
| | | | | | | |
| | | | | | | |
| | | | | | | |
| | | | | | | |
| | | | | | | |
| | | | | | | |
| | | | | | | |
| | | | | | | |
| | | | | | | |
| | | | | | | |
| | | | | | | |
| | | | | | | |
| | | | | | | |

* Fill in after votes have been totalled.

# Figure 9.2—Group Worksheet for Values Prioritization (concluded)

| Final* Order | Selected Value | Page 2 of 2-as needed Individual Points Received | Total Points | % of Total Points | # Voters | # First-Place Votes |
|---|---|---|---|---|---|---|
| | | | | | | |
| | | | | | | |
| | | | | | | |
| | | | | | | |
| | | | | | | |
| | | | | | | |
| | | | | | | |
| | | | | | | |
| | | | | | | |
| | | | | | | |
| | | | | | | |
| | | | | | | |
| | | | | | | |
| | | | | | | |
| | | | | | | |
| | | | | | | |
| | | | | | | |
| | | | | | | |
| | | | | | | |

* Fill in after votes have been totalled.

during the course of the activity. In this way, everyone's votes are conveniently captured. After all of the vote-points have been tabulated and the rest of the form has been completed, the facilitator can make copies of the master summary for each participant so that it is not necessary for everyone to take detailed notes.

## Explanation of the Values Prioritization Form

The following explains the purpose of each column on the form, working by column heading from left to right, and describes how they are used.

**1. Final Order**   This column is for clearly establishing the hierarchy of the group's values. Once all the points have been tabulated in the fourth column (*Total Points*), rank them from "1" to whatever number of values you have recorded. If two values end up in a tie, assign them identical positions. For example if they tie for second place, put a "2" under *Final Order* for each. Since they are the second and third values counted, the next value you would rank "4," not "3." This column has been placed first so that it is easy to spot the top vote-getting values after the worksheet has been completed.

**2. Selected Value**   This box is filled in for every new value that receives a vote for the first time by a contributing participant. The *second* time someone votes, say, for "Responsiveness" with 3 points, you would not write Responsiveness on the form a second time, but simply place a "3" for 3 points in the second small block under the column *Individual Points Received*.

**3. Individual Points Received**   This column provides little boxes per selected value for recording the vote-points of up to ten participants. If more than ten people vote for a value, carefully improvise in a nearby white space.

**4. Total Points**   This column is for the sum of a value's vote-points. Add up the *Individual Points Received* by each value and place in each box as a total. It is the *Total Points* figure that determines the *Final Order*.

| | |
|---|---|
| **5. % of Total Points** | You may find it interesting to add up the total vote-points (it should always be 15 [5+4+3+2+1] times the number of voting participants) and divide into the number of points cast for each value. What you will find is some form of the 80-20 rule (usually more like the 70-30 rule), where 70%-80% of the vote-points are cast for 20%-30% of the values, usually the top 4 or 5 vote-getters. This is important because it helps you determine the degree of values commonality (or variety) among the group partici-pants. |
| **6. # Voters** | This column is derived by adding up the number of filled-in boxes (the number of voters voting on a given value) in the *Individual Points Received* column. Here you are not adding up the points, but simply the number of small *boxes* with points to get the number of *voters*. The more voters, the greater commonality of shared belief in the importance of that value. |
| **7. # First-Place Votes** | What value a person selects as the most important should be carefully noted. To count the number of first-place votes, review the entries down the *Individual Points Received* column, looking for any "5's," which signify a first-place vote. Add up the first-place (5) votes for each value and post the total number in the box in the far right column. As an audit check, the total number in your first-place votes column should equal the total number of parti-cipants taking part in the values exercise of the session. |

Two pages are provided for the Values Prioritization because participants in groups of over ten often will generate more than twenty values, and the form is designed for up to twenty values per page.

Now that the group's values have been identified and prioritized via the above process, it may prove helpful in a group setting to post on a flip chart the top seven to ten values in order of the votes they received. My experience with prioritized values is that to reach such a point on a group level is quite useful because *out of hundreds of possible alternatives in a language of hundreds of thousands of words, the planning group has selected a specific handful they feel are of special importance to them and that reflect their enterprise. It is to these beliefs they aspire, and by which they wish to measure themselves, the organization, and all of its aspects and activities.*

But there is a real shortcoming to leaving values at the level of a short prioritized list. Why? Such a list communicates what values are important, *but does not clarify what relationship these and other values have in relationship to each other.* My Enterprise Values Matrix (Figure 9.4) was developed gradually, client by client from 1989 through 1991, in order to address this important issue.

## The Enterprise Values Matrix

Your clear, prioritized order of unit or company values having been developed, the next step is to determine how they and other identified values interrelate to one another. A good question to ask is this: "What consecutive, cause-and-effect, logical relationship do our selected values have to each other?" For the purpose of building an Enterprise Values Matrix for your team, you first need to classify each of your major selected values in one of the following four categories, using the Preliminary Categorization sheet shown in Figure 9.3.

1. **First Category: Foundational Values**—defined as those values which are the fundamental, preconditional cornerstones upon which all other values stand. These values are like a tea bag in hot water; they osmose and filter into all parts of the enterprise. They are generally deep, subjective *traits,* not action-oriented. They are generally intrinsic elements needed *before* a company opens its doors, sets its course, and does or is anything. Examples of Foundational Values are integrity, respect for the individual, and social responsibility.

2. **Second Category: Service Features Values**—defined as those values which are the major characteristics of your enterprise, products, and/or services. These are the true action values or catalytic values that operate in execution of your enterprise's vision and mission. Examples of Service Features Values include innovation, efficiency/effectiveness, responsiveness, and reliability. These should be filled into your Enterprise Values Matrix from left to right, in logical order. For example, using the Service Features Values above: Innovation breeds productive people...breeds highest efficiency/effectiveness...breeds responsiveness...breeds reliability."

## Figure 9.3—Preliminary Categorization for Enterprise Values Matrix

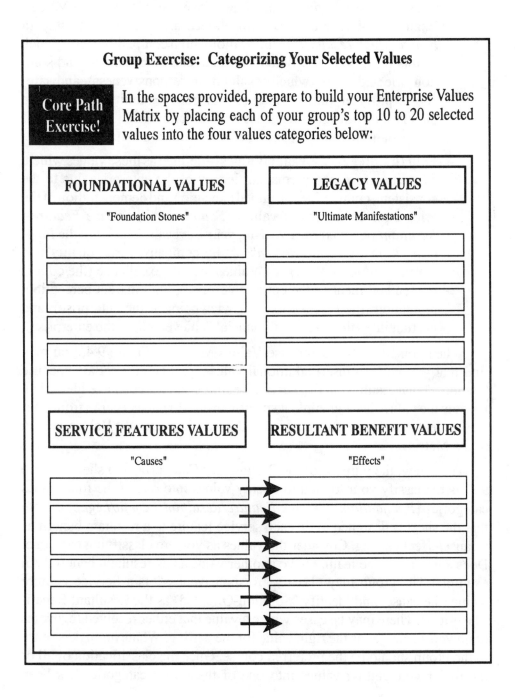

**Group Exercise: Categorizing Your Selected Values**

**Core Path Exercise!**

In the spaces provided, prepare to build your Enterprise Values Matrix by placing each of your group's top 10 to 20 selected values into the four values categories below:

**FOUNDATIONAL VALUES**

"Foundation Stones"

**LEGACY VALUES**

"Ultimate Manifestations"

**SERVICE FEATURES VALUES**

"Causes"

**RESULTANT BENEFIT VALUES**

"Effects"

3. **Third Category: Resultant Benefit Values**—defined as the benefits that result when the Service Features Values are exhibited. These are the true *outcome* values of your Service Feature Values. Examples of Resultant Benefit Values are market leadership (a *benefit* which *results from* innovation), high competitiveness (which results from highest efficiency/effectiveness), customer- and solution-oriented value (which results from responsiveness), and safe-choice provider value (which results from reliability). Do you see the clarity of insight this cause-and-effect ordering may bring? (If not, wait until you see your enterprise values in matrix format!)

4. **Fourth Category: Legacy Values**—defined as those values which, over time, form the permanent legacy of the enterprise due to the consistent, cumulative, sustained execution and demonstration of the prior three categories of values (*Foundational, Service Features, Resultant Benefits*) on a year-in, year-out basis. These are the *long-term, ultimate manifestations* of the company's true quality and worth. Examples of Legacy Values include excellence (the collective embodiment of the entire enterprise), high market perception, reputation (the positive external viewpoint of the enterprise), and profitability (the sustained financial achievement of the enterprise).

When you fill in the Enterprise Values Matrix in Figure 9.4, you may find that you wish to insert additional values, particularly certain specific "Benefits" that result from the Service Features Values you have identified. Review the values list and think of specific results that may accrue from your service features. These can be added in the Resultant Benefit Values section of the Matrix.

To review, the purpose of the Preliminary Categorization sheet (Figure 9.3) is to classify your top ten to twenty values into one of the four values categories (*Foundational/Service Feature/Resultant Benefit/Legacy*). Note that the sheet is designed to tie each service feature to a resultant benefit as a cause/effect pairing. Consider the values as you are classifying each one: Does a given service feature have another value as its resultant benefit? An example: The group may classify "Responsiveness" as a Service Feature Value (the cause) and identify "Solution-Oriented" as the Resultant Benefit (the effect). There may be cases where a value that either received few votes or no votes emerges as the right value for the pairing. Whatever makes sense to the group should be the preferred course. Once the classification of all or the major vote-getting values into one of these four categories has been

## Figure 9.4—Enterprise Values Matrix

**Group Exercise: Enterprise Values Matrix**

Core Path Exercise!

**Legacy Values**

- _____
- _____
- _____
- _____
- _____

**Resultant Benefit Values**

**Service Feature Values**

**Founda- tional Values**

- _____
- _____
- _____
- _____
- _____

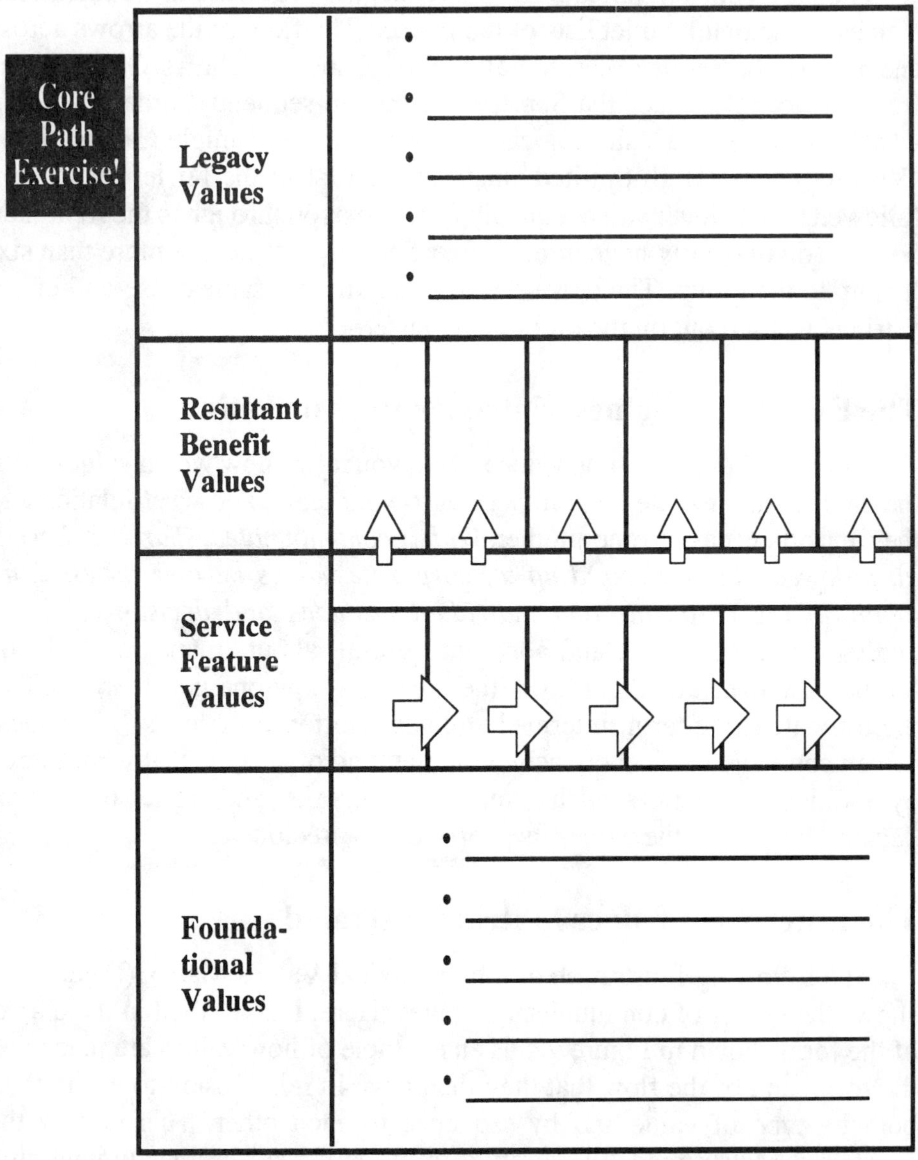

Note: More spaces have been provided than you may need. If you need yet more spaces, please feel free to draw them in!

completed, it is time to fill in the Enterprise Value Matrix itself, which is easy to do.

## Filling Out the Enterprise Value Matrix

Transfer your classifications of the Legacy Values and Foundational Values to the blank bullet lists of the matrix. The flow of the arrows across and up from the Service Feature Values is explained as follows. Going across from left to right, place the Service Features in sequential order, deciding what Service Feature Value logically comes first. For example, "Innovation," "Visionary," or "High-Spirited" may be the first in the far left-hand box, followed by whatever value logically flows next, on through to the right-side boxes. You may only have three or four Service Features, or more than six. It is up to the group. The upward arrows signify the same cause-and-effect pairings worked out on the preliminary sheet.

## The Enterprise Values Matrix: Values in Action

After all of this base-line values work, you now know which values from the values universe are most important to your team, and what relationship they and others have to one another. *Widely communicated, shared, believed-in, followed, and measured up to, corporate values become an essential factor in the corporate and individual attitudes and decisions.* Values cultivation, expectation, and adherence are all about "managing well the journey." Values are about how "the means"—how one gets there—affect the ultimate, long-term, intermediate, and shorter-term "ends." A values-driven company cares about achieving the kind of success that is measured by traditional yardsticks, such as market share, sales, and profits, but it cares *because* it upholds the values its people deem precious.

## The Enterprise Values Matrix Illustrated

The following illustration of a hypothetical Values Matrix (Figure 9.5) shows the power of communicated values. Here, I have filled in the blanks of the form shown in Figure 9.4 as an example of how values are placed on the form, and of the flow that they then have in relationship to each other, both by type of value and by sequence to each other. This is how the Illustrated Matrix reads in narrative form, as if read by the summarizing consultant or CEO:

# Figure 9.5—Enterprise Values Matrix Illustrated

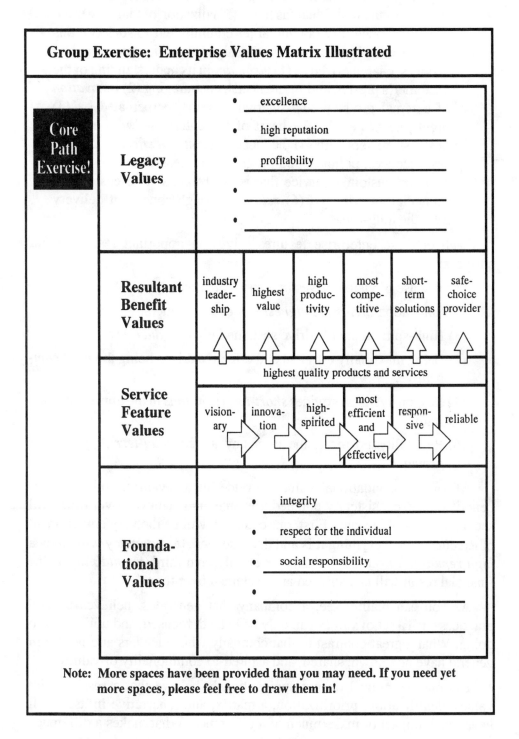

**Group Exercise: Enterprise Values Matrix Illustrated**

**Core Path Exercise!**

**Legacy Values**
- excellence
- high reputation
- profitability
- 
- 

**Resultant Benefit Values**

| industry leader-ship | highest value | high produc-tivity | most compe-titive | short-term solutions | safe-choice provider |

highest quality products and services

**Service Feature Values**

| vision-ary | innova-tion | high-spirited | most efficient and effective | respon-sive | reliable |

**Founda-tional Values**
- integrity
- respect for the individual
- social responsibility
- 
- 

Note: More spaces have been provided than you may need. If you need yet more spaces, please feel free to draw them in!

Based upon a foundation of integrity (as the moral commitment), respect for the individual (as the externalization of that trust), and social responsibility (as the larger commitment to society), this enterprise aspires to provide the highest quality products and services, characterized as (1) *visionary* in its understanding of the customer's present and future needs, encouraging (2) *innovation* of external products and internal systems, perpetuated by (3) *high-spirited* people, the heart of the enterprise, who execute business matters with (4) the most *efficient and effective* processes, practices, policies, and programs, all geared to deliver outstanding customer service that is (5) *responsive* to customers' immediate needs, and (6) *reliable* through consistent delivery over the long-run.

Each of these enterprise features drives an important result for our business:

(1) A sense of vision drives *industry leadership.*

(2) Innovation drives the *highest value* to customers.

(3) High-spirited people drive sustained *high productivity.*

(4) Being maximally efficient and effective drives being the *most competitive.*

(5) Responsiveness provides *short-term solutions* in the immediate time frame.

(6) Reliability positions the company as the *long-term, safe-choice provider.*

All of our foundational values, service-feature values, and resultant-benefit values, consistently pursued, fostered, and achieved over time, will secure a three-fold legacy: First, our company will be the very embodiment of *excellence* in everything it is and does; second, the company will enjoy a *high reputation* from the industry externally; and third, *profitability* as the financial result will be achieved and sustained over time."

As you can plainly see, a company that generates, believes in, and practices such a set of values can only be helped, focused, and uplifted in so doing. What a great contrast to that company whose leaders and people in general have no known, shared, and aspired-to commonality of values.

But one warning: I do not superstitiously believe that a session with values identification, prioritization, a matrix, and a narrative in itself will have much impact or make much of a difference. What makes a difference is a ccmplete dedication by the leadership to "walk the talk," to meet the challenge and communicate within a set of embraced values and dare to live by them and be measured by them.

## Final Values Observations

When done well, values selection helps unify the team members by securing under them a solid common foundation and frame of reference for conducting business. There are also side benefits. One side benefit is the clarity of meaning that results when vague values terms, such as "excellence" or "quality," are explicitly defined and a common understanding of what they specifically mean is established. In Figure 9.5, "quality" has six feature characteristics under it. "Excellence" has the entire underpart of the matrix defining and producing it. Another side benefit is that by clearly defining values, audits on adherence to values can be held in future years to see to what degree the company's values are known and, most importantly, manifested throughout the organization.

All in all, values are a great place from which to launch the enterprise on its strategic journey, much in the same way as the development and documentation of the Constitution launched the United States on its new journey as a nation. And from a personal and group-dynamics standpoint, working and agreeing on a set of shared values not only galvanizes the team, but releases the flow of creative, channeled, congruent energy to develop the successive phases of the strategic plan, which are to be covered in the upcoming chapters.

# Chapter Ten

# Setting the Vision

You may share my discomfort with business fads. Whenever nouns become verbs, take notice. "Visioning" has been liberally bandied about the national corporate landscape in recent years. The need for companies and individuals to have a clear and meaningful vision is an unarguable necessity, for as the Book of Proverbs succinctly warns: "Without a vision the people perish, "or "run wild." Such is true of the modern enterprise. The key is to assert the need for a crystal-clear vision and to elevate the quality of that vision above the level of a trendy activity which, performed in ad hoc fashion, causes inadequate communication within an organization thereafter. The vision should be lucid and impactful, and should permeate the organization as an inspiring, focused message that lives and breathes, directing the course of today's business on an inexorably straight path toward the desired end.

Under this general Vision category, three pieces of information interconnect to provide a complete picture of the enterprise. First, the *Business Definition* of the enterprise is determined, answering the question: *"What business are we in?"* Second, the *Long-Range Vision* of the enterprise is identified, answering the question: *"Where are we going?"* Determining Long-Range Vision is like firing a bow-shot across the extending horizon to connect the desired future with the actual present. Third, the *Mission Statement* for the enterprise is generated, answering the question: *"Who are we in light of our defined business and vision?"* This question produces a linking statement, bridging the present to the far future.

For many well-established companies, the Business Definition exercise will be a brief documentation of the obvious. For a new company (or mission) or for a company fundamentally questioning its present scope, this section causes participants to address some fundamental matters.

For companies' planners who want to keep it simple by starting the vision work now and expanding upon it later, I recommend that time and effort primarily be spent on the long-range vision statement. Why? The mission statement, a tactical adaptation of the vision statement, can be developed at a later time. If there are ever any fundamental questions about the structure or foundation of the business, then spending time on the Business Definition is warranted. A brief perusal of the items addressed there will let you know whether or not you need to invest time on Business Definition to address some basic issues.

## The Business Definition

Before an enterprise sets its future course, it must determine specifically what business it is in, like checking the soil underneath before laying the foundation. This usually is a very straightforward process, although it can get complicated (or at least more interesting) when there are different feelings within the group, such as when one or more persons believe that their retail company should also be a wholesaler. The Enterprise Definition Worksheet (Figure 10.1) is straightforward and self-explanatory, as seen on the following pages.

The members of the planning group individually complete their worksheets, then their inputs are ready to be compared. You may find some disparity of inputs, particularly when people think they are in different businesses. For example, someone may respond: "We're in the transportation business." Another may respond: "We are primarily a manufacturer because we make the rail car containers for 30% of the entire market." Or, for an international company, people may not know sales percentages by global geographic region. What can get interesting is when people believe the enterprise should be in activities different than those it presently is in. At the very least these basic matters should be nailed down, or purposely left open for later strategic consideration. Once this business definition work has been done, the planning group can set its sights on its long-term dream, its expectation, aspiration, and ultimate realization: the vision.

## The Need for a Vision Statement

In antiquity, Moses did not merely lead the children of Israel out of Pharaoh's Egypt to escape the harshness and bitterness of life there. He had a driving vision that propelled him and approximately two million people through the wilderness's perils, obstacles, and interim defeats to "a land flowing with milk and honey." This "promised land" was Moses' and the peoples' governing, long-term vision. It was such a distinct, attractive, and compelling vision that it drew them like a powerful magnet through enormous difficulties toward the goal.

As I mentioned earlier, setting a long-term vision should not be approached in a frivolous, episodic (one-time, event-driven) manner. Many of us have been through very disappointing planning sessions, where time was used poorly and the opportunity to make significant progress was missed. Furthermore, when the plans are neglected afterwards, and they usually are, this gives rise to suspicion, then eventually to cynicism and the belief that

## Figure 10.1—Enterprise Definition Worksheet

---

### Personal Exercise: Enterprise Definition Worksheet

1. **Classification:** ☐ For Profit     ☐ Not for Profit

2. **Business Type:** ☐ Incorporated     ☐ Partnership     ☐ Sole Proprietorship

3. **Ownership:** ☐ Publicly Traded     ☐ Privately owned
   (Exchange: _____ )

4. Identify the **Industry Sectors** in which your company participates:

   ☐ Manufacturing    ;   Specifically: 1) _____ 2) _____
   ☐ Services    ;   Specifically: 1) _____ 2) _____
   ☐ Retail Trade    ;   Specifically: 1) _____ 2) _____
   ☐ Finance/Ins./RE    ;   Specifically: 1) _____ 2) _____
   ☐ Transportation/Util. ;   Specifically: 1) _____ 2) _____
   ☐ Wholesale    ;   Specifically: 1) _____ 2) _____
   ☐ Other [1]    ;   Specifically: 1) _____ 2) _____

5. Identify the Enterprise's **Revenue Generation Sources** (Prior Year):

   ☐ Services;      Approx. Percent: ☐ %
   ☐ Consumer Products Mfg.;      Approx. Percent: ☐ %
   ☐ Indus./Commer./Gov't. Products Mfg.;      Approx. Percent: ☐ %

6. Do you know approximately what percentage of your Corporate Sales Revenue is **Value Added** by your Enterprise? [2]

   ☐ % (Note: Finance is a good source for this information)

[1] Agriculture/Forestry/Fishing/Mining/Construction, Misc.
[2] Value Added = Total sales revenues minus outside purchases (for resale).

---

## Figure 10.1—Enterprise Definition Worksheet (concluded)

---

**Personal Exercise:  Enterprise Definition Worksheet (concluded)**

7.  Where are your Enterprises' **Geographic Revenue Bases**?

| | | | |
|---|---|---|---|
| ☐ U.S. & Canada | [ % ] | ☐ Middle/Near East | [ % ] |
| ☐ Europe | [ % ] | ☐ Australia/New Zealand | [ % ] |
| ☐ Central/So. America | [ % ] | ☐ Far East | [ % ] |
| | | ☐ Other Country(ies)[3] | [ % ] |

8.  What is your Product/Service **Life-Cycle Mix**?

Approx. % of Revenue

☐ Introductory Stage        [ % ]
    (New Products/New Markets)

☐ Growth Stage        [ % ]
    (High Change; $\geq$ 10%  Annual Growth)

☐ Maturity Stage        [ % ]
    (Mature Products/Mature Markets)

☐ Decline Stage        [ % ]
    (Aging Products/Shrinking Markets)

9.  **Narrative Summary Draft:**

In your own words, in light of the above, how would you define your enterprise in one to three sentences?

_____

_____

_____

_____

[3] Other = India & Pakistan, Africa, USSR.

---

"this soft planning stuff does not work." Yet we can observe successful companies of many different types and easily see that in one way or another, they are driven by a very clear, overarching vision, especially when effective leadership is at work. How to develop this kind of major, driving, focused vision is what this section addresses.

## The Positioning of the Vision Statement

This part of strategic plan creation is the bluest slice of blue sky you will traverse using my planning technology. Simply stated, the challenge is, *"What is your long-range vision for this enterprise?"* Traveling through the far blue sky can be done via two staightforward steps:

Step 1.   Fill in answers to some helper questions to stir your creative thinking and to form specific thought patches about your future vision for the enterprise.

Step 2.   Weave these patches together to formulate a succinct 25-to 45-word statement that crystallizes, in your leadership team's own words, your long-term vision.

When the planning group locks in on a vision statement, the statement combined with the Values Matrix already developed will generate a tremendous surge of momentum that will launch the enterprise headlong into strategic thinking and planning, paving the way for development of the specific goals and actions that will comprise the heart of the plan. You are in for a special experience if you have not yet tapped the latent and enormous energy that invigorates an organization which formulates and shares vibrant values and vision statements. The energizing effect of doing so is like putting a turbo-charger inside the corporate engine!

Ideally, every team "down and across" the enterprise should have its own vision and values for the particular business goals it is responsible for and must accomplish, all in concert with the overall vision and values set. At every level of the business, there needs to be vision and values involvement and synergy. This is an important point, which is reflected on a smaller scale by the following illustration. If twenty people in a leadership planning session each developed a vision statement on their own and then, one by one, read them to the group, the degree of diversity and the varying focus and content of their individual visions would contribute to teambuilding; but if the activity was left at that stage, the team would not reach closure to the degree necessary for it to achieve the larger team synergy that enables the enterprise to move forward together as one entity.

One can make a good case for the idea that the flow from business definition to mission to vision are steps toward corporate self-actualization. The company starts out in the present, doing what it does here and now. It has a vision of the eventual destination, its corporate fulfillment. It has a mission that acts as a tactical ladder, building upon the present and reaching into the near-future, taking "the next steps." *But out of tens of thousands of companies "out there," how many take the first step of really understanding the business they are in? Of these, how many have clear long-term vision statements? Of that group, how many have clear, documented mission statements for their short-term direction?* When developed and used well, these "advanced degrees of corporate self-consciousness and far-seeing direction" absolutely are strategic weapons, or, in more benign terms, actual differentiators which distinguish the company who uses them from other companies in the same industry and markets who do not use them. Additionally, many positive cultural benefits derive from genuine vision development, such as high-spiritedness, morale, an exciting and enjoyable workplace, and a sense of professional meaning and purpose.

## Long-Range Vision Determination Worksheet

The worksheet in Figure 10.2 asks a series of questions, answerable by brief phrases, to help you zero in on your individual sense of vision for your organization. Each group participant should complete this worksheet.

*Primary product(s) or service(s)* addresses what your major deliverable(s) will be in the long-term future. It may be the same as today's, slightly changed, or altogether different. *Primary market(s)* addresses in what sphere you will compete. *Primary customer(s)* addresses who is the primary recipient of your products and/or services. The *exclusive, differentiating benefit* identifies what you do that is special, different, and better than the competition. *Geographic coverage* answers the important questions: Are you primarily local, regional, multi-regional, national, or international? Exactly where will you be operating? How big the enterprise will be in five years is a very important matter, for it implies how fast you envision growth in sales, people, and locations. *Competitive position* addresses your anticipated standing among your competitors in five years, as leader, pioneer, niche specialist, middle-of-the-pack member, or follower. *Special factors* addresses any

**Figure 10.2—Long-Range Vision Determination Worksheet**

---

**Personal Exercise:  Long-Range Vision Determination Worksheet**
**page 1 of 2**

1.  Long-Range Vision elements:

    **Directions:**  For each of the following, develop a brief, simple phrase.

    a.  What will your **primary product(s) or service(s)** be in five years?

    _____

    b.  What will be your **primary market(s)** be in five years?

    _____

    c.  Who will your **primary customer(s)** be in five years?

    _____

    d.  What will your **exclusive, differentiating benefit** be in five years?

    _____

    e.  What will the **geographic coverage** of your enterprise (local/regional/national/multinational/global) be in five years?

    _____

    f.  How big do you see the enterprise in five years in:

    i.   Total Sales:              $  _____
    ii.  Total # Employees          _____
    iii. Total # Locations          _____
    iv.  Types of Locations:        _____
         (Mfg., Distrib., Sales,    _____
         Service, HQ, etc.)         _____

---

**Figure 10.2—Long-Range Vision Determination Worksheet
(concluded)**

---

**Personal Exercise: Long-Range Vision Determination Worksheet** (concluded)
**page 2 of 2**

---

    g.  What do you perceive your **competitive position** will be in five years
        (leader, middle pack, follower, pioneer, niche specialist, etc.)?

        _____

    h.  What kind of **special factors** (culture/unique approaches) will make
        the far-future enterprise a very special work experience?

        _____

2.  Long-Range Vision Determination:

    **Directions:**  Selecting from any combination of the above inputs, please list your
                 Long-Term Enterprise Vision. Be simple and brief in expressing
                 the concept.

    a.  Long-Term Vision Draft:

        _____

        _____

        _____

    b.  Long-Term Vision Final Personal Version:

        _____

        _____

        _____

additional considerations not covered above that are important. This may include unique cultural or other organizational characteristics.

Five years is the recommended frame of reference for the determination of a long-range vision because if your time frame is too close to the present, your thinking will extrapolate from the status quo, carrying forward the same kind of business that you now have. If it is set too far in the future, for instance at seven or ten years, your mind will have difficulty grasping the time frame, and your thinking will be clouded by a sense of the unreal or the unimaginable. *Between these extremes, five years is a reasonable planning time frame, dislodging the participant from the realm of today while focusing him or her on an imaginable future.*

After answering these first eight vision-positioning questions, you can pull your thoughts together via a Long-Term Vision Draft. Once you have gotten your basic thoughts together, space is provided for your Final Personal Version.

## The Group's Long-Range Vision Statement Development

Once the group participants have drafted their own vision statements to whatever degree of final vision or completeness, their vision drafts can be shared. The group worksheet in Figure 10.3 captures helpful phrases from the various participants' answers and statements. Then, through considerable dialogue, the collective vision draft is hammered out. This can be done by voting on the contributed phrases in order to determine which phrases are most expressive of the group's vision definition. Eventually, the final group vision statement is formulated. I recommend that the final organization vision statement be between 25 and 45 words—no longer than that overall length. Why? Long, rambling statements are usually so because they have not been molded enough. The words do not carry enough weight or bear enough freight, and/or there is excessive detail or redundancy. I have found that excessive words add little more than "smoke," not elucidation or clarification. With sufficient creativity and labor, a final vision statement of the recommended length is possible.

Some final notes: You may find that the formats covered in the upcoming Mission Statement sections are helpful in your Vision Statement work. Why? Because these sections provide prescriptive help with how to structure the statement phrase by phrase; although Vision and Mission Statement *content* may differ, the sentence *structure* may be similar.

### Figure 10.3—Long-Range Vision Group Selection Worksheet

---

**Group Exercise: Long-Range Vision Group Selection**

| | |
|---|---|
| Exercise Directions:<br><br> | Now that each session participant has drafted his or her Long-Range Vision Statement, the next step is to go around the participant group, and, one by one, each person who has a Long-Range Vision drafted can read it to the group. After each reading, the group can highlight any aspects or phrases that capture the greater group sense as being part of the ultimate Vision. The Facilitator then writes these key phrases for all of the group to see. Then, after all have read their Vision Statements and key thoughts have been recorded, the group is to hammer out an inclusive Long-Term Vision Statement that conveys the group's collective view for the future enterprise. |

1. Key Vision Phrases from Fellow Participants:

    a. _____

    b. _____

    c. _____

    d. _____

    e. _____

    f. _____

    g. _____

---

## Figure 10.3—Long-Range Vision Group Selection Worksheet (concluded)

**Group Exercise: Long-Range Vision Group Selection (concluded)**

2.  Draft Combined Statement:

_____

_____

_____

_____

_____

_____

_____

3.  Final Long-Term Vision Statement:

_____

_____

_____

_____

_____

_____

_____

Also, remember that it is only the degree to which you *use* your developed Vision Statement that will have a living and lasting effect on your organization. If the vision statement is not communicated, not referenced in day-to-day life—written, internalized, integrated, and institutionalized (treated as more than a "museum artifact" in the corporate lobby)—the likelihood of the vision being fulfilled is highly unlikely. Treat your organization vision statement as the precious and powerful down-payment on your collective future that it truly can be if utilized properly.

## The Mission Statement

With the formation of a vision statement, the bulk of your "visioning" work is now completed. You have defined the context of your business and sketched a blueprint for the future. The mission statement is the logical connecting bridge between where you are at this time and where you want to be in the eventual future. It too should be "short and sweet" and specific, neither broad and fluffy on one extreme nor narrow and restrictive on the other. *Hence, your enterprise mission statement should have the ring of authenticity and specificity, capturing who you are and what you do in the short-term tactical period (2 to 3 years).*

## Mission Statement Generation

On an individual basis, your task is simply to chart out a phrase or two for each of the mission aspects requested on the Mission Statement Components Worksheet (Figure 10.4). Then, the group will discuss the material generated by the worksheets, selecting and combining the most useful phrases into one coherent statement.

Since the approach for building the mission statement can also be used for developing the vision statement, we will provide the details for how to construct a statement from scratch. First of all, I can tell you from many hours of experience facilitating the building of vision and/or mission statements that the process is not a simple one. There are several reasons for this overall difficulty: (1) Each person has his or her own style, way of thinking, and choice words and phrases; (2) as words express people's concepts, so the variety of ways people think is reflected in a wide variety of written statements; (3) some people have great difficulty putting their thoughts into words, and in doing so quickly; (4) many people have a hard time moving out of the framework of "today" into the far future (vision) and mid-future (mission); (5) some people feel very strongly about their own way of stating things, to the point where they become stylistically inflexible and rigid, expecting that their statement draft will be the basis, or model, for the group; (6) some people tackle only a small part of the vision, which, as valuable as that part may be, can pose problems; (7) because people spend so little time considering the future, there is a very significant variety of, even fundamentally different views about, the future, from size, to content, to priority and focus issues.

In light of these factors, building a statement seems daunting. I literally use a "divide and conquer" method to get the job done in a time- efficient manner. By this I do not mean that I divide the group to conquer it, but that I divide the statement's creation up into manageable pieces. The approach has two aspects. I highly recommend that whether you are an executive, manager, professional leader, or external resource, you consider the following approach for many kinds of group discussions and projects.

First, get as many participants as possible to provide "simple, brief phrases" that they really like. Collect these phrases by writing them down on a flip chart. Second, after collecting a good list (10 to 15 long) of phrases (or items of any kind for that matter), give each participant 3 or 5 votes for selecting the phrases that the person most likes. Go from phrase to phrase, asking for total votes for each one. The phrases with the highest votes can form the heart of, a part of, or all of the mission or vision statement. This method: (1) breaks the ice in creative thinking; (2) gets many people to participate; (3) "lowers the bar" from generation of a complete statement draft to contribution of a small phrase, focusing on a more attainable level; (4) isolates small chunks, not long thoughts; (5) gives everyone votes for selecting their favorites, and (6) narrows the total list of candidates to a short list of attractive phrases for continued discussion as the team moves toward formation of a coherent statement.

## Using the Components Worksheet

The Mission Statement Components Worksheet (Figure 10.4) is divided into three sections so that individuals can develop phrases for three important aspects of the statement.

The first aspect of the mission statement identifies "what your company does." You can see from the details under that section and the following two sections that the assistance is very prescriptive, right down to sentence syntax. Why? Because of the difficulty most people have with honing their ideas to produce a *short* statement, compressing so many thoughts, ideas, opportunities, and word options into just a few phrases. I am sure many readers share a concern of mine that phrases or words used in statement development will sound too generic or clichéd. But remember, as less than 5% of people have goals and less than 3% have written goals, so *very few companies, departments, or work teams have anything written down and used as a commonly held vision or mission statement.* Therefore, even if you feel your team's statement draft is a bit too non-specific or general, remember that it is a start, a draft, and brings you to a much better place than if you "held things up in committee" or did nothing at all! Of course, your aim should be to describe those special, unique, differentiating sparks, essences, or directions that communicate your true corporate individuality.

The second and third sections of the Components Worksheet address what the results are for all concerned and, if appropriate, what the underlying values or beliefs are. The generic example would then read:

> *XYZ Company delivers performance technologies and profitability systems, resulting in enhanced performance for our clients and proper returns for our stockholders, based upon a foundation of integrity and respect for the individual.*

This statement is 32 words in length, meeting the 25- to 45-word rule. You can see the density and economy of the message: (1) 13 nouns are used, supported by specific modifications; (2) these words cover many bases, including what the company's business is, who all of the beneficiaries are and how they benefit, and what intrinsic values are most important to the company's people. This single sentence delivers a message that indicates purpose, balance, and uniqueness, which is the goal of both the mission statement and vision statement.

It is useful to tie these points together with those made in the prior section on Vision, and to compare the Statement Vision and the Mission Statement so that each can be further distinguished. *By comparison, the Vision Statement is more long-term, more broad, more overarching, more grand, inspiring, and ultimate. The Mission Statement, in contrast, is more short-term, more narrow or specific, more incremental, more practical, descriptive, and focused.*

## Mission Statement Generation

With all of the matters on constructing useful statements now covered, you and your team have the tools to generate a solid mission statement. The personal preparatory work has been completed and you should have a list of

## Figure 10.4—Mission Statement Components Worksheet

---

**Personal Exercise:  Mission Statement Components Worksheet**

Fill in a phrase or two answering each of the following:

1.   What your company does: ("Your Enterprise") (verb) (adjective and noun) "and" (adjective and noun).  (EG: "XYZ company delivers performance technologies and profitability systems")

 a.   _____

 b.   _____

2.   What are the results to your customers, company, and/or others (society, owners, etc.)? ("resulting in") (noun benefit) "for" (first constituency) "and" (noun benefit") "for" (second constituency).  (EG: "resulting in enhanced performance for our clients and proper returns for our stockholders")

 a.   _____

 b.   _____

3.   Optional:  What are the underlying values or beliefs upon which the above is made? ("based upon a foundation of") (value #1) "and" (value #2).  (EG: "based upon a foundation of integrity and respect for the individual")

 a.   _____

 b.   _____

---

phrases that were "voted in" from the Mission Statement Components Worksheet. The two-page group worksheet, Mission Statement Generation (Figure 10.5), serves simply to log in the most attractive phrases from that list in parts 1, 2, and 3 of the worksheet's first page. Then, parts 4 and 5 provide spaces for the draft and final mission statements.

## Final Thoughts

Of all that has been said regarding Vision and Mission Statements, the netted-out message is simply: *These statements are not easy to develop, but if done patiently and used well, they provide a major, meaningful influence to set and pursue an organization's strategic and tactical direction.*

## Figure 10.5—Mission Statement Generation

---

**Group Exercise:  Mission Statement Generation**

Exercise Directions:  Utilizing the categories of phrases generated by individual participants, the strategic team may now forge the Enterprise Mission Statement.  Phrases of like kinds should be gathered, then discussed.  The goal is a simple yet descriptive and unique statement describing your company.

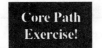

---

**Group Exercise:  Mission Statement Generation Worksheet**

1.  Good "What your enterprise does" phrases:

    a. _____

    b. _____

    c. _____

2.  Good "What are the results..." phrases:

    a. _____

    b. _____

    c. _____

3.  Good "What are the underlying values..." phrases:

    a. _____

    b. _____

    c. _____

---

## Figure 10.5—Mission Statement Generation (concluded)

| Group Exercise:  Mission Statement Generation Worksheet (concluded) |
|---|
| 4.   Draft Mission Statement (less than 30 words): <br><br> _____ <br><br> _____ <br><br> _____ <br><br> _____ <br><br> _____ <br><br><br> 5.   Final Mission Statement: <br><br> _____ <br><br> _____ <br><br> _____ <br><br> _____ <br><br> _____ |

# Chapter Eleven

# An Introduction to Environmental Variables

We have now covered the Valuation, Values, and Vision components of Venue One, the Origination Venue. The last major component of Venue One, a component that can have an effect on all the elements of the Venue, is appropriately named *Variables*. Variables encompass a variety of major and complementary internal and external factors, one or more of which may be a significant driving force to the enterprise. They are defined as follows:

### Definition of a Driving Force Variable

*A driving force variable is defined as that internal or external factor which has the executive attention, significant influence, and pronounced effect upon the enterprise.*

In addressing driving forces, I have replaced the old, widely known, and (I believe) inadequate "eleven driving-force types" used for decades (one of which was "natural resources," a major dependency of the industrial revolution) with twelve clear, complementary, and intuitive environmental factors, each of which may or may not be a driving force depending upon the company.

In this section on environmental variables, first we will identify the twelve major kinds of factors—six of them internal and six of them external to the enterprise. Then you will be introduced to an analysis that helps first the individual and then the group determine which of these factors are driving forces having the greatest influences upon the enterprise.

This first section provides you with a set of wide-angle binoculars through which to view your corporate environmental landscape in general. In future chapters several very important environmental arenas will be explored in greater detail. Remember the purpose and context of this Variables step: to take complete stock of where your organization is in the "here and now" before making plans for the future. Because many companies have the tendency not to see much of what is beyond "their four walls," this stage of the process is the right time to utilize the "sky hook" to lift the strategic participants out of their personal, departmental, or corporate walls in order to view the bigger picture. Directly after our coverage of Variables, when there is a clear understanding of the entire "environmental waterfront" facing the company, we move to the stage of selecting the optimal strategic opportunities for the enterprise.

## The Twelve Environmental Factors

With the passage of time, business life seemingly becomes more complicated. Just the thought of sifting through the unordered myriad of factors operative in an enterprise's internal and external environment is wearisome, quickly inspiring the wise planning participant to seek a good aerial vantage point! This section introduces a complete driving force assessment system that in a brand new way classifies the universe of factors (and potential driving forces) into twelve categories—six internal and six external—which can then be prioritized and analyzed in light of their relative value to and impact on the enterprise.

### The Internal Factors

The first group of environmental elements I call the Internal Factors. They are

1. **Human Resources: The *people* of the enterprise as factor**
   This factor includes executive, management, and employee capability, functional capabilities (sales, marketing, production, service, research and development, purchasing, finance and accounting, human resources, distribution, and so forth), motivation, compensation, loyalty, morale, culture, productivity, professional-ism, labor, training, education, skills, subcontracted support, and development.

   Essentially, the human resources factor includes anything directly related to *people* that has an influence upon the organization.

2. **Products and Services: The *deliverables* of the enterprise as factor**
   This factor includes all products and services of all kinds and stages intended for, marketed to, sold to, and supported after sale to customers of all kinds, from the stages of research, development, introduction, growth, middle life, renovation, extention, decline, replacement, and retirement. This section also includes the specific ways in which products and services are affected by aspects of industry, niche, market, mix, role, and share dynamics, as well as diversification, divestment, and acquisition.

   Essentially, the products and services factor includes anything related to the *deliverables* of the organization that has an influence on the organization.

3. **Organizational Culture and Climate: The *values* of the organization as factor**

   This factor includes everything to do with the intrinsic essence, the heart and soul of the enterprise, including the beliefs, norms, standards, expectations, people policies, political realities, myths, ways, rules, traditions, customs, recognition, rewards, and mores.

   Essentially, the organizational culture and climate factor includes anything related to the *values* of the organization that has an influence on the organization.

4. **Policy: The *objectives* of the enterprise as factor**

   This factor includes all internal policies, principles, priorities, plans, assumptions, strategies, programs, audits, and controls related to business and financial matters. Key targets and measurements include sales, expense, profit, asset, liability, equity, cash flow, and tax matters, and capital, return-on-investment, stock, risk, market, and historical actuals, plans, objectives, and performance.

   Essentially, the policy factor includes anything related to the *objectives* of the organization that has an influence on the organization.

5. **Technology: The *internal investment* of the enterprise as factor**

   This factor includes anything put into the business of a greater than annual expense nature, including new research and development, equipment, capital, major software, hardware, telecommunications, and any other capitalizable, multi-year, large-sum business inputs.

   Essentially, the technology factor includes anything related to the *internal investment* of the organization that has an influence on the organization.

6. **Infrastructure: The *internal operating capability* of the enterprise as factor**

   This factor includes anything that contributes to the internal corporate "skeleton," the existing operational systems, information systems structure, software, programs, procedures, practices, protocol, technical processes, functional organizations, interfaces, technical communications, engineering, manufacturing, distribution, robotic processes already in operational use, all cumulatively forming the basic internal capability of the enterprise.

   Essentially, the infrastructure factor includes anything related to the *internal systems and operations* of the organization that has an influence on the organization.

## The External Factors

The second group of environmental elements I call the External Factors. They are

1. **Customers: The *buyers* of the enterprise as a factor**
   This factor includes everything related to that individual who is first a prospect and eventually a purchaser of the enterprise's products or services. On one side, this factor includes all customer micro-demographics (as contrasted with large-market, macro-considerations), micro-psychographics, preferences, research, trends, tastes, and expectations; on the other side, it includes contacts, compliments, complaints, follow-ups, communications, cross-selling, and complete servicing.

   Essentially, the customer factor includes everything related to the *buyers* of the organization's products and services that has an influence on the organization.

2. **Markets: The *external strategies* of the enterprise as factors**
   This factor includes everything related to the aggregate territory or territories in which the enterprise's products and/or services are made available for purchase, including all of the ways they can be channeled, such as geographic, segmentation, differentiation, specialization, concentration, vertical and horizontal integration, positioning, and strategy dimensions.

   Essentially, the markets factor includes everything that is related to the *external strategies* of the organization as a factor.

3. **Social: The *societal needs* as an enterprise factor**
   This factor includes everything related to overall social trends, macro-demographics, macro-psychographics, lifestyles, niches, ages, preferences, interest and pressure groups, population categories, moral, spiritual, recreational, leisure, environmental needs and directions on international, national, regional, and local levels.

   Essentially, the social factor includes everything that is related to the *societal needs* as an organization influence.

4. **Public Sector: The *government* as an enterprise factor**
   This factor includes everything related to international, national, state, and local laws, politics, legislation, regulation, and judicial activity.

Essentially, the public sector factor includes everything that is related to all forms of the *government* as an enterprise factor.

5. **Competition: Your *market's participants* as an enterprise factor**
This factor includes everything related to those entities in your markets that vie for the same buyers that you do and includes their characteristics, strengths, weaknesses, successes, failures, leadership, product and service features, organization, market share, strategies, track record, opportunities, threats, market share, innovations, and your various responses to them in the market, including growth, attack/retreat/differentiation/marketing strategies and options.

Essentially, the competition factor includes everything that is related to your *market's participants* as an enterprise factor.

6. **Economy: The *business environment* as an enterprise factor**
This factor includes everything related to international, national, regional, and local economies, policies, and trends, including inflation, deflation, monetary policy, employment, unemployment, macro-market cyclicality, interest rates, credit availability, bank strength, exchange rates, currencies, tax policies, financial markets and exchanges.

Essentially, the economy factor includes everything that is related to the *business environment* as an enterprise factor.

## The Linkage of Internal and External Factors

The twelve environmental factors we have just reviewed—six internal and six external—can be paired off logically in complementary fashion, as shown below:

| Pair # | Internal Factor | External Factor | Linkage |
|---|---|---|---|
| 1. | Human Resources | Customers | The *Human* Factor |
| 2. | Products and Services | Markets | The *Delivery* Factor |
| 3. | Culture and Climate | Social | The *Psychological* Factor |
| 4. | Policy | Public Sector | The *Agenda* Factor |
| 5. | Technology | Competition | The *Alternatives* Factor |
| 6. | Infrastructure | Economy | The *Structural* Factor |

141

These factors do not mirror each other in an abstruse, academic kind of way, but in actuality. When I ask my clients to rank these twelve factors in order to determine which of the twelve truly are driving forces for the enterprise, often the strategic planning participants rank human resources and customers in the top two to four places of the twelve. Why? The human factor is unique and special because people drive all of the other ten factors, and hence, are the primary factors in the eyes of many strategic participants.

The other pairs of internal and external factors all reinforce in their own ways the point made with this first pair: *The inside and the outside of an organization are in specific ways symmetrical to each other. The enterprise is a microcosm of the business world. Both the enterprise and the business world have human, delivery, psychological, agenda, alternative, and structural factors. The main difference is one of scale and scope, not of nature or essence.* Accordingly, what drives the business world generally may often drive the individual enterprise specifically. For example, the nationwide decrease of available talent in certain business skills actually may be felt by an individual enterprise's human resource executive who, responsible for fulfilling the company's hiring needs, is having difficulty finding a skill type identified in the overall shortage.

Recognizing that each of these twelve environmental factors has some influence and effect upon an organization is important in itself. How much influence each one has sends certain messages. Learn always to ask why. Also, whether a company has a preponderance of internal driving forces or external driving forces is significant, as well as if one or two factors are of preeminent importance. How these factors' importance shifts over time due to internal and external changes is yet another important trend to track year-by-year.

## The Factor Analysis Exercise

The following exercise helps first the individual and then the group generate a ranking of what factors are driving forces, ordering the twelve from top to bottom.

*The concept of the Environmental Factor Analysis exercise (Figure 11.1) is to choose each factor against every other factor.* The exercise is completed by going down the left-hand side of the matrix row by row and placing an "X" in every box where the item to the left is more important than the item on the top. If the item on the left is *not* more important than the item on the top, leave it blank. Notice that this matrix is logically set up so that if you

## Figure 11.1—Environmental Factors Analysis Worksheet

| Personal Exercise: Environmental Factors Analysis Worksheet | | | | | | | | | | | | | | | |
|---|---|---|---|---|---|---|---|---|---|---|---|---|---|---|---|
| **Factor** | Human Resources | Product & Services | Culture & Climate | Policy | Technology | Infrastructure | Customers | Markets | Social | Public Sector | Competition | Economy | | Total "X's" | Ranking | |
| **Human Resources** | ■ | | | | | | | | | | | | | | | |
| **Products & Services** | | ■ | | | | | | | | | | | | | | |
| **Culture & Climate** | | | ■ | | | | | | | | | | | | | |
| **Policy** | | | | ■ | | | | | | | | | | | | |
| **Technology** | | | | | ■ | | | | | | | | | | | |
| **Infrastructure** | | | | | | ■ | | | | | | | | | | |
| **Customers** | | | | | | | ■ | | | | | | | | | |
| **Markets** | | | | | | | | ■ | | | | | | | | |
| **Social** | | | | | | | | | ■ | | | | | | | |
| **Public Sector** | | | | | | | | | | ■ | | | | | | |
| **Competition** | | | | | | | | | | | ■ | | | | | |
| **Economy** | | | | | | | | | | | | ■ | | | | |
| | | | | | | | | | | | | | ■ | | | |
| | | | | | | | | | | | | | | ■ | | |

(Note: Notice that in the logic of the way this matrix is set-up, if you mark one item "*a* over *b*" the first time, when the two are paired again (*b* with *a*) then that second time you would leave a blank in that space.)

mark item *a* with an "X" the first time that it is compared with *b,* when those two are compared again (*b* with *a*) you would leave the space blank. For example, you will begin using the matrix by moving across the horizontal row of boxes that extend to the right of "Human Resources," marking your choices as you proceed to link this factor with those that head the vertical columns of boxes. If you choose "Human Resources" over "Products and Services" and place an "X" in the appropriate box, your choice is made. If you later, when working through the "Products and Services" row, mark the box that links this factor with "Human Resources," you will contradict yourself and your matrix will not present a clear picture of your preferences. Also, note that the two triangles formed by the descending diagonal from the top left to the bottom right are the exact opposites of each other. In other words, if you were to fold the matrix on the black diagonal line, the "X's" placed on either side of the diagonal will fill in every box. All said, the simple rule of thumb is that if the pair has an "X" in the top combination's space, it has a blank in the bottom combination's space.

After you have filled out the matrix according to the above directions, add up the "X's" in each row and place the sum in the **Total "X's"** column. After each row has been added up, rank the factors from "1" for first place (greatest sum of "X's") to "12" for twelfth place (lowest sum of "X's").

## A Shortcut Method

If you do not wish to spend the time ranking the twelve environmental factors in the rigorous method described above, where each factor is brought up for selection with every other, you can perform a simple ranking. The method is to select the first, most important factor, asking yourself: "If I only had *one* factor to select among the twelve, which one would I select above all others as the greatest driving force to the organization?" Then ask yourself: "If I had a *second* environmental factor to select among the remaining eleven, which one would it be?" You can continue this process down to the eleventh factor. If you get stuck, you can continue in reverse, asking: "What is the twelfth, the least pressing or consequential, environmental factor?" Then, continue with the eleventh, the tenth, and so forth. Your scores can be posted in the large, far right-hand column. I have found this method to be efficient and effective as a quick exercise if time is limited for the group planning process.

## Group Factors Consensus

When participants in the planning group have completed their individual factors analysis, their scores can be posted on the following Group Factors Consensus Worksheet (Figure 11.2). Each individual's ranked factors are posted as numbers from one to twelve, each placed in his or her own column. The form has ten columns, but if your planning session has more than ten participants, you can draw additional lines from top to bottom to create more input columns. Once all participants' rankings are filled in, simply add up the numbers row by row, factor by factor. Enter the total number in the *Totals* column to the right. Once each factor's totals have been added up, you can either divide those totals by the number of participants and then rank them from first (lowest points) to twelfth, or rank them directly from the vote totals, whichever you prefer. The ranking is done like the results from a cross-country race: The lower score is better because first place is only 1 point, second is 2 points, down to twelfth, which is 12 points.

## Analyzing the Group Environmental Factors Data

You have now clearly identified which environmental factors have a driving-force impact upon your enterprise. The question to ask regarding your top drivers is *why* each plays the important role it does. In an executive strategic planning session, a client of mine, one of the large national residential real estate brokerage companies, voted "human resources" as its primary driving force. Its second driving force was "customers." It became clear to what extent this company truly is in the people business: Externally, it is driven by its end-customers; internally, it is driven by its employees and associates. The healthy fact of the matter is that the executives *realize* how important the human dimension is to its company and in its industry.

There are several very useful ways to assess the environmental factors' group rankings:

1. Determine as a group *why each factor was prioritized as it was.* Address issues and differences among individuals' rankings if participants want to discuss their own rankings.

2. Look at the amount of *points* (or tenths of points if you divided by the number of participants) *between each factor.* Usually, you will find that the twelve factors cluster into anywhere between four to six tiers of data. The next question is, "Why did each group cluster together in the same tier of results?" Usually, there are some enlightening reasons underneath the surface results.

## Figure 11.2—Group Factors Consensus Worksheet

| Group Exercise: Factors Consensus | |
|---|---|
| Exercise Directions:<br><br>**Core Path Exercise!** | Now that each individual has completed the Factors Analysis, summarize your findings to determine the group's aggregate inputs. Write in each individual input below and summarize. |

| Participants'<br>Priorities<br><br>**Factor:** | 1 | 2 | 3 | 4 | 5 | 6 | 7 | 8 | 9 | 10 | Totals | ÷ By # | Rank |
|---|---|---|---|---|---|---|---|---|---|---|---|---|---|
| **Human Resources** | | | | | | | | | | | | | |
| **Products & Services** | | | | | | | | | | | | | |
| **Culture & Climate** | | | | | | | | | | | | | |
| **Policy** | | | | | | | | | | | | | |
| **Technology** | | | | | | | | | | | | | |
| **Infrastructure** | | | | | | | | | | | | | |
| **Customers** | | | | | | | | | | | | | |
| **Markets** | | | | | | | | | | | | | |
| **Social** | | | | | | | | | | | | | |
| **Public Sector** | | | | | | | | | | | | | |
| **Competition** | | | | | | | | | | | | | |
| **Economy** | | | | | | | | | | | | | |
| | | | | | | | | | | | | | |
| | | | | | | | | | | | | | |

3. The third angle of analysis is also a very helpful one: Which group of factors ranked as more of an *aggregate driving force: internal or external?* Remember that, of the twelve environmental factors, six are internal factors and six are external. Go down the list of twelve factors (on the Factor Analysis Worksheet, the first six are internal and the second six are external). Which group of factors ranked as more of an aggregate driving force: internal or external?

In the case of my residential real estate client, the findings were striking. Four of the top six factors, including the second, third, and fourth, were external drivers. It was clear that the company recognizes its preeminent need to attract and retain the topmost human talent to meet the aggregate *external* demands placed upon it.

Some companies are more self-absorbed, more internally driven, while others are more externally oriented, and yet others are evenly driven. Over dozens of clients, I have seen that trends occur by industry. For example, to continue with my earlier reference, companies in the real estate industry typically rate the economy much higher than most other companies outside of real estate would rate it. This seems logical enough, because real estate, along with the automobile industry, has long been a bellwether of the overall direction of the economy, and it invariably experiences the undulatory peaks and valleys much more dramatically than many other industries.

## Driving Forces Summary

What at the beginning of this chapter may have seemed like a fairly academic exercise is, in the end, an invaluable determination of the most pressing, real-life issues of the individual company's own business. What starts out as a generic bunch of *"environmental factors"* is sorted out, converted, and reduced from one to four true *"driving forces."* Once identified and understood, the major strategic question is, "How can our strategies best accommodate or leverage these known driving forces?" The answers to that question may well contribute to the major strategic goals to be locked in later during the upcoming Venue Two Goals Section.

# Chapter Twelve

# Deeper Internal
# Environmental Analysis

In Chapter Eleven, you were introduced to an entirely new way of looking at the total environment via six internal and six external macrofactors; yet beyond this initial layer of factors are deeper matters on the internal and external fronts that can be explored by any organization whose leadership desires a better understanding of the *core* factors that affect its business. Let us start with a deeper inspection of the internal environment, beginning with the identification of the *stakeholders* in your organization.

## Stakeholder Analysis

Stakeholders of your enterprise are defined exactly as the word implies: those who *"hold"* a *"stake"* in your business for one of many legitimate reasons. The job of the leadership is to ensure that all stakeholders are identified, that their orientation, objectives, and needs are clearly understood, and that the appropriate proactive strategies are developed accordingly. The following Stakeholder Analysis exercise provides the individual and team with a method to identify your enterprise's stakeholders, to determine their relative criticality to your company, and to highlight what special focus is needed to accommodate your primary stakeholders.

## Group Stakeholder Identification and Analysis

To carry out this exercise, use the Stakeholder Analysis Worksheet (Figure 12.1). As a group (or individually if you like), go down the list of potential stakeholders, checking those that pertain to your company and adding any others that you may have to the bottom of the list. Give each a "criticality measure" of from 1 (lowest) to 10 (highest), and determine if there is the need for special focus during the later goal-setting section of the planning session (Venue Two).

Obviously, each company will have its own set of stakeholders, uniquely weighted from a criticality standpoint. What may be a primary stakeholder for one company, such as a labor union to an automobile manufacturer, may not even be on the list of another company, such as one in banking.

Why, you may ask, is this exercise in the category of internal environment when only two of the twelve identified stakeholders are internally rooted ("employees" and "management/executives")? The other ten are from external sources. The answer is that the focus is not primarily upon the *source* of the stakeholder but of the necessarily internal-centered *response* to that

## Figure 12.1—Stakehold Analysis Worksheet

| Group Exercise:  Stakeholder Analysis Worksheet | | | |
|---|---|---|---|
| **Potential Stakeholder** | **Criticality Measure (0-10)** | **Special Focus Needed?** | **Why?** |
| 1.  Creditors | ☐ | | |
| 2.  Customers | ☐ | | |
| 3.  Employees | ☐ | | |
| 4.  Financial Institutions | ☐ | | |
| 5.  General Public | ☐ | | |
| 6.  Government(s) | ☐ | | |
| 7.  Industry(ies) | ☐ | | |
| 8.  Investors/Stockholders | ☐ | | |
| 9.  Local Community | ☐ | | |
| 10.  Management/Executives | ☐ | | |
| 11.  Suppliers | ☐ | | |
| 12.  Unions | ☐ | | |
| 13.  _____ | ☐ | | |
| 14.  _____ | ☐ | | |

stakeholder. The company should be proactive, initiating conscious strategies and policies to achieve effective partnerships with these constituencies. Remember that the goal of the entire Venue One of the Strategic Planning Technology is to inspect thoroughly every background aspect and nail down basic vision elements. In that light, the question of most importance is, *"What strategic goals are needed to optimize the relationships with our primary stakeholders?"* Throughout each phase of the process, as the question is repeatedly asked and answered, more pieces of the strategic mosaic are found, to be fitted into a complete picture in the Venues to come.

## Pluses and Minuses Analysis

The second major field to plow for more detailed inspection of the environment is the entire realm of the positives and negatives of the organizational experience. By this point the planning participant has become deeply immersed in thinking about the enterprise in relation to time—past, present, and future—and to space—internal and external. It is the right time for some summarizing analysis about how the organization is doing from several performance standpoints. Again, although this section involves consideration of some arenas external to the organization, it belongs in this section because the frame of reference is absolutely from an internal company perspective, viewed through the inside eyes of the leaders of your enterprise. The key question for this entire section is, *"What are the major things we are doing right, our strengths, and our opportunities, and what are the major areas for improvement, the weaknesses, and the threats?"*

## Group Exercise:  The "SF SWOT" Team

Experience teaches us with its own unique sense of humor the lesson that in real life things are not always as they appear to be. Such is the case with the title of the following exercise. Not a simulation of a northern Californian (SF) drug raid (SWOT [*sic*]), the exercise bears significant strategic relevancy:

- SF means          **Success and Failures**
- SWOT means      **Strength and Weaknesses;
   Opportunities and Threats**

Many people have heard the acronym SWOT through prior educational or business seminar exposure. SWOT analyses are the particular favorite of business school case-study methodologies. But I do not believe that these classic four criteria are enough. First of all, no one would argue that the OT part, "opportunities and threats" is not valuable, as that pairing addresses the *future* of the enterprise. But "strengths and weaknesses" (SW) are not enough in assessing the *present*. Why? The aspect of strengths and weaknesses covers the basic *condition* of the enterprise from the recent past to the present time.

An excellent analogy is when the balance sheet is used to understand a company's financial condition. The balance sheet is an excellent instrument to understand assets, liabilities, and equity within the enterprise and via ratio and industry benchmarking. However, the balance sheet only gives some of the information needed. The income statement, showing not the condition but the *performance* of the enterprise over a given period, provides another key piece of data. This additional aspect is covered by analyzing the company's "success and failures." Whereas strengths and weaknesses address the *condition, the being* of the company, successes and failures address the *actions, the doings* of the company. Therefore, SWOT is not nearly enough, failing to adequately address the present. Once you see the complementarity and comprehensiveness of the "SF SWOT" Team Exercise performed for your company, you may well agree that its expanded format adds noticeable value.

## Conducting the "SF SWOT" Team Exercise

For this exercise you will need the "SF SWOT" Team Exercise sheet (Figure 12.2). Your job as a group is to brainstorm the identification of major items, category by category, as part of your complete environmental scanning.

When each of the six categories has been filled in, review them as a group to determine which identified items constitute significant opportunities or exposures/risks that must be addressed in the goal-setting section of the planning process (Venue Two). Circle any items that you feel must be pursued and begin to think about how to convert each circled item into a strategic goal. Don't forget to revisit them later!

## Internal Environment Summary

This deeper inspection of the internal environment covers two complementary and major matters: who and what is important to the enterprise. Together, they focus strategic thinking from a wide universe of past and present data and future expectations to some specific, important factors. The

## Figure 12.2—"SF SWOT" Team Exercise

---

### Group Exercise: "SF SWOT" Team Exercise

Identify key lists for the following categories:

**1. Enterprise Successes and Failures (SF)**

    a. Successes:                    b. Failures:

       (1) _____       (1) _____
       (2) _____       (2) _____
       (3) _____       (3) _____
       (4) _____       (4) _____
       (5) _____       (5) _____

**2. Enterprise Strengths and Weaknesses (SW)**

    a. Strengths:                    b. Weaknesses:

       (1) _____       (1) _____
       (2) _____       (2) _____
       (3) _____       (3) _____
       (4) _____       (4) _____
       (5) _____       (5) _____

**3. Enterprise Opportunities and Threats (OT)**

    a. Opportunities:              b. Threats:

       (1) _____       (1) _____
       (2) _____       (2) _____
       (3) _____       (3) _____
       (4) _____       (4) _____
       (5) _____       (5) _____

---

key to strategy is focused thinking, planning, and implementation. *The challenge, in effect, is to gather specific arrows of emergent opportunity into the strategic quiver, to sort them out in the goal-preparation stage (Venues Two and Three), and to launch them in the implementation sections (Venues Four and Five).*

# Chapter Thirteen

# Deeper External Environmental Analysis

There are three external arenas so important to the majority of companies that they each deserve deeper inspection: (1) the *customer,* (2) the *competition,* and (3) the *markets, products,* and *services.* Each of these topics will be addressed in order, with helpful analytical tools provided to bring to the surface the major strategic opportunities.

## Customer Analysis

The century that began with the industrial revolution has shifted at its conclusion to the service revolution, turning away from an internal-product-feature mentality to an external-customer-benefit mindset. More and more, there is common talk that "everybody has a customer," and that there are "internal customers" and "external customers." As recently as the late 1970s and early 1980s, the vast majority of people would have been very confused by the word "customer" being used for anyone other than the actual external buyer of their goods or services. But every person is, in effect, getting goods or services from someone else. This universal principle needs particular application to your enterprise throughout the strategic process. For external assessment purposes, our focus is on the external customer, answering the questions:

- Who are our customers?
- What are their needs?
- How are they best met?
- How can we prove it?

## Customer Buying Criteria Analysis

The following exercise serves to answer the more specific question: *"What are our customers' prioritized buying criteria?"* Regarding customer assumptions, remember that the *best* way to ensure accuracy is to *ask* directly a number of your current customers and prospects about their preferences. Their data is the best data! The matrix in Figure 13.1, organized like the Environmental Factors Analysis Worksheet we covered earlier (Figure 11.1), provides you with the opportunity to weigh each criterion against every other. Note that the matrix allows each participant to delete and add any criterion as desired.

## Figure 13.1—Customer Buying Criteria Worksheet

| Personal Exercise: Customer Buying Criteria Worksheet | | | | | | | | | | | | | | | |
|---|---|---|---|---|---|---|---|---|---|---|---|---|---|---|---|
| **Criterion** | Product/Svc. Quality | Price | Terms | Delivery | Support | Purchase Size | Purchase Frequency | Industry | Geography | Ability to Pay | Function/Use | | | Total "X's" | Ranking | |
| **Product/Service Quality** | ■ | | | | | | | | | | | | | | | |
| **Price** | | ■ | | | | | | | | | | | | | | |
| **Terms** | | | ■ | | | | | | | | | | | | | |
| **Delivery** | | | | ■ | | | | | | | | | | | | |
| **Support** | | | | | ■ | | | | | | | | | | | |
| **Purchase Size** | | | | | | ■ | | | | | | | | | | |
| **Purchase Frequency** | | | | | | | ■ | | | | | | | | | |
| **Industry** | | | | | | | | ■ | | | | | | | | |
| **Geography** | | | | | | | | | ■ | | | | | | | |
| **Ability to Pay** | | | | | | | | | | ■ | | | | | | |
| **Function/Use** | | | | | | | | | | | ■ | | | | | |
| **Additional Criterion:** | | | | | | | | | | | | ■ | | | | |
| | | | | | | | | | | | | | ■ | | | |
| | | | | | | | | | | | | | | ■ | | |

(Note: Notice that in the logic of the way this matrix is set-up, if you mark one item "*a* over *b*" the first time, when the two are paired again (*b* with *a*) then the second time you would leave a blank in that space.)

Questions that will help you define and judge each criterion on the matrix are provided below:

| Criterion | Question |
|-----------|----------|
| • **Product/Service Quality** | How important is quality to the buyer? |
| • **Price** | To what degree is the actual price a factor? |
| • **Terms** | Are the accompanying terms and conditions a significant factor? |
| • **Delivery** | How important are delivery arrangements? |
| • **Support** | How critical is the support surrounding the sale of the product and/or service? |
| • **Purchase Size** | Is the quantity of the purchase important? |
| • **Purchase Frequency** | Is the frequency of the purchase—how often purchases are made—important? |
| • **Industry** | How important are the type of industry and the industry dynamics to the customer? |
| • **Geography** | How important are the location of the buyer and seller and their proximity to each other? |
| • **Ability to Pay** | How much is the customer's ability to pay for the product or service a buying factor? |
| • **Function/Use** | How significant are the actual features, functions, and benefits of the product or service? |

The scoring for this matrix is performed in exactly the same manner as the scoring for the Environmental Factors Analysis Worksheet (Figure 11.1). The computation of the Customer Buying Criteria Consensus scores (Figure 13.2) is also exactly the same as that for the Group Factors Consensus Worksheet (Figure 11.2).

After you have developed a group ranking of the customer buying criteria, you now should ask: *"Are we performing well in these key criteria? If not, what major measures can be done to enhance our effectiveness?"* Discovered needs in this customer buying arena provide additional material to be placed into your strategic goals' wish list for future address in Venue Two.

## Figure 13.2—Customer Buying Criteria Consensus

| | | **Group Exercise:** |
|---|---|---|
| | | **Customer Buying Criteria Consensus** |
| Exercise Directions: | | Now that each individual has completed the Customer Buying Criteria Worksheet, summarize your findings to determine the group's aggregate inputs. Write in each individual input below and summarize. |
| **Core Path Exercise!** | | |

| Participants' Priorities<br><br>Criterion: | 1 | 2 | 3 | 4 | 5 | 6 | 7 | 8 | 9 | 10 | Totals | ·/· By # | Rank |
|---|---|---|---|---|---|---|---|---|---|---|---|---|---|
| Product/Ser. Quality | | | | | | | | | | | | | |
| Price | | | | | | | | | | | | | |
| Terms | | | | | | | | | | | | | |
| Delivery | | | | | | | | | | | | | |
| Support | | | | | | | | | | | | | |
| Purchase Size | | | | | | | | | | | | | |
| Purchase Frequency | | | | | | | | | | | | | |
| Industry | | | | | | | | | | | | | |
| Geography | | | | | | | | | | | | | |
| Ability to Pay | | | | | | | | | | | | | |
| Function/Use | | | | | | | | | | | | | |
| Additional Criterion: | | | | | | | | | | | | | |
| | | | | | | | | | | | | | |
| | | | | | | | | | | | | | |

## Your Typical Customer Attribute-Power Worksheet

Although the new paradigm for selling and support is the non-manipulative, consultative, win-win partnership (contrasted with the manipulative, one-sided, and transactional selling of the first three-quarters of this century), *there are still legitimate and actual sources of power that affect the buyer-seller relationship.* The upcoming Customer Attribute-Power Worksheet (Figure 13.3) lists ten attributes in which the "power" is held in varying degrees by the customer or by you. Before introducing the worksheet, the following definitions of its key terms are provided.

- **Concentrated Buyer Group:**

  This means that there are only a few large customers. The fewer and larger your customers are, the more power they have and can harness when working with you.

- **Large Purchase Volumes:**

  The bigger the physical volume, the larger the dollar transaction and the fewer the absolute number of transactions, all of which make the customers feel more selective and careful in awarding the business they consider a "plum" to the winning supplier. That converts to higher customer power.

- **Big Purchase Item:**

  The focus here is on the "big item": that large, one-time purchase which must be rigorously reviewed and evaluated by the buyer before he or she renders a decision. The larger the buyer company and the larger the purchase price tag, the more complex and bureaucratic are the capital approval procedures in order to minimize risk and spread accountability around. All of these internal buyer processes, in which the seller, in most cases, has limited influence or effect from the outside, convert to customer power.

- **Undifferentiated/Commodity:**

  If your product or service is relatively generic and undifferentiated, or is considered an off-the-shelf commodity or readily available service, then your prospect or customer has a wide set of available options and can readily go elsewhere. The more this is so, the greater the power your customer has.

- **Low Product Seller-Switching Costs:**

  If, from the buyer's standpoint, there is relatively little to no cost of switching from one seller to another, then the buyer is given considerable power. The switch is inexpensive, and indicates that if there is not a solid partnership-relationship between you and your buyer, it is convenient for him or her to do business elsewhere.

- **Low Profit Margins:**

  The lower the financial profits of the buyer, the greater the internal pressures on the buyer to negotiate the price down. This tough bargaining posture reflects greater power on behalf of the buyer.

- **They Can Make, Not Buy:**

  This decision, called a "sourcing decision," means that the buyer does not *have* to buy at all. The buyer can pull the "source of manufacture" (or service provision) in-house, done within its own premises by its own people instead of by an outside third party. When a buying company has this alternative as a viable option, it translates into a major source of power and legitimate leverage in the relationship.

- **Non-Criticality for Perfect Quality:**

  The classical definition of quality is "conformance to your requirements." The implication of that definition is profound: *If* the customer's requirements for product or service quality are *less* than the specifications of your product or service quality, that customer may well go to another seller who has lower quality than yours but who meets customer requirements at better price or terms. That buyer flexibility converts to significant power in the relationship.

- **Customer Knows You Well:**

  In the buyer-seller relationship, "knowledge is power" indeed. The more the customer knows you and the more information he/she has, the more power is available to be exerted in the buying negotiation, not just once, but on an ongoing basis.

## Figure 13.3—Your Typical Customer Attribute-Power Worksheet

| **Personal Exercise:  Your Typical Customer Attribute-Power Worksheet** | | |
|---|---|---|
| (Note that these attributes, when present in your customers, signify customer power. Hence, the higher the scores, the more powerful are your customers.) | | |
| **Customer or Your Product Attribute (Explanation)** | **Applicability Grade (0-10)** | **Rank** |
| 1.  **Concentrated Buyer Group**  (e.g., a few large customers) | ☐ | ☐ |
| 2.  **Large Purchase Volumes**  (fewer transactions, bigger $) | ☐ | ☐ |
| 3.  **Big Purchase Item**  (your customer is price-conscious) | ☐ | ☐ |
| 4.  **Undifferentiated/Commodity**  (can they easily go elsewhere?) | ☐ | ☐ |
| 5.  **Low Product Seller-Switching Costs**  (easy to go elsewhere) | ☐ | ☐ |
| 6.  **Low Profit Margins**  (makes tougher bargainer) | ☐ | ☐ |
| 7.  **They Can Make, Not Buy**  (vertical integration real option for them) | ☐ | ☐ |
| 8.  **Non-Criticality for Perfect Quality**  (**their** product has wide preferences) | ☐ | ☐ |
| 9.  **Customer Knows You Well**  (information is leverage) | ☐ | ☐ |
| 10.  **Strong "Purchasing" Capability**  (a tougher sell) | ☐ | ☐ |
| 11.  _____ | ☐ | ☐ |
| 12.  _____ | ☐ | ☐ |

Thanks to Robert A. Stringer for his basic Buyer Group criteria in his book, *Strategy Traps and How to Avoid Them,* (1986), Lexington Books.

- **Strong "Purchasing" Capability:**

  The stronger the buyer's purchasing capability is, the greater power the buyer can exert. A purchasing department or function that is extremely adept in its profession can make the selling process rigorous and demanding, placing the seller on the defensive.

You may have additional power attributes to add to this list, and you may wish to delete a couple of the existing ones if they are entirely inappropriate. The benefit of maintaining ten separate factors is to keep a 100-point scale (10 items of 10 points each). This way, if you have different sets of customers or wish to trace this power index over time, you can do so on the same 100-point scale. The Customer Attribute-Power Worksheet in Figure 13.3 is to be filled out by each individual involved in the strategic planning process. One note on scoring: You can score each item either on its own merits from 0 to 10 or you can prioritize each of the 10, from 10 points for #1 to 1 point for #10 if you want to force-rank them and do not need a 100-point scale. The key is that all participants use the same scoring method.

After each individual has completed the Power Worksheet, each set of scores can be posted on the group Priorities Worksheet shown in Figure 13.4. The scoring of the group inputs can be done either by adding up the scores and ranking directly or adding them up, dividing the score number by the number of participants and then ranking them (if you like dealing with smaller numbers). After the group rankings have been calculated, you then need to figure out what the rankings mean, for it is your use of information that is emphasized in this system, not mere analysis. The second part of the group Priorities Worksheet, the *Customer Power Summary* provides a format for learning from the data you have gathered from the group power rankings.

The format and questions are self-explanatory. The point is to crystallize what you know about your customers, and what both their and your greatest sources of power are. Again, the ultimate intention is to convert important insights into major goals. You should be thinking about how to enhance your effectiveness in working with your customers over the long haul.

## Product, Service, and Market Analysis

Now that you have a fresh concept about your key customers' characteristics, sources of power, and buying criteria, you can shift your attention to the wider contextual scope: where to reach your customers—the *market,* and with what deliverables—and your *products* and/or *services.* The purpose

## Figure 13.4—Customer Attribute-Power Priorities Worksheet

| Group Exercise: Customer Attribute-Power Priorities | | | | | | | | | | | | | |
|---|---|---|---|---|---|---|---|---|---|---|---|---|---|
| Exercise Directions: | Combine the individual responses on the following group worksheet as a basis for further discussion. | | | | | | | | | | | | |

### Group Exercise: Customer/Attribute/Power Priorities

| Customer Attribute | Indiv. | Individual Participant's Rankings | | | | | | | | | | Totals • By # • | Rank |
|---|---|---|---|---|---|---|---|---|---|---|---|---|---|
| | | 1 | 2 | 3 | 4 | 5 | 6 | 7 | 8 | 9 | 10 | | |
| 1. _____ | | | | | | | | | | | | | |
| 2. _____ | | | | | | | | | | | | | |
| 3. _____ | | | | | | | | | | | | | |
| 4. _____ | | | | | | | | | | | | | |
| 5. _____ | | | | | | | | | | | | | |
| 6. _____ | | | | | | | | | | | | | |
| 7. _____ | | | | | | | | | | | | | |
| 8. _____ | | | | | | | | | | | | | |
| 9. _____ | | | | | | | | | | | | | |
| 10. _____ | | | | | | | | | | | | | |
| 11. _____ | | | | | | | | | | | | | |
| 12. _____ | | | | | | | | | | | | | |
| 13. _____ | | | | | | | | | | | | | |
| 14. _____ | | | | | | | | | | | | | |
| | | | | | | | | | | | | | |

**Figure 13.4—Customer Attribute-Power Priorities Worksheet
(concluded)**

| Group Exercise: Customer Power Summary |
|---|
| Based upon the above findings, answer the following: |
| Give a brief narrative summary about your key customer: <br><br> _____ <br> _____ <br> _____ |

What are this key customer's three greatest sources of power?

| | Source | How can you best address this power? |
|---|---|---|
| 1. | _____ | _____ |
| 2. | _____ | _____ |
| 3. | _____ | _____ |

What are your enterprise's three greatest sources of power in light of the above analysis?

| | Source | How can you best utilize this power? |
|---|---|---|
| 1. | _____ | _____ |
| 2. | _____ | _____ |
| 3. | _____ | _____ |

of this section is to generate ideas on optimal market strategy so that your products and/or services can be positioned for maximal effect in those markets.

## "Crash-Course" Market Theory

No strategic planning process would be complete without the proper address of that most traditional cornerstone of strategic planning: market and portfolio analysis. But so as not to step onto that steep and slippery slope of "the academically abstruse or the theoretically obscure," we will keep it simple and practical. The intent in supplying a basic understanding of vital market aspects is to stimulate your best thinking about *"where* you should be, in *what* markets, *with what* products and services, and *how."*

## The Basic Market Portfolio Thesis

The matrix in Figure 13.5, which has long been known as the Boston Consulting Group's Market Portfolio model, provides a simple and helpful overview of the market portfolio concept.

**Figure 13.5—The Basic Market Portfolio Thesis Matrix**

### The Basic Market Portfolio Thesis
### Boston Consulting Group

**Market Share & Business Strength**

| Market Growth & Industry Attractiveness | | High | Low | |
|---|---|---|---|---|
| | **High** | "Stars" | "Question Marks" | **High** |
| | **Low** | "Cash Cows" | "Dogs" | **Low** |
| | | **High** | **Low** | |

**Principle:**
An enterprise's products/ services can be shown as a portfolio with varying share and growth conditions/potentials.

The governing principle of the Market Portfolio Thesis is that the products and/or services of an enterprise can be shown as a portfolio with specific subcategories reflecting various combinations of share, growth, and potential capabilities.

The vertical part of the matrix addresses the realm of future *potential,* whereas the horizontal part of the matrix addresses the realm of present *reality.* Upside potential is via growth of the market and attractiveness of the industry. Realities of the present include existing market share and existing business strength of your products and/or services. Obviously, those products and services that feature high share/strength *and* high growth/attractiveness market potential are "stars"; their double-low opposites are "dogs."

When share/strength is high and growth/attractiveness is low, the conventional wisdom says to milk the "cash-cow." When share/strength is low and growth/attractiveness is high, there is uncertainty—hence a "question mark" as to whether or not that product/service should be maintained. You may have seen this matrix and its variations used in interesting ways, filled with X's or O's that plot certain companies' portfolio of products and services, indicating how they fall into these four categories in general, and fall specifically within each category or quadrant. Used in this way, this market portfolio matrix has made a big contribution to pioneer the once new territory of market analysis. Since its introduction decades ago, the concept has been expanded and complemented with a wide array of additional market assessment approaches. There are a couple of other basic ways to look at markets and their products and services, covered next.

## Current and New Products and Markets

The Products and Markets matrix in Figure 13.6 charts the state of the products and services (existing, modified, and new) on the vertical axis and the state of the market on the horizontal axis (current, expanded, and new).

The matrix reads from lower left to upper right. An existing pro- duct in a current market is classified as a *"status quo" strategy.* Pushing into modified products/services in current markets and expanded markets for existing products means a *modest adjustment strategy.* The next level is an *incremental growth strategy,* which can be achieved through three combinations:

1. You can place a *new* product/service in an *existing* market.
2. You can *modify* a product in an *expanding* market.
3. You can place an *existing* product in a *new* market.

## Figure 13.6—Current and New Products and Markets Matrix

CURRENT AND NEW PRODUCTS AND MARKETS

**Principle:**
From life-cycle and stability standpoints, enterprises should consider the mix of products/services they have in various market categories.

The next layer of policy aggressiveness is an *expansionist strategy,* with either new products/services in expanded markets or modified products/services in new markets. The fifth level of policy aggressiveness is an entrepreneurial strategy, aptly named for when a new product or service is launched in a new market. Obviously, most products and services can be categorized into one of these nine boxes, and therefore, into one of the five identified market strategies. Why is this kind of classification process helpful? Because it shows how your overall mix looks across the board. Is it a balanced or tilted mix? A preferred, optimal mix? An un-optimized, under-performing mix? Seeing *where you are* with your product/services portfolio crystallizes your thinking of *where you want to be.*

## Price-Versus-Quality Product Competitiveness

The third basic cut at understanding products and markets addresses the price and quality positioning of the product or service, as illustrated in the matrix shown in Figure 13.7.

## Figure 13.7—Price-Versus-Quality Product Competitiveness Matrix

How do your products and services slot into these categories? The vertical axis addresses the pricing-position strategy, from low to medium to high. The horizontal axis classifies the product or service quality as average, good, or outstanding. Going again from lower left to top right, five positioning strategies cover the spectrum:

1. If price is low and quality is average, the positioning reflects a basic *commodity strategy.*

2. If pricing or quality moves up a notch, it still reflects a *low-end market strategy.*

3. If price is high with average quality, or price is low with outstanding quality, or price and quality are slotted carefully in the middle, these reflect *niche-market selection strategies.*

4. High pricing with good quality or medium pricing with outstanding quality reflects a push upwards into a *high-end market strategy.*

5. High pricing with outstanding quality products or service reflects a *premium market strategy.*

## Group Product/Market Matrix Analysis

Now that a number of product and market criteria and dimensions have been introduced, the application of these principles to your company's products/services portfolio can give your team considerable insights about the adequacy of your positioning. Individually or in a group setting, the first step is to identify the major products and/or services you wish to assess strategically. Then, fill in the Product/Market Matrix Worksheet (Figure 13.8) by reaching consensus on each product/service by columnar section. Note that this matrix includes all of the major aspects, or criteria, covered in the three prior theory matrixes, placing the entire analysis on one page for your focus and convenience.

Lastly, review the filled-in matrix to look for trends or areas of strength or weakness. When looking at your completed matrix, ask yourself if you would consider it to be strategically ideal. If not, what strategic goals would you develop to improve the standing and performance of your portfolio?

## Competitive Analysis

Competitive analysis is the third and final aspect of our deeper exploration of the external environment.

*As the realities of day-to-day business bear out, product and service providers do not operate in a vacuum wherein prospects flock to them, eager to sign up as new customers who will gladly support their offerings in ever-growing, predictable markets. Enter the competition.* And in today's business climate, one cannot either underestimate or "under-know" the competitors. Rather, sufficient competitive knowledge and attendant proactive strategies can combine to form an extremely powerful competitive advantage.

## Competitive Analysis and Competitive Advantage Policy Matrix

There are three aspects of competitive analysis:

- Positioning
- Market Attractiveness
- Degree of Advantage

## Figure 13.8—Product/Market Matrix Worksheet

| Product or Service Name: | Check the box in each section that pertains: | Product/ Service | | | Market | | | Price | | | Quality | | | Market Growth Industry Attrac. | | | Market Share &/or Business Strength | | |
|---|---|---|---|---|---|---|---|---|---|---|---|---|---|---|---|---|---|---|---|
| | | Existing | Modified | New | Current | Expanded | New | Low | Medium | High | Average | Good | Excellent | Low | Medium | High | Low | Medium | High |
| 1. | | | | | | | | | | | | | | | | | | | |
| 2. | | | | | | | | | | | | | | | | | | | |
| 3. | | | | | | | | | | | | | | | | | | | |
| 4. | | | | | | | | | | | | | | | | | | | |
| 5. | | | | | | | | | | | | | | | | | | | |
| 6. | | | | | | | | | | | | | | | | | | | |
| 7 | | | | | | | | | | | | | | | | | | | |
| 8. | | | | | | | | | | | | | | | | | | | |
| 9. | | | | | | | | | | | | | | | | | | | |
| 10. | | | | | | | | | | | | | | | | | | | |

**Group Exercise: Product/Market Matrix Worksheet**

The Competitive Advantage Policy Matrix (Figure 13.9) indexes the degree of competitive advantage and the number of sources of competitive differentiation.

**Figure 13.9—Competitive Advantage Policy Matrix**

| COMPETITIVE ADVANTAGE POLICY MATRIX | | | |
|---|---|---|---|
| | (Can be done by product, service, in general, or other criteria) | **Enterprise Sources of Competitive Advantage/Differentiation** | |
| | | Few/None | Several | Numerous |
| **Degree of Competitive Advantage** | Substantial | Preserve/Protect Differentiator and Hold On | Strengthen Differentiation and Grow | Maintain Differentiation &Preserve Position |
| | Some | Hyper-Exploit Differentiator or Withdraw | Expand Differentiation and Grow | Strengthen Differentiation Activity to Grow |
| | Minimal to None | Abandon | Hyper-Exploit Differentiators or Withdraw | Prepare Differentiation Strategy & Launch |

When the determination is made between the *degree* of competitive advantage and the amount of *sources* of competitive differentiation, the obvious extremes are as follows: (1) If there are *minimal* to no competitive advantages and *few* to no sources of potential competitive differentiation and advantage, then *abandon* the product/service in that market; (2) if there is *substantial* competitive advantage with *numerous* sources of differentiation, *maintaining* differentiation and preserving position is necessary. The basic challenge here is to preserve the present competitive advantage a product/service has while launching new differentiation strategies according to its potential untapped sources. Note that this analysis calls for a grasp and appreciation of even slight differences in existing advantage and potential differentiation. *Winners in the competitive marketplace are masters of the details and the subtleties of successful differentiation.*

## Competitive Market Matrix

The second cut at competitive analysis is to determine your company's competitive position in light of the market's relative attractiveness. The Competitive Market Matrix (Figure 13.10) can help you do this. The vertical axis covers the company's competitive capabilities (from weak to average to strong). The horizontal axis covers the degree of market or business sector attractiveness (from unattractive to average to attractive).

### Figure 13.10—Competitive Market Matrix

**COMPETITIVE MARKET MATRIX**

| Company's Competitive Capabilities "/" Position | | Degree of Market or Business Sector Attractiveness | | |
|---|---|---|---|---|
| | | Unattractive | Average | Attractive |
| | Strong | Use as Cash, or Reputation, Leverage | Press for Dominance or Growth | Maintain, or Enhance Leadership |
| | Average | Phased Withdrawal | Grow or Maintain | Press for Growth |
| | Weak | Abandon | Maintain, or Phased Withdrawal | Strengthen or Out! |

*Source:* Further adaptation of "Directional policy matrix," Lester A. Digman. (1986). *Strategic management,* p. 65. Plano, Texas: Business Publications.

When you look at a couple of the extreme scenarios, like the top left box contrasted with the bottom right box, you can see the continuum of strategic competitive options. On the top left, when the company has *strong* competitive capabilities/position *but* is in an *unattractive* market, the competitive market strategy may be to use that existing position as *leverage.* On the other extreme, on the bottom right, when the company has *weak* competitive capabilities/position *but* is in an *attractive* market, the competitive market strategy likely should be to either *strengthen* its position in the market *or get out* altogether!

## Competitive Position Matrix

The third dimension of competitive strategy policy, represented by the competitive Position Matrix (Figure 13.11), connects your company's strength of competitive position (particularly the specific product or service) with the life-cycle stage of your product or service.

On the vertical axis is the "strength of competitive position" gauge, from weak to uncertain, to favorable, to strong, to dominant. On the horizontal axis is the stage of the life cycle, with four basic stages, from introductory (start-up/embryonic), to growth (expansion), to maturity (saturation), to decline (aging/fall-off).

Continuing our illustration-by-contrast approach, let us take two scenarios that are more subtle than those we have used previously: first, a *strong* competitive position in the growth stage of the life cycle, and second, an *uncertain* competitive position in the *mature* stage of the life cycle. The product or service that has a *strong* competitive position in a *growth* stage essentially should consolidate its "beachhead gains," improving its position and pushing for additional points of market share. On the other hand, a product or service with an *uncertain* competitive position in the *mature* life cycle stage—a substantially different scenario—may call for a strategy to hold on to certain niche areas where it has relative strength. Implicitly, this increased rifle-shot focus may mean winding down activity in lackluster or lagging areas of the market. Here, the "80-20" Rule applies: *Hit hard those 20% of considerably stronger niches that achieve 80% of the top- and bottom-line results,* thus minimizing relatively wasted or low-return efforts in other areas.

## Figure 13.11—Competitive Position Matrix

**Competitive Position Matrix**

| Strength of Competitive Position | Stage of Life Cycle | | | |
|---|---|---|---|---|
| | Introductory (Start-up/ Embryonic) | Growth (Expansion) | Maturity (Saturation) | Decline (Aging/ Fall-Off) |
| Dominant | Hold Position Hold Share | Hold Position Grow w/Indus. | Hold Position Delay Decline | Hold Position |
| Strong | Strengthen Position Push for Share | Improve Position Push for share | Hold Position Grow With Industry | Hold Position or Harvest |
| Favorable | Selective/Niche Improvement | Selective/Niche Improvement | Protect Niche Preserve Base | Protect, Then Phased Withdrawal |
| Uncertain | Highly Selective Improvement | V. Selective Niche Focus | Hold on to Niche(s) | Phased WD or Abandon |
| Weak | Up or Out! | Turn Around or Abandon | Turn Around or Abandon | Abandon |

*Source:* Adapted from "Business profile matrix," Lester A. Digman. (1986). *Strategic management,* p. 164. Plano, Texas: Business Publications.

## The Competitiveness Audit

In light of the three competitive matrices shown on the prior visual templates, the following Competitiveness Audit (Figure 13.12) provides a simple, straightforward, and comprehensive overview of the competitive posture of your company's products and/or services. To fill in the form, list your salable products/services down the left-hand column. Then check off one box in each of the four competitive analysis categories from left to right.

## Figure 13.12—Competitiveness Audit

| Group Exercise: Competitiveness Audit | | | | | | | | | | | | | | |
|---|---|---|---|---|---|---|---|---|---|---|---|---|---|---|
| Product or Service Name: | Strength of Competitive Position/Advantage | | | | | Stage of Life Cycle | | | | Degree of Mkt. Attrac. | | | Sources of Comp. Adv. | | |
| | Weak | Uncertain | Favorable | Strong | Dominant | Introduction | Growth | Maturity | Decline | Unattractive | Average | Attractive | Few to None | Several | Numerous |
| 1. | | | | | | | | | | | | | | | |
| 2. | | | | | | | | | | | | | | | |
| 3. | | | | | | | | | | | | | | | |
| 4. | | | | | | | | | | | | | | | |
| 5. | | | | | | | | | | | | | | | |
| 6. | | | | | | | | | | | | | | | |
| 7. | | | | | | | | | | | | | | | |
| 8. | | | | | | | | | | | | | | | |
| 9. | | | | | | | | | | | | | | | |
| 10. | | | | | | | | | | | | | | | |
| | | | | | | | | | | | | | | | |

Please note that the four assessment categories (*competitive position, life-cycle stage, market attractiveness,* and *competitive-advantage services*) consolidate the prior matrices onto one handy worksheet.

## Analyzing the Audit

There are many ways you can assess what you have before you, now that the portfolio has been audited product by product (or service by service) for competitiveness. Several major angles of analysis include the following:

1. **Review the *total portfolio's big picture*.** What is the general read-out? What overall grade would you give the entire portfolio? Why?

2. **Analyze *each of the four matrix categories*.** Rank your portfolio's performance in each arena. Where is it strongest? Weakest? In which arenas are there the most palpable opportunities? What aspects must be shored up across the portfolio? How can you push the "portfolio's water level" up to the next higher mark in areas where it is depressed?

3. **Analyze *each of the products/services* one at a time.** What are its strengths and weaknesses? What is the next step for this product or service from its current position in the market? How can the product or service be more competitive? Where is the greatest opportunity to make a move on the field? From a corporate profitability standpoint, what is the most responsible strategy for this product or service?

4. **Compare *individual products'/services' greatest strengths and weaknesses*.** How can lessons or strong points from one product help another product? Here, you are the matchmaker, determining if and where a certain strong point of one product can provide insight and be applied to help another product that is weak in that regard.

You have now been introduced to, and perhaps participated in, a time-efficient yet thorough analysis of your portfolio's competitive posture. The next complementary analysis is to determine the level of competitiveness within the industry.

## "Competitiveness Within the Industry" Analysis

This exercise further explores the topic of the competition by focusing upon the prime competitors in your market(s) as a group. If you compete in multiple markets, this analysis can be replicated for every different cluster of competitors you have.

Before using the Overall Competitiveness Matrix (Figure 13.13) which this exercise focuses on, consider the brief one-sentence definitions of each competition-inducing criterion below:

1. **Large number of firms competing:** Usually, the greater the number of firms competing, the greater the degree of competition (competitive intensity) is present.

2. **Growth in the market is slow:** The less the market pie is increasing, the more fiercely contended is the existing business.

3. **Fixed costs are high:** When the fixed costs of doing business are high, the unrelenting pressure to "cover your overhead nut" increases the competitive fervor within the industry.

4. **Storage costs are high:** The higher the inventory carrying costs, the higher the pressure there is to maintain or increase inventory turnover, foisting more product on the market and placing great pressure on winning the business against others.

5. **Customer switching costs are low:** As we covered earlier, the less financially vested a customer is, the more easy it is for it to switch from one competitor to another.

6. **Differentiation is low:** The less differentiated the products/services are in the eyes of the customer/buyer, the more pitched is the battle to get and keep the business by utilizing other than feature/benefit selling strategies.

7. **Competitors look alike:** Not only if the products or services look similar, but also if the competitors themselves look alike, competitiveness within the industry is increased.

8. **Stakes are high for all:** If the market you and your competitors are in is crucial to those firms, or if in any other way the stakes are high to win in that market with that product/service, competitiveness will be greater.

9. **Market exit costs are high:** If companies have a tremendous investment in the market and the cost of getting out of that market is high, the psychological and financial pressure is to stay, even when you are "stuck" and must fiercely fight it out to make the best return on your sunken costs and anchored position.

10. **Barriers of entry are low:** On the other side of the market, if it is easy for new competitors to enter the market at low initial cost and start-up effort, the competitive intensity will significantly increase.

## Figure 13.13—Overall Competitiveness Within the Industry Matrix

| Group Exercise: Overall Competitiveness Within The Industry | | | | | | | | | | |
|---|---|---|---|---|---|---|---|---|---|---|
| Reminder: Ideally, this exercise should be performed for every major, distinct industry or product when a different cluster or mix of competitors (and conditions) is involved. | | | | | | | | | | |

| Competition-Inducing Criterion: | Degrees of Competition Present (Please Circle One:) | | | | | | | | | |
|---|---|---|---|---|---|---|---|---|---|---|
| | 0 (none) | | | 3 (little) | | | 6 (extensive) | | | 10 (total) |
| 1. Large # Firms Competing | 0 | 1 | 2 | 3 | 4 | 5 | 6 | 7 | 8 | 9 | 10 |
| 2. Growth in Market is Slow | 0 | 1 | 2 | 3 | 4 | 5 | 6 | 7 | 8 | 9 | 10 |
| 3. Fixed Costs are High | 0 | 1 | 2 | 3 | 4 | 5 | 6 | 7 | 8 | 9 | 10 |
| 4. Storage Costs are High | 0 | 1 | 2 | 3 | 4 | 5 | 6 | 7 | 8 | 9 | 10 |
| 5. Cust. Switching Costs are Low | 0 | 1 | 2 | 3 | 4 | 5 | 6 | 7 | 8 | 9 | 10 |
| 6. Differentiation is Low | 0 | 1 | 2 | 3 | 4 | 5 | 6 | 7 | 8 | 9 | 10 |
| 7. Competitors Look Alike | 0 | 1 | 2 | 3 | 4 | 5 | 6 | 7 | 8 | 9 | 10 |
| 8. Stakes are High for All | 0 | 1 | 2 | 3 | 4 | 5 | 6 | 7 | 8 | 9 | 10 |
| 9. Mkt. Exit Costs are High | 0 | 1 | 2 | 3 | 4 | 5 | 6 | 7 | 8 | 9 | 10 |
| 10. Barriers of Entry are Low | 0 | 1 | 2 | 3 | 4 | 5 | 6 | 7 | 8 | 9 | 10 |

Total, Degree of Competitiveness:
(0% = None; 100% = Total)    _____ %

Now you are ready to fill in the Overall Competitiveness Matrix (Figure 13.13). To use the matrix, circle the appropriate number to score each competitive criterion. Then, you can simply add up the item scores to generate a total score on a 100-point scale.

This matrix can be filled out not only for every market/customer-set you have, but can be done at least every year to chart the changing competitive dynamics in your market on an annual basis. Make sure that you carefully analyze the results to determine which criteria provide opportunities for strategic action planning to bolster your competitiveness.

## Individual Competitor Analysis

In the prior group exercises, you have assessed the overall competitiveness of your company and industry. However, those inspections are not in themselves sufficient for two reasons: First, the earlier analyses were at a broad macro-level; second, they were internally generated based largely on the subjective feelings of the the individual or the planning team. The Individual Competitor Analysis provides a template for examining your primary competitors. You may choose to perform all or part of this analysis during the strategic planning session, although many teams will find it preferable to perform the analysis in a separate session. If you choose to devote some time to this assessment during the overall session, I recommend taking one of three prime competitors and performing a "rough cut" during the planning session itself, to be followed up with a more detailed analysis later.

The Individual Competitor Analysis System (Figure 13.14) has seven separate components and then a summary section. While the seven categories are fairly self-explanatory, their purpose is summarized as follows:

1. *Basic Demographics* addresses the fundamental matters of competitor size and identification.

2. *Products/Services/Markets* identifies what the competitor provides and where it provides it.

3. *Business/Financial Performance* addresses the important financial and performance data.

4. *Sales Strategy* covers sales/marketing approaches and account performance.

5. *Differentiators* addresses what is unique and different about that competitor.

## Figure 13.14—Individual Competitor Analysis System

| Group Exercise: Individual Competitor Analysis System | | | |
|---|---|---|---|
| **Competitor:** <br><br> **Data Element:** | Competitor #:____ <br><br> Name:_____ | Competitor #:____ <br><br> Name:_____ | Competitor #____ <br><br> Name:_____ |
| **1. Basic Demographics** | | | |
|   a. Total sales | | | |
|   b. Number of employees | | | |
|   c. Number of offices & locations | | | |
|   d. Name of chief executive | | | |
|   e. How owned (private/public subsidiary, etc.) | | | |
|   f. HQ location/parent company | | | |
|   g. _____ | | | |
| **2. Products/Services/Markets** | | | |
|   a. Major products | | | |
|   b. Major services | | | |
|   c. Major industries penetrated | | | |
|   d. Major market niches | | | |
|   e. Reputed prod./service quality | | | |
|   f. _____ | | | |
| **3. Business/Financial Performance** | | | |
|   a. Net profits | | | |
|   b. Debt to equity ratio | | | |
|   c. Est. sales by product/service | | | |
|   d. Historical performance | | | |
|   e. Other background information | | | |
|   f. Approximate market position | | | |
|   g. _____ | | | |

## Figure 13.14—Individual Competitor Analysis System (continued)

| Group Exercise: Individual Competitor Analysis System (continued) | | | |
|---|---|---|---|
| **Competitor:**<br><br>**Data Element:** | Competitor #:____<br><br>Name:_____ | Competitor #:____<br><br>Name:_____ | Competitor #____<br><br>Name:_____ |
| **4. Sales Strategy**<br> a. Type of sales organization/ structure<br> b. Targeted markets<br> c. Sales presentation approach<br> d. Marketing collateral materials<br> e. Use of advert./other promotions<br> f. Major new accounts<br> g. Major lost accounts<br> h. Major vulnerable accounts<br> i. Won/lost vs. competitors<br> j. _____<br><br>**5. Differentiators**<br> a. Use of technology<br> b. Pricing strategy<br> c. Unique features/benefits<br> d. Vert./horiz. integration?<br> e. Overall industry reputation<br> f. _____ | | | |

## Figure 13.14—Individual Competitor Analysis System (concluded)

| Group Exercise:  Individual Competitor Analysis System (concluded) | | | |
|---|---|---|---|
| **Competitor:** | **Competitor #:___** | **Competitor #:___** | **Competitor #___** |
| **Data Element:** | **Name:_____** | **Name:_____** | **Name:_____** |
| **6. Infrastructure**<br>  a. How organized?<br>  b. Mfg. capacity<br>  c. Distribution methods<br>  d. Critical suppliers<br>  e. Corporate culture<br>  f. Quality of human resources<br><br>**7. Strategic Elements**<br>  a. Vision/mission<br>  b. Known alliances/JV's<br>  c. Strategic thrusts/goals<br>  d. Financial goals<br>  e. Growth (niche/mkt. focus)<br>  f. Prods./svcs. in development?<br>  g. Prod./svc. enhancements?<br>  h. _____ | | | |
| **Evaluation Summary**<br><br>For each category, give a<br>0 to 15 score:     0 = Lowest<br>                    15 = Perfect<br><br>1. Demographic strength<br>2. Product/service/mkt. strength<br>3. Business/financial strength<br>4. Sales strategy strength<br>5. Differentiator strength<br>6. Infrastructure strength<br>7. Strategic direction strength<br><br>**Total Score:**<br>(Out of Possible <u>105</u>) | (Note:  Even if you only have partial data for above, what is your intuitive feeling for each item below?) | | |

6. *Infrastructure* covers how the company is structured internally, including its culture and human resources capability.

7. *Strategic Elements* address what is known about that competitor's vision, strategies, and major activities.

The *Evaluation Summary* is filled in by assigning a grade of zero (0) to fifteen (15) for each of the seven categories, for a 105-point scale total (7 sections x 15 points/section = 105 points).

## Using the Individual Competitor Analysis Results

There are several major ways in which this data can be used:

1. **You can compare and contrast all of the totals** and sectional scores to determine each competitor's strengths and weaknesses.

2. **You can fill this form out for your own company**—at least scoring the Evaluation Summary, in order to compare and contrast the totals and sectional scores to determine your and each competitor's relative strengths and weaknesses.

3. **You can retake this analysis for your competitors on an annual basis** to determine shifts in overall and specific areas of strengths and weaknesses.

4. The goal of all of these sets of analyses is to determine what **major steps you should take to enhance your competitiveness** across your product/service lines.

# Chapter Fourteen

# Venue Two—
# All About Strategic Goals

## Venue Two Overview

In Venue One, we covered:

- How to perform a comprehensive *valuation* of the present condition of the enterprise

- How to identify and integrate your corporate *values*

- How to develop a clear *vision* for the enterprise

- How to undertake a complete scan of your internal and external environmental *variables*

By doing this fourfold review via Venue One, the origination point of the strategic planning effort, you have uncovered a number of key opportunities that, along with any others you may choose to add, form the content of Venue Two.

In this Venue of Opportunities, we will:

1. Identify your enterprise's *goal categories*
2. Present a systematic and simple process to make thorough *identification* of the enterprise's *major strategic goals*
3. Present a process for these major strategic goals to be *prioritized*
4. Identify those strategic goals that need *action plans* in order to be implemented.

## Strategic Goal Categories' Identification

You may recall from the Valuation section of Venue One that the Written Pre-Interviews and Strategic Enterprise Assessment each utilize four strategic quadrants with sixteen total sections, each section covering a slice of complementary strategic territory. The Enterprise Strategic Goal Categories Wheel (Figure 14.1) uses the same kind of circular template as the one used for the SEA (Figure 8.2). Please note the Strategic Goal Wheel's sixteen strategic goal categories.

The most obvious feature of the wheel is the one-to-one correspondence between its section and the sections introduced in Venue One. In fact, if any of these categories is not intuitively clear to you, please review each of the seven key phrases back in the appropriate Strategic Enterprise Assessment

## Figure 14.1—Enterprise Strategic Goal Categories Wheel

**ENTERPRISE STRATEGIC GOAL CATEGORIES**

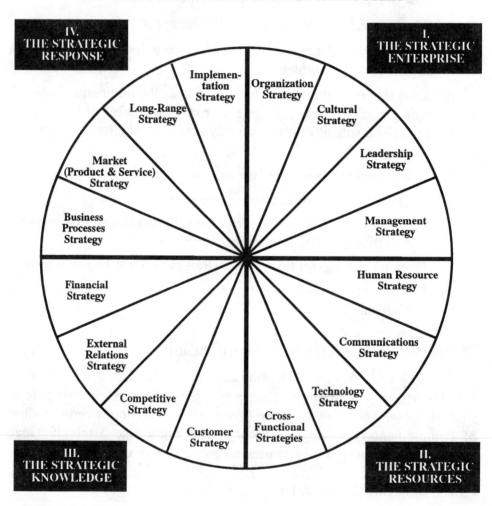

category in Chapter Eight. These seven descriptive terms will help you understand the nature and impact of each category.

To help you become more comfortable with these sixteen strategic goal categories and, most importantly, with how they relate to *your* enterprise, the following succinct scope-definitions are provided for each category.

## Strategic Goal Category Scope—Definitions

### Section I. The Strategic Enterprise

1. **Organization Strategy**: structure, roles, responsibilities, reporting relationships.

2. **Cultural Strategy:** atmosphere, style, what is rewarded, what is discouraged.

3. **Leadership Strategy**: executive development, training, succession, compensation, ability, effectiveness, leadership.

4. **Management Strategy:** management development, training, succession, compensation, ability, effectiveness, empowerment, autonomy.

### Section II. The Strategic Resources

5. **Human Resource Strategy:** total HR headcount requirements, development, training, efficiency, effectiveness, capacity, motivation, involvement, empowerment, support, loyalty.

6. **Communications Strategy:** information flow up, down, out, in; communication systems, methods, effectiveness, teamwork, synergy.

7. **Technology Strategy:** understanding of, leverage of, investment in, use as exclusive differentiator.

8. **Cross-Functional Strategies:** each organization's and function's specific plans, integration, cross-pollination, coordination, synergy in unison.

### Section III. The Strategic Knowledge

9. **Customer Strategy:** commitment, focus, knowledge, support, systems, communication, problems, quality.

10. **Competitive Strategy:** knowledge, strengths and weaknesses, opportunities and threats, major strategies, pricing, key responses.

11. **External Relations Strategy:** market, economy, government, social forecasts, public/market perception, public relations, vendors, suppliers, industrial relations.

12. **Financial Strategy:** financial resources, cost/expense management, budgets,targets, measurement of actuals, reviews, cash flow, financial statement goals.

### Section IV. The Strategic Response

13. **Business Processes/Systems Strategy:** total quality management, critical processes, identification and plans, regulatory policies, effectiveness of processes, continuous improvement of systems, other infrastructural systems.

14. **Market (Product & Services) Strategy:** products, services, markets, plans, performance, development, mix, differentiation.

15. **Long-Range Strategy:** addresses uncertainty, risk, conflicts, agendas, needs, critical success factors, investments, resources.

16. **Implementation Strategy:** plan, implement, quantify/qualify goals, tracking, action plans, completion, adjustment, flexibility, updates, new iterations.

## About These Categories

The four major sectors—concerning the strategic *enterprise, resources, knowledge,* and *response*—are complementary to and distinct from each other. In the same way, the four categories within each of the four major sections are also complementary to and distinct from each other. But there are also natural interconnections, dependencies, and thematic overlaps in places. For example, the Cross-Functional Strategies (#8), may well contain human resource, communications, and technology strategies that tie in with goals covered in other categories, such as Human Resource Strategy (#5), Communications Strategy (#6), and Technology Strategy (#7).

## Flexibility and Tailoring

Due to a unique situation or special characteristic of your enterprise, you may wish to add a new and different category to this list using the extra forms provided in Addendum A and Addendum B. Secondly, the "granularity," or specific identification, of sixteen separate categories does not mean that your goal-setting process needs to be complex, laborious, or complicated! Rather, *consider the four major sections and sixteen total categories as a checklist that serves to trigger your thinking in all aspects of the business, so that you think of and select the truly most significant strategic goals.* In addition, you will have an opportunity to change, add, or delete strategic goal categories later on in the formats section.

## A Further Word on Cross-Function Strategies

There is a reason why "strategy" is used in the plural for Cross-Functional Strategies (#8). The "functions" are the various departments or activities generic to any enterprise of any size, such as manufacturing, engineering, sales, marketing, accounting, human resources, purchasing, and so forth. Each function needs its own strategy, with a particular focus on implementing its part of the overall strategic plan. Secondly, each functional strategy needs to be interconnected with the others so that clear communication and crisp execution is ensured. This interconnection among units (or functions, departments, etc.) is what is meant by *"cross-functional strategies"—the effective, coordinated fusion of complementary organizational plans to execute the big, corporate one.* The chart in Figure 14.2 illustrates the tie-in between these cross-functional strategies and the overall plan categories.

## The Three Different Types of Strategic Items

Before beginning the strategic item identification process, it is necessary to define clearly the three major types of strategic elements, all of which are germane for your upcoming strategic item lists. During my decade in twelve assignments at IBM, mostly in the planning arena, I heard many different definitions for strategy, objectives, goals, and other planning-type words. While I am not claiming these to be the right and final definitions, time and again my clients have found them to be intuitively logical, easy to remember, and helpfully distinctive from one another.

## Figure 14.2—Cross-Functional Strategies and Strategic Goal Categories Chart

| Enterprise Strategic Goal Category | Illustrative Cross-Functional Strategies for Strategic Goal Categories | | | | | | | |
|---|---|---|---|---|---|---|---|---|
| | Manufacturing | Engineering | Sales | Marketing | Accounting | Administration | Support | Purchasing |
| Organization | | | | | | | | |
| Cultural | | | | | | | | |
| Leadership | | | | | | | | |
| Management | | | | | | | | |
| Human Resource | | | | | | | | |
| Communications | | | | | | | | |
| Technology | | | | | | | | |
| Customer | | | | | | | | |
| Competitive | | | | | | | | |
| External Relations | | | | | | | | |
| Financial | | | | | | | | |
| Business Process | | | | | | | | |
| Market | | | | | | | | |
| Long-Range | | | | | | | | |
| Implementation | | | | | | | | |

What fills in these slots are action plans that people in various functions will do (see Venues IV and V). Also, how to **coordinate** functional plans into the enterprise plan is addressed.

- **Strategic Results:**
  These are the *"why"* or *"how much"* items, the typically *quantitative* long-range targets or *desired outcomes* as the issuance of successful execution of strategic goals.

- **Strategic Goals:**
  These are the *"what"* items, the *objectives,* the major *initiatives* needed to fulfill the desired strategic results.

- **Strategic Means:**
  These are the *"how"* items, the *implementational actions*, the ways in which the strategic goals are achieved in order to attain the desired results.

A visual depiction of how these three strategic elements flow "down and up" is shown in Figure 14.3.

**Figure 14.3—Flow of Strategic Elements**

FLOW OF STRATEGIC ELEMENTS

Planning Mode   Executing Mode

Strategic Results

Strategic Goals

Strategic Means

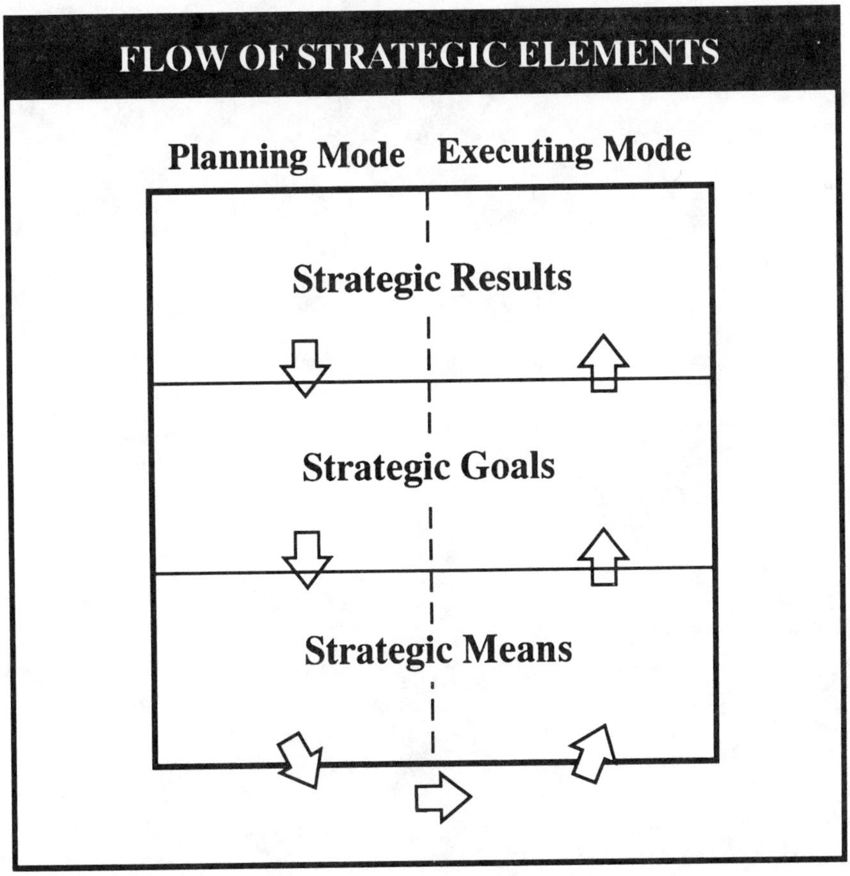

## Flow of Strategic Elements

The Flow of Strategic Elements (Figure 14.3) reads as follows: "In the *Planning Mode, strategic results,* or targets, are set as the long-term focus (serving as the *"eyes"* or the focuses of the strategic plan). These strategic results drive the identification and pursuit of *strategic goals* (serving as the *"heart"* of the strategic plan), which in turn are implemented by the development of *strategic means,* the practical year-one action plans (serving as the *"hands"* of the strategic plan).

In the *Executing Mode,* the *strategic means,* once implemented, drive the fulfillment of the *strategic goals,* and these strategic goals, when fulfilled, drive the achieving of *strategic results,* the pre-established long-term targets of the enterprise.

# Chapter Fifteen

# Strategic Goal Identification and Prioritization

In this chapter, first we will cover the process by which the individual strategic planning participant identifies his or her major strategic goals for the organization. Second, we will identify and explain the method by which all of the individuals' goals are merged and then prioritized to generate the group's consensus strategic goals.

At this very point, at the edge of the planning precipice and ready to launch out on strategic flight, the participant stands upon an accumulated large mound of strategic material, analysis, and brain activity that was built up from nearly all aspects of the company. *Now, in by far the most crucial input the individual will make in strategic plan formulation, the planning participant has a completely clean canvas upon which to brush in the shapes and colors from the palette of his or her strategic thinking.*

The section is all about each individual taking ownership. In the entire spectrum of the planning process, now is the actual time to set forth the participant's best ideas. "Later" is too late. *The necessary ingredients for this exercise are creativity, originality, freedom, and above all, acceptance of complete personal responsibility.* Each person needs to think boldly and express honestly, with creativity, having the inferred permission to make a complete contribution. At the same time, each participant should represent his or her areas of business, technical, market, and financial expertise, all of which are needed to build a good final plan.

Before finalizing your goals list, look back at every section that has been completed in Venue One, including the pre-work, values, vision, and internal (stakeholder and "SF SWOT") and external (customer/market/competitor) analyses. Make sure that any lights or triggers set off by these prior sections are remembered, in order to convert your insights into strategic goals.

## Individual Major Strategic Goals Identification

In Addendum A, sixteen individual participant Strategic Goals Identification Sheets are provided to capture each participant's strategic goal ideas. It is very important that individuals take the sufficient time to do an adequate, thorough job to provide their inputs. It is the individuals' contributions that literally drive the rest of the planning process!

It should be no surprise to you that the identification sheets provided are one page per each of the sixteen strategic goal categories identified in Chapter Fourteen. Additional sheets are included in case you have a strategic goal that does not fit into one of these sixteen categories, an unlikely yet possible eventuality. The participants should not feel pressed to create goals in each of the sixteen categories, but only to use those categories for which there is a specific major goal in mind. The sample form in Figure 15.1 shows the first of the sixteen strategic goal category input sheets.

### Figure 15.1—Individual Major Strategic Goals Identification Sheet

| Personal Exercise: Individual Major Strategic Goals Identification | | |
|---|---|---|
| **Section I: The Strategic Enterprise**<br>**Category 1: Organization Strategy**<br>Includes areas such as: structure, roles, responsibilities, reporting relationships. | | |
| **Strategic Item** | **Check One:**<br>Result  Goal  Means | **Explanation/Notes**<br>**(Why, How Measured, Etc.)** |
| 1. _____ | ☐  ☐  ☐ | |
| 2. _____ | ☐  ☐  ☐ | |
| 3. _____ | ☐  ☐  ☐ | |
| 4. _____ | ☐  ☐  ☐ | |
| 5. _____ | ☐  ☐  ☐ | |

## Explaining the Individual Goals Sheet

1. First, note that *clear referencing* is provided at the top of each form: first the Section (from I through IV), and then the Category (from 1 to 16), accompanied by their appropriate names.

2. Next, note that a *brief description* of the category is provided underneath the category's number and name, in order to provide a convenient reminder of each one.

3. The input categories involve *three basic columns*. The first, *Strategic Item,* gives a title to the strategic idea that the participant has. There is room provided for five strategic items per page. The second column identifies whether the item the participant has written in is a strategic result (a quantitative outcome), a strategic goal (a directional objective), or a strategic means (an implementational action). You should have no pre-set preference for one of these three types of strategic items above another. Each has its role and its place in the overall strategic plan. The third column is a convenience section, a space for the participant to write in any explanatory notes and to record any thoughts about the strategic item.

## Major Strategic Goals Summarization

After all individual participants have completed writing their major strategic items on the worksheets, *summarization* at a group level needs to occur. This is done by the facilitator proceeding category by category, asking for and collecting all the items that the individuals have written down for each of the sixteen categories. This step is taken by using the Major Strategic Goals Summarization Sheet (Figure 15.2). Some facilitator side-notes: (1) The first person to give a strategic goal will have that goal posted. If three or four others have that same goal, there is no need for them to re-submit or re-discuss it. It is covered! "Non-redundant first-mentioning" saves a lot of time in the goal-collection stage; (2) when individuals are giving their inputs category by category, that time is not the time for debate about that goal, but for ensuring that the meaning and scope of each goal is *understood.* This keeps the input flow going and the atmosphere proactive, conducive for the surfacing of new and different ideas.

If the participants have generated strategic items that they believe do not belong in the sixteen categories but in new and different ones (something that has never happened with my clients but that theoretically could), and the group agrees that the goal cannot be accommodated by one of the sixteen

## Figure 15.2—Major Strategic Goals Summarization Sheet

| Group Exercise: Major Strategic Goals Summarization | | | | | | | |
|---|---|---|---|---|---|---|---|
| Section I: The Strategic Enterprise<br>Category 1: Organization Strategy<br>Includes areas such as: structure, roles, responsibilities, reporting relationships. | | | | | | | |
| | | | | Refer to Section: D | | | E |
| Strategic Item | Check One: | | | Individual Prioritization Votes | Vote Totals | Category Priority | Total Plan Priority | Year-One Action Plan |
| | Result | Goal | Means | | | | | |
| 1. | ☐ | ☐ | ☐ | ☐ ☐ ☐ ☐ | ☐ | ☐ | ☐ | ☐ |
| 2. | ☐ | ☐ | ☐ | ☐ ☐ ☐ ☐ | ☐ | ☐ | ☐ | ☐ |
| 3. | ☐ | ☐ | ☐ | ☐ ☐ ☐ ☐ | ☐ | ☐ | ☐ | ☐ |
| 4. | ☐ | ☐ | ☐ | ☐ ☐ ☐ ☐ | ☐ | ☐ | ☐ | ☐ |
| 5. | ☐ | ☐ | ☐ | ☐ ☐ ☐ ☐ | ☐ | ☐ | ☐ | ☐ |
| 6. | ☐ | ☐ | ☐ | ☐ ☐ ☐ ☐ | ☐ | ☐ | ☐ | ☐ |
| 7. | ☐ | ☐ | ☐ | ☐ ☐ ☐ ☐ | ☐ | ☐ | ☐ | ☐ |
| 8. | ☐ | ☐ | ☐ | ☐ ☐ ☐ ☐ | ☐ | ☐ | ☐ | ☐ |
| 9. | ☐ | ☐ | ☐ | ☐ ☐ ☐ ☐ | ☐ | ☐ | ☐ | ☐ |
| 10. | ☐ | ☐ | ☐ | ☐ ☐ ☐ ☐ | ☐ | ☐ | ☐ | ☐ |
| 11. | ☐ | ☐ | ☐ | ☐ ☐ ☐ ☐ | ☐ | ☐ | ☐ | ☐ |
| 12. | ☐ | ☐ | ☐ | ☐ ☐ ☐ ☐ | ☐ | ☐ | ☐ | ☐ |
| 13. | ☐ | ☐ | ☐ | ☐ ☐ ☐ ☐ | ☐ | ☐ | ☐ | ☐ |
| 14. | ☐ | ☐ | ☐ | ☐ ☐ ☐ ☐ | ☐ | ☐ | ☐ | ☐ |
| 15. | ☐ | ☐ | ☐ | ☐ ☐ ☐ ☐ | ☐ | ☐ | ☐ | ☐ |

categories, then a seventeenth can be added, and so forth, until all submitted items find a categoric home.

Not all categories may collect goals. The key is to ensure that there is no need for any major strategic goals in that category. Specific discussion should occur as to why these categories did not collect goals, and what should or should not go in one of these previously blank categories.

After all goals have been collected on the summary sheets, the next phase, Item Prioritization, can occur. If appropriate, the facilitator can appoint a person to record the group data, then copy it for all. Another method is that the goals, when collected, can be written down on flip charts on two or three pages of lined entries for all to be able to view. Category and Total Plan priority will be done a bit later, after the "voting" is completed. A description of the Summarization Sheet follows.

## Description of the Summarization Sheet

Please note that, once again, there is a one-page form for each of the strategic goal categories, sixteen pages in all. Also, as mentioned earlier, there are extra Summarization Sheets if the group has decided to add a seventeenth or eighteenth category. You can find all of these Major Strategic Goals Summarization Sheets in Addendum B in the last part of this book.

Regarding the form itself, essentially it is a group summary mechanism for the individuals' goal sheets. Remember that the facilitator is to take the group through these summary sheets category by category, writing on the sheets or on flip charts the *Strategic Goals* (first column) for as many identified goals the individuals may have. Also, remember that you do not want to have redundancy or overlap on the goals. They should be separate, distinct, and complementary.

The *Result/Goal/Means* section is a simple "check one" format. Over 90% of these items will be goals, with at most a handful of Results and Means. The third column, *Individual Prioritization Votes*, is the place where individuals' votes will be written in when the time comes. However, the voting process does not take place until after all of the sixteen categories are completed, because the voting will be done on the entire population of strategic goals that have been submitted.

## The Prioritization Process

Once all of the major strategic items have been generated and summarized in their appropriate categories, it is important to find out what the group's sense of priorities are and extract them from the large total goals list. This is accomplished by each person casting a set number of votes on certain goals from the entire list. Through much trial and error with strategic goal-voting methodologies through the years, I have settled upon some guidelines that have worked well for me with my clients. The principle I use is called *"meaningful voting coverage."* The entire process is, at its front-end, an inherently democratic one, wherein each participant has the freedom to contribute every item that he or she deems to be important. Then, at the next stage of democratic due-process, each person has the right to cast a given number of votes to bring priority, focus, and order to the substantial and assorted list that has been collected.

*The opportunity for each individual to invest in strategic planning causes him or her to take ownership in the process and then in the outcome. That sense of intensified, enhanced teamwork, of consensus, of unified buy-in, is a big ancillary benefit of all individuals in the group participating in the strategic planning process.* This idea lies at the least of my "meaningful coverage" voting philosophy. I like to see enough votes given to cover at least 40% of the strategic planning items. For example, if there are 45 goals, then at least 20 votes should be cast per person; if 60 goals, then at least 25 votes; if 75 goals, then at least 30 votes, and so forth. What I typically direct participants to do is place no more than five (5) votes per any one given goal, but they can mix up the number of votes they give an item from one (1) to five (5). I also remind them of their responsibility to wear their "largest" corporate hat, and to vote accordingly (not for any self-serving or parochial interest a participant knows to be subordinate to other goals or strategic needs/opportunities).

## Casting Votes

Each strategic planning participant should review all of the group exercise Major Strategic Goals Summarization Sheets for each of the sixteen categories. Consider which strategic items are the most important to you on an *individual* basis. In fact, I have found it most helpful if individuals place an "X" by or circle the numbers of any strategic goals that strike them as being particularly important *while* they are being consolidated on the group worksheets category by category. This saves time in the review process later.

Focus more on the "Goals" and "Means" items rather than on any "Results" items, which typically will result if a number of goals and means are identified and performed.

Once you have selected your top goals, prioritize them in your own mind, and determine how many votes each should get. I have found through the years that individuals employ a variety of ways to divide their votes. For example, if they have 30 votes on 75 goals, some individuals will narrow their voting to 6 major goals at 5 votes each. Others will vote for 30 separate items! Most fall inbetween, for example casting 5 votes for 1 item, 3 votes for 3 items, 2 votes for 5 items, and 1 vote for 6 items (5 x 1 = 5, + 3 x 3 = 9, + 2 x 5 = 10, + 1 x 6 = 6, = 25 votes in all), and so forth. The key is "to thine own self be true." *This flexibility of voting is another important dimension in further heightening the sense of personal ownership each participant has in developing his or her own strategic agenda for the enterprise.* Once the individual has selected the goals and determined how many votes each should receive, the votes should be written in on one of the small boxes in the *Individual Prioritized Votes* for that particular item.

The facilitator or other designated person should start with Category 1, Goal #1, and collect votes for each item. A very simple and easy way to do this is to call out the item number and ask for all participants to indicate their votes by immediately raising the number of fingers on one hand that corresponds to the number of votes being cast, from one finger for one vote to five fingers for five votes. Then, with a quick count of raised "fingers on hands," the total number of votes is collected very quickly. The person counting the votes should then write down the total number of votes item by item in the *Vote Totals* boxes to the right of each item in the fourth major column.

With votes gathered and totaled for all strategic items, each category's items can be ranked *within* the category, with the ranking shown in the *Category Priority* column to the right of the *Vote Totals* category. But the most important next step is to rank all of the strategic items from all 16 categories, ranking at least the "Top 10" or "Top 20" in the *Total Plan Priority* column to the right of the *Category Priority* column. These results—the overall priorities of the group—are very important, as they form the very heart of the strategic plan. These priorities as a group are all the more significant in that, out of a universe of options and alternatives, the participants have identified the major opportunities and crucial needs of the enterprise for the upcoming years.

The final activity to be done for Venue Two's Goals Identification and Prioritization is to determine, particularly for the top 20 to 30 vote-getters, which strategic items will require the development of specific action plans for their implementation or commencement within the next six to twelve months. I have found that the vast majority of top-prioritized goals require first-year action plans, while only a few are out-year items that will be addressed from year two onward. The space provided for this action plan designation is the right-most column on the summarization worksheet, marked *Year-One Action Plan.*

## Venue Two Summary

Because of the comprehensive preparatory work performed in all of the sections of Venue One, at the beginning of Venue Two—the second major stage of our strategic sojourn—"we were all dressed up" but still had "nowhere to go" as yet. What Venue Two has served to do is to bring to the surface *all* of the goal candidates for *consideration* for inclusion in the core strategic portfolio, then *facilitation* of certain important, commonly held and agreed-to strategies. Now, at the end of Venue Two, the enterprise's agenda has gone from previously unknown to distinctly clear. The remaining Venues add definition, depth, and development and deployment to the firm foundation the planning team has laid through this goal-setting process.

# Chapter Sixteen

# Venue Three—Setting Your Multi-Year Financial Objectives

We have covered Venue One as the *origination* point of the strategic planning session, and Venue Two as the identification of *opportunities* to maximize the future of the enterprise. In this chapter, we address the third station of our strategic journey: *Venue Three—the quantification of the major directions of the organization into objectives.*

This section focuses on the act of quantification into "units" and "dollars," making tangible milestones out of the overall strategic directions. In Venue Three, first the key financial and business assumptions will be charted. Then these criteria will be utilized to formulate summarized, top-down income statements for future years, that will chart the annual stair-steps of the company's strategic future.

One contextual observation: Traditional strategic planning has been fixated on crunching out "five-year financials" based upon a few assumptions, reducing a potential holistic strategic effort into a financial, "bean-counting" exercise. It is extremely important to recognize that the financials produced in Venue Three are driven and calibrated by all of the work already completed in Venues One and Two.

## Key Business and Financial Assumptions and Rates

*Overview*

All of the output that your strategic planning team will have generated to this point in the process is a large set of assumptional material. Our focus at the onset of Venue Three is on specific "hard-data" assumptions useful in setting your "Strategic P & L (Profit and Loss)" or Income Statement. The focal question is, *"What are the important financial and business variables we need to identify in order to set our quantified business objectives?"*

*Enterprise Revenue Structure*

The first step of assumption setting is to identify the actual revenue structure of your organization. What are your enterprise's revenue building blocks? Do you measure revenue by corporate divisions? By product or service type? By both? As one total number? By other formats? The upcoming exercise helps the strategic participants identify the ideal manner in which they would like the company's strategic revenues, costs, and profits to be charted.

### Group Exercise: Forming a Simple Strategic Revenue Structure

Remember that the goal of this Venue is the generation of major, annual, product/service financial targets. You are not generating some kind of full-blown operating budget. No, far more preferably for these purposes, you are setting up a simple structure through which to calculate basic revenue flows into the "out-years." The following exercise is ideally suited for the planning team to answer as a group. Remember the "keep it simple" rule. Ideally, plans are made to be comprehended, referred to long after the session, and updated periodically. Detailed over-complexity will not serve you well here. You are now ready to fill in, on an individual or group basis, the first sheet of the Strategic Revenue Structure exercise (Figure 16.1).

## The Enterprise Strategic Revenue Matrix—Matrix Column Definitions

The next phase of assumption setting, The Enterprise Strategic Revenues Matrix (Figure 16.2), builds on the previous step we have just completed. The following definitions are provided to help you understand each column of the matrix:

- **Name of Enterprise Function/Division:**
  If your enterprise has multiple functions or divisions that generate revenues, you can name each one with its respective strategic time frame (typically, the upcoming five years), with the products or services itemized to the right of the division or function, in the next column. If your enterprise does not have distinct organizational revenue centers/functions/divisions, simply skip this column altogether.

- **Name of Major Product or Service:**
  If your enterprise has distinct products or services that are revenue centers, they can be itemized accordingly.

- **If New Product/Service, 1st Full Year of Sales:**
  Often, companies will introduce new products or services over the future five-year time frame. If so, the first *full* year of revenues should be noted. This is done so that future revenues will be conservatively projected and not overstated, unless the enterprise has a proven track record of exact prediction of the time frame and revenues of new product introductions. According to my observation of dozens of new product and service introductions to the market, most are later in timing and lower in revenues than originally planned.

## Figure 16.1—Your Strategic Revenue Structure: Sheet 1

| | |
|---|---|
| **Group Exercise:  Your Strategic Revenue Structure—Sheet 1** | |
| **Check the boxes that pertain.  Fill in the blanks as appropriate.** | |

1.  What structure do you use to calculate your
    overall revenues today?

    a.    By functional division/geographic unit/
          organization                                      ☐

    b.    By type of product or service                     ☐

    c.    By product or service within each
          functional division                               ☐

    d.    Simply as "total sales"                           ☐

    e.    By another method:_____             ☐

                                                    Yes      No

2.  Does your revenue-summary system work for you now?   ☐    ☐

    If yes, will it work for your strategic plan?        ☐    ☐

    If no, which of the above systems **will** work (a. - e.)?   ☐

    Why?  _____

          _____

Figure 16.2—Your Strategic Revenue Structure: Sheet 2

| Group Exercise: Your Strategic Revenue Structure—Sheet 2 | | | | | | | | | |
|---|---|---|---|---|---|---|---|---|---|
| Enterprise Strategic Revenue Matrix | | | | | | | | | |
| | | | | Check one box per category | | | | | |
| | | | | Revenue Unit of Volume Measure | | | Annual % Changes | | |
| Item # | Name of Enterprise Function or Division | Name of Major Products or Services | If new prod/svc, 1st full year of sales | # of Units | # of Transactions | Other | Annual % Price Inc. | Total Vol. % Increase | Volume Will Vary |
| 1. | | | | | | | | | |
| 2. | | | | | | | | | |
| 3. | | | | | | | | | |
| 4. | | | | | | | | | |
| 5. | | | | | | | | | |
| 6. | | | | | | | | | |
| 7. | | | | | | | | | |
| 8. | | | | | | | | | |
| 9. | | | | | | | | | |
| 10. | | | | | | | | | |
| 11. | | | | | | | | | |
| 12. | | | | | | | | | |
| 13. | | | | | | | | | |
| 14. | | | | | | | | | |
| 15. | | | | | | | | | |

- **Revenue Unit of Volume Measure:**
  This section addresses how you count volume quantities: by unit, by transaction (TX) or by some other means.

- **Annual Volume Changes (%'s):**
  This column addresses the question of how much you anticipate unit or transaction prices will go up (or down) annually, and how much total sales volumes will go up (or down) annually. There are two options here: you can simply set an "escalation factor" of "X"% every year as an increase, *or* have different percentage changes each year if you have an accurate and reasonable basis for being that fine-tuned. In many cases, as a product ramps up or winds down dramatically, or is in a predictable cyclical (macro-economic-cycle) business, this especially will be the case.

Again, as always, avoid the planning pitfall of "analysis paralysis," which tends to rise up and bite the planners particularly during annual preparation of the out-year financial plan. You mainly are establishing general directions that do not need surgical precision, and you will update these plans every year anyway. So be *strategic,* not myopic and incremental, in your thinking.

## Other Business and Financial Assumptions

Besides the various revenue component variables we have already addressed, there are other assumptions that the planning team may wish to state. One major assumption is what the organization's Net Profit Before Taxes (NPBT) will be. Once that rate is established, you may wish to back into your total costs line (Total Revenues Minus Net Profits). Total Cost includes "Cost of Goods" (or Services "Direct Selling Expenses," and "General and Administrative Expenses" [Indirect]). You may choose to itemize these as well, but always remember to keep your strategic plan "workably simple." Lastly, you may wish to set some *general assumptions* about the following (and other) arenas:

- Headcount Levels and Staffing

- Technology and Investment Levels

- Annual General Inflation Rates

- Geographic/Territorial Alignment

- Organization Structure and Philosophy

- Major Physical Expansion Plans

- Major Acquisition and Divestment Strategies
- Major Product/Service Sourcing Assumptions
- Major Joint-Venture Agreements
- Any Other Special Assumptions

The third sheet of the Your Strategic Revenue Structure exercise (Figure 16.3) provides a space for you to document these additional assumptions.

**Figure 16.3—Your Strategic Revenue Structure: Sheet 3 (conclusion)**

| Group Exercise:  Your Strategic Revenue Structure—Sheet 3 |
|---|
| What Are the Enterprise's Other Business/Financial Assumptions? |
| 1. |
| 2. |
| 3. |
| 4. |
| 5. |
| 6. |
| 7. |
| 8. |
| 9. |
| 10. |
| |

## Generating Your 5-Year, Top-Down Profit and Loss Statement

After your identification of key business and financial assumptions, at last the enterprise planning team is ready to construct the five-year P&L statement. The governing question is, *"What are our enterprise's annual summarized revenues and profits, given our stated business and financial assumptions for the strategic period?"*

## Individual Product or Service Revenue Calculation

The format for building the enterprise strategic income (P&L) statement is straightforward. The first step is to develop mini-profit-and-loss sheets for each separate product or service. The second step is to summarize these individual product/service P&L's using the Strategic Income Statement Summary (Figure 16.5). Note that you are not *required* to perform out-year financial plans at a product or service level; you may go directly to the summary form if you have a simple revenue structure. In case you need to use the detail sheets first, the Strategic Income Statement Detail form (Figure 16.4) will allow you to do so. For additional forms for up to 10 separate product and service revenue categories, please refer to Addendum C at the back of the book.

## Explaining the Individual Product or Service Revenue Calculation Form

### The Headings

Note that the headings at the top of this form are the same as the first two column headings of the Enterprise Strategic Revenue Matrix, which was used to gather key business and financial assumptions. These same two sections (*Organization Function or Division* and *Product or Service Name*) also appear on the upcoming Strategic Income Statement Summary. For smaller companies, divisions, or products/services, you may wish to plan in thousands, whereas for larger companies, you may wish to plan in millions (actually, in tenths of millions, such as $1.0M, $2.5M, etc.). Check the appropriate box at the top accordingly.

### Assumption Variables

The first item in this column calls for the *Unit* (for products) *or Transaction* (for services) *Annual Volumes.* On the Enterprise Strategic Revenue

## Figure 16.4—Strategic Income Statement Detail

| Group Exercise: Strategic Income Statement Detail | | | | | | | |
|---|---|---|---|---|---|---|---|
| **Individual Product or Service Revenue Calculation** | | | | | | | |

**Organizational Function or Division:** _____
**Product or Service # and Name: 1.** _____
(Note: The product or service # above correlates to the row
numbers on the Strategic Income Statement Summary)
**(Check One: ☐ Millions ☐ Thousands)**

| Assumption Variables: | Prior Year Actual: 199__ | Current Year Estimate: 199__ | Strategic Period Time Frame | | | | |
|---|---|---|---|---|---|---|---|
| | | | Year 1 199__ | Year 2 199__ | Year 3 199__ | Year 4 199__ | Year 5 199__ |
| 1. Unit or Transaction Annual Volume: | ☐ | ☐ | ☐ | ☐ | ☐ | ☐ | ☐ |
| 2. Price Per Unit or Transaction: | ☐ | ☐ | ☐ | ☐ | ☐ | ☐ | ☐ |
| 3. Total Revenue by Year: | ☐ | ☐ | ☐ | ☐ | ☐ | ☐ | ☐ |
| Optional: | | | | | | | |
| 4. Total Expenses: | ☐ | ☐ | ☐ | ☐ | ☐ | ☐ | ☐ |
| 5. Total Profits: | ☐ | ☐ | ☐ | ☐ | ☐ | ☐ | ☐ |

Notes: _____
_____
_____

Matrix, the basic assumptions were settled. Simply lay your volumes in and escalate or change them according to your prior assumptions. Next, lay in your base-line price per unit, or transaction, and plug in, or change, the annual price according to your prior assumptions. The third step is simply to multiply #1 (Volumes) by #2 (Price) to generate #3 (Total Revenue by Year). Steps #4 and #5 involve the insertion of estimated total expenses by year. When #4 (Total Expenses) are subtracted from #3 (Total Revenues), that results in #5 (Total Profits).

Now that we have covered the columns from top to bottom, we need to focus on the columns that cover all of the years from left to right. The first column, *Prior Year Actual: 199___,* is the total annual number for all of the rows of your last full prior (not partial or current) year. Why this column? The historical year's "actual" provides a real benchmark, hopefully not to promote extrapolative thinking, but to serve as a helpful frame of reference. The second column, *Current Year Estimate: 199___,* is dedicated to reflect the plan or estimate you have in place for the current year. The next five columns (*Year 1, Year 2,* etc.) cover the up to five out-years that represent your company's strategic future. At the very bottom of the worksheet is a *Notes* section where you can write in any special considerations, assumptions, or information that contribute to the above compilations.

Once you have filled in individual worksheets for each product and/or service you have, you are ready to post your sheet totals on the Strategic Income Statement Summary (Figure 16.5).

The purpose of this sheet is to summarize the individual product/service worksheets. The revenue totals should be laid in row by row from the *Total Revenue by Year* line (#3) of each individual worksheet. After entering all of the individual total revenues, the next step is to add up all of these to calculate the *Total Revenues* lines by year for the entire enterprise.

Note that the *Total Expenses* line is either something you compute separately and insert, or if you developed expenses on an individual product/ service basis, simply add up the total expense lines for individual worksheets by year and write in your total on the *Total Expenses* line of the summary worksheet. Your final step is a mathematical one: to subtract *Total Expenses* from *Total Revenues* to compute the *Total Profits,* or *NPBT* (Net Profit Before Taxes). Remember that the individual and summarized expenses and profits are not mandatory items. You may wish to focus only on the "top line," total revenues.

## Figure 16.5—Strategic Income Statement Summary

| Group Exercise: Strategic Income Statement Summary | | | | | | | | |
|---|---|---|---|---|---|---|---|---|
| (Note: Please refer to following pages for individual product or service revenue calculations. This shows summary data only.) | | | | | | | | |
| REVENUES: $ in ☐ Millions or ☐ Thousands (Check One) | | | | | | | | |
| Organi- zation or Division | Product or Service Name | Prior Year Actual: 199___ | Current Year Estimate 199___ | Strategic Period Time Frame | | | | |
| | | | | Year 1 199___ | Year 2 199___ | Year 3 199___ | Year 4 199___ | Year 5 199___ |
| | 1. | | | | | | | |
| | 2. | | | | | | | |
| | 3. | | | | | | | |
| | 4. | | | | | | | |
| | 5. | | | | | | | |
| | 6. | | | | | | | |
| | 7. | | | | | | | |
| | 8. | | | | | | | |
| | 9. | | | | | | | |
| | 10. | | | | | | | |
| | 11. | | | | | | | |
| | 12. | | | | | | | |
| | 13. | | | | | | | |
| | 14. | | | | | | | |
| | 15. | | | | | | | |
| Total Revenues: | | $ | $ | $ | $ | $ | $ | $ |
| Total Expenses: | | ( ) | ( ) | ( ) | ( ) | ( ) | ( ) | ( ) |
| Total Profits (NPBT): | | $ | $ | $ | $ | $ | $ | $ |

All in all, *you have a great deal of latitude for how thoroughly you build year-to-year financials.* On one extreme, you can utilize only this summary sheet and focus on total revenues. That simplifies the yearly financials, reducing them to as few as seven numbers for seven years of revenues. Or, you can build total mini-P&L's with revenues, expenses, and profits for seven years (past, present, and the next five years) for every product and/or service. In addition, if your planning team does not wish to generate year-to-year financials during the planning session itself, several people can be appointed by the group to develop yearly strategic financials via an after-session action plan.

The main focus of Venue Three—*objectives*—is on developing quantified financial benchmarks for future years. These out-year financial plans should be updated on an annual basis. This is why they should not be developed with an undue level of detail. The plans beckon the enterprise to launch toward and hurdle over them, and serve the important purpose of setting tangible future markers by which to measure the performance of the enterprise. They are also like directional torches that project the future, and with the lighting of these torches comes the recognition of how far the organization has already come in the strategic planning process—from the vagueness of pre-launch possibilities in Venue One, onward to the distinct goal priorities of Venue Two, and further forward to the clear financial targets of Venue Three.

"What remains?" you may ask. Two Venues to meet two needs: Venue Four, to set vital year-one action plans that convert all of the "what's" into "how's," and Venue Five, to ensure that the entire strategic plan and attendant actions are implemented, on time and well! And after these final two Venues, I have added a final chapter by Dr. Ellen Domb that addresses the crucial matter of how front-end strategic planning integrates smoothly into a total-quality-management (TQM), ongoing-change-management way of life for a company.

# Chapter Seventeen

## Venue Four—Developing Your Year-One Action Plans

Venue One addressed all matters concerning plan *Origination,* Venue Two identified the most important strategic *Opportunities,* and Venue Three developed future year *Objectives;* now Venue Four focuses on *Operations.* It concentrates on an arena that the great majority of strategic planning programs and processes fail to address: the need to focus the entire plan on very specific, measurable, person-responsible, time-bounded actions that serve as its critical success factors.

In the introduction to the Strategic Planning Technology, we discussed the concept of leverage—the kind that occurs when operational, reactive individuals (functions, departments, divisions, etc.) become coordinated into a strategic, proactive team that synchronously addresses the truly important long-term agenda. This leverage cannot, and in actual business life does not, occur without disciplined, conscious action planning and implementation. Therefore, the focal question to be asked and answered in Venue Four is, *"How should we implement the vital year-one actions needed to lay the foundation for our strategic future?"*

## Defining the Effective Action Plan

There are several characteristics of an effective action plan that should be clearly defined and appreciated, as the action plan is the real "beast of burden" that carries the plan from concept to reality:

1. **Specific Activity:** This is neither something too general or fuzzy, nor something too pedestrian or minor. It is a specific, major action, which may involve three to six subactivities in order to complete.

2. **Measurable:** The test of what a "specific activity" is is simple: Can you tell that the activity was done? Can it be defined as a unique, specific task or event with a tangible, clear result, where some aspect of the business is different than before the activity was performed? If it is not measurable, it does not pass the "specific activity test," indicating that the item is not yet an action, and that you are not yet clear about what precisely must be done.

3. **Time-Bounded:** This "specific, measurable activity" must be one that has clear timing, with a specific beginning and ending, taking a specific number of hours, days, weeks or months to do. Time-bounding means that the activity seldom is ongoing, or that if it is ongoing, some feature of the activity is still usually checked or monitored on a monthly, quarterly, or some other regular basis. A commitment is

made for an activity to be done by a certain deadline. The date is not too general, such as "1993." When the committed time comes due, there should be completion of the tasks or a *very* good reason why not!

4. **Person-Responsible:** This time-bounded, specific, measurable activity is not performed by the "royal we," or by "them," or by "that function." It must be done by an actual person or persons—by real human beings, not left in limbo or in the vagaries of the organizational bureaucracy. When the due-date comes, this actual person (or persons) must give specific account. And this person must be the right one, having the *authority* as well as the responsibility to carry out the task. It should not necessarily be a person too high up who will automatically delegate the task, perhaps to oblivion. Neither should the assignee be that poor soul, the over-delegated one, who does not have the authority, but only the responsibility to get the job done! It is very important to match the right person(s) in the organization to the right task if you want the right result!

5. **Follow-Up on Status/Completion:** This time-bounded, specific, person-responsible, measurable activity must be monitored via a clear implementation system to maintain tracking of the task's status on a regular, ongoing basis to ensure the timely completion of the action plan. This step is so very important that the entire Venue Five (*Outcomes*) is devoted to the all-important aspect of developing an effective implementation system.

## Developing Vital Action Plans by Business Function

As you may recall from the Group Strategic Goals Worksheets of Venue Two (Chapter Fifteen), after the identification and prioritization of all major strategic goals, the last activity performed by the planning team was the identification of all items needing specific year-one action plans. For thorough action planning, those prioritized goals that need implementational actions must be considered, and the approach is to go in the order of "Top 10" or "Top 20" priorities as established in the Venue Two process.

By this point in the strategic planning process, the focus has become 100% real-world and practical: to convert ideas into actions, to shift from "planning the work" to "working the plan." It is here that most strategic planning systems and activities fail miserably, and where, without exaggeration, millions of dollars of enterprise opportunity evaporate through non-action and neglect! It is an enormous waste of time and talent to "bookshelf" the plan. How can you avoid this—the ultimate strategic trap? By taking the two steps of Venue Four and Five, the first of which is taken at this point, and by answering the question: *"How can we convert this strategic plan into a meaningful set of actions?"*

## The Process of Developing Year-One Action Plans

The process starts by referring to Venue Two, Major Strategic Goals Summarization Sheet (Figure 15.2), Column E, which contains the list of strategic items requiring year-one action plans. I recommend working on action-plan development in the order in which the strategic goals were prioritized. Why? Because your planning team may develop a large number of strategic goals, and there may not be sufficient time during the planning session to address all of them.

## Combining Like Goals

There is one important step to take before producing action plans from your Top 10 or Top 20 prioritized goals. The top-prioritized goals likely will be very significant, large, multifaceted strategic items. What this indicates is that there are a number of other strategic goals, smaller and more specific in nature, that received fewer votes and that can be *included* in one of the high-ranking major goals. Simply look at your Top 10 or Top 20 prioritized goals, and then carefully scan all of the other goals, looking to see if any of the smaller ones can be categorized under any of the larger ones. In this way, you may be able to consolidate low- and high-priority goals, logically integrating the smaller with the larger wherever they fit best, at the same time adding dimensionality to the larger goal. Why is all of this necessary? Because the importance of goals follows the 80/20 rule, *wherein 20% of the strategic items derive 80% of the strategic benefits, business results, and profits.*

You may be wondering what happens to all of the remaining strategic goals that were neither the top-prioritized nor consolidated ones. In the event that the planning group has anywhere from ten to forty of these remaining strategic goals and you have run out of time in your planning session, I recommend that a team of three or four people be assigned the task of meeting one more time in the coming weeks after the planning session in order to determine what should be done with each of these smaller items. Because these goals (1) did not receive many votes or (2) did not fit for consolidation under one of the larger goals does not mean that each could not conceivably bring substantial value to the enterprise. In addition, please do not fail to remember that each one of the planning participants contributed an item. It was important enough to that person to bring it forward to the group. This follow-up, inclusionary step brings appropriate address, and then closure, to the entire docket of contributed goals.

I have found that a very practical way of doing this post-planning session work is to go through each remaining action-plan item, classifying it as a priority 1, 2, or 3. Then, assign each to the appropriate person(s). The lower the priority, the later the due-date will be in most cases. This mop-up phase does not mean that every goal must be implemented, but rather that a *position* must be taken on whether or not to implement each item, and if so, when.

## Building Action Plans—Preliminary Notes

The Year-One Strategic Action Plan Form (Figure 17.1) provides thorough action-plan generation. Please note that Addendum D includes six additional pages of action-plan forms for you to use and make additional copies from. You have all of the forms that you need to write action plans that will sufficiently address your strategic goals. These completed action-plan forms tie in with the "Implementation System" that will be covered in Venue Five, and draw directly from the Major Strategic Goals Summarization Sheets filled out in Venue Two, as was pointed out earlier.

One last, very important preliminary point bears noting: There will be occasions when a given strategic item will require more than one action plan in order to be carried out adequately. This is done by repeating the same strategic goal identification information for each different action plan, a simple process that will become clear as you read on and look more closely at the action-plan form.

## Year-One Strategic Action-Plan Form Explanations

The action-plan form in figure 17.1 is both easy to understand and to use. Each section is described below:

- **Category #:** This is the Strategic Goal Category from #1 to #16 that you used in Venue Two for goal-setting.

- **Category Title:** This is the name of the Strategic Goal Category that corresponds to the category number. For example, Category #1 is titled *Organization.*

## Figure 17.1—Year-One Strategic Action-Plan Form

| Year-One Strategic Action Plan |
|---|

Category #: _____    Category Title: _____

Strategic Item #: _____    Item Description: _____

Implementational Action: _____

Person(s) Responsible:

Due-Date: _____/_____/_____    Actual Date: _____/_____/_____

How Measured/Notes: _____

- **Strategic Item #:** This is the item number from your Venue Two Major Strategic Goals Summarization Sheet, which is the left-most column on that worksheet, that numbers each strategic item within each of the 16 categories.

- **Item Description:** This is the description you gave to the right of the Strategic Item # on the Major Strategic Goals Summarization Sheet.

- **Implementa-tional Action:** This is the name that you choose to give each action plan. *Note that you can have multiple action plans for the same strategic item* by writing different implementation actions on the action-plan forms. This description should be very succinct and clear, such as "Develop a Competitive Analysis Report."

- **Person(s) Responsible:** This is the person (or persons) that has the full responsibility and authority to fulfill this action plan. It is this person to whom the entire organization looks for results and to whom accountability is held for the action plan's successful completion.

- **Due-Date:** _/ / This space is to be filled in with MM/DD/YY, where "MM" = month, "DD" = day, and "YY" = year. The due-date should be neither too far off nor too aggressive, especially in light of the fact that the same people may be responsible for quite a few action plans. You want the Due-Dates to reflect priority, logical sequencing, and the overall balance between a sense of urgency and solid, steady defect-free progress on the plans.

- **Actual Date:**
  _/_/_  This is the date you fill in later on when the given action plan is finally completed and totally implemented, and you are officially closing out the item.

- **How Measured/** This space is for you to write in any other points
  **Notes:** about the action, such as how you will measure its progress or completion and test its effectiveness. Also, note any relationship the action may have with other action plans or any dependencies it may have upon certain other things being done or upon people required to assist. It is an overflow space for noting any important thoughts you now may have that would be useful for future reference.

## Summary

*If prioritized strategic goals are the "heart" of the planning process, action plans are its "hands and feet," because they enable the plan that was developed to be transformed from a state of being to a state of doing.* Sadly, seldom does this ever happen with strategic plans. But, as is self-evident, action planning is a logical, practical continuation of the process. Coupled with a clear implementation system to coordinate all of these developed action plans, you have a system so workable it needs *only one ingredient to succeed: "monthly discipline."* How to set up the implementation system is covered in the final part of the Strategic Planning Technology.

# Chapter Eighteen

# Venue Five—The All-Criticality of Implementation

When the plan-generating exercises that comprise Venues One through Four are completed, the basic strategic plan has been developed. The final stage of the initial strategic planning process is to develop a clear implementation plan for your strategy. The overriding question for this step is, *"How can we ensure that, now that we have planned our work, we will work our plan successfully?"*

In Venue Four, we defined success in planning as a simple two-step process:

1. Strategic action plans must be *set*.

2. Action plans must be *done*.

*In combination, these two steps harness the strategic plan to achieve the actual leverage needed to drive the actions and realize the potential return-on-investment opportunities which the strategic plan has identified.*

## The Last Frontier: Implementation

I have spent a considerable amount of time researching strategic planning approaches and models. One of the most dramatic findings was this: *It is shocking how little, and most of the time how barely any, emphasis is placed on implementation of the strategic plan!* Frequently (and I offer the following example with not a little amazement and dismay), implementation receives only token notice, afforded an afterthought on the strategic planning systems' flow charts or on conceptual templates, appearing in the form of a little box, slanted to the far right, entitled something like "Delegated to Respective Business Units." In other words, the failure of the majority of strategic planning approaches is due to the presumption that somehow the considerable work that has been planned will get done by being pushed down into the vague and amorphous domain of day-to-day operations by some kind of executive decree. Or, even worse, the strategic plan never really gets out of the bound report and atrophies, its rich potential dissipating with every passing day of neglect. *I believe one of the fundamental reasons for this problem is that executives and their hired consultants are hesitant to drive the group to deeply practical, specifically responsible, time-driven "next steps." As a result, the good start is aborted.*

How many times you and I have seen it: Well-meaning but busy executives, re-emersed in fire-fighting chaos, soon forget the "important but inconvenient," "out-of-sight, out-of-mind" strategic agenda. Hence, dust collects on the "bookshelved" plan. (Ironically, in many cases I've seen, not much was lost because the plans that were developed did not get beyond the stage of vision, culture, market analysis, and general objectives anyway!) Regardless of the actual quality, holism, and practicality of the developed plan, the one major logic problem remains: If the strategic thinking of a given plan is on target, millions of out-year revenues and other important, less measurable business benefits are lost by not implementing the developed plans—lost simply by the leadership team's benignly unintentional but costly reversion from the realm of potential new initiatives back to the grind of day-to-day operations—the unwitting habit of perpetuating the status quo.

This final Venue is devoted to making sure the strategic plan gets done. I strongly recommend that the enterprise's strategic planning team finish its strategic planning session by developing clear, specific plans for how the plan will be implemented.

## Maximizing Your Strategic Success Potential

Strategic success potential is achieved in direct proportion to the degree to which both strategic planning and operational implementation are performed well, as illustrated by Figure 18.1, the Strategic Success Potential Template. When working through this template, please note that the vertical axis measures the enterprise team's *Quality of Strategic Planning,* while the horizontal axis measures the enterprise team's *Quality of Operational Implementation.* Both measures contain three performance gradations: "Poor to Average," "Good," and "Excellent."

On the two quality extremes, *excellent* strategic planning combined with *poor to average* operational implementation, or the converse of *poor* strategic planning and *excellent* operational implementation, will cause significant lost opportunities. In the worst case, both poor to average strategic planning and operational implementation will cause the very survival of the enterprise to be called into question. At the other extreme, the stronger both planning and implementation become, the more competitive the enterprise is likely to be.

The chart makes the point that merely "good" planning and implementation often are not enough. Why not? Because of the ferocity of the competitive global marketplace across the majority of industries. Companies achieve a relatively strong chance for strategic success when their leaders and teams are not only good at both planning and implementing, but excellent in one

## Figure 18.1—Strategic Success Potential Template

or the other. Of course, the company that excels in both is on the road to maximizing its potential.

## The Centerpiece of Successful Strategic Implementation

Drawing on my experience at IBM (where I eventually was responsible for the planning, tracking, and summarization of hundreds of millions of dollars of resources and projects), on my strategic consulting practice with dozens of corporate clients (of many shapes, types, sizes, industries, markets, classifications, services, and products), and on my responsibility as CEO and President of one of the international training and development companies, I have designed and honed a time-tested tool that I have found to be of great help for successful strategic implementation: the Monthly Executive Review (MER) process.

The Monthly Executive Review is the means by which the enterprise team can monitor and review its progress toward implementing its strategic plan on a regular basis. The Monthly Executive Review is held monthly for several reasons:

- Reviewing the action plans *less* often will cause a *loss of focus.*

- Reviewing the plan *more* often is unnecessarily excessive, as it is a long-range plan.

- Enough action plans come due each month to make a *monthly check-up* just the right timing.

- People responsible for certain action plans have *enough time* to make substantial progress toward completion on action plans that come due month by month.

- Review of the strategic action plans can be held at the *same time* that the monthly enterprise "business operations" results are reviewed (assuming your company has a monthly operations meeting).

## The Basic Monthly Executive Review Agenda

Done well, the MER is a very efficient and effective meeting that reviews the action plans' status in a regular, systematic manner. Since my approach was implemented, adjusted, tested, and refined during the 1980s in a variety of organizations, it has developed the following four performance characteristics:

1. It stimulates getting the planned job *done.*

2. It is extremely *time-efficient.*

3. It ensures that the strategic plan becomes a *living* plan, continuously updated with new action plans as necessary.

4. The *right people are kept up-to-date with the right information at the right time,* with the right level of executive focus and individual accountability.

The Monthly Executive Review format in Figure 18.2 provides a guideline that has proven to be very useful to a variety of types and sizes of organizations. Note that there are two major parts of the Monthly Executive Review:

I. Review of Monthly Operational Performance, and

II. Review of Strategic Action Plans.

## Figure 18.2—Monthly Executive Review

---

[Enterprise Name]

**Monthly Executive Review**

Month of:  June, 1993                                    Date:  7/15/93

### AGENDA

I.  **Review of Monthly Operational Performance**

   A.  **Operations**

      1.  Customer and Employee Satisfaction
      2.  Functional Performance Highlights

   B.  **Financials**

      1.  Sales by Area/Product/Service
      2.  Expenses by Category
      3.  Profits/Other
      4.  Other Financial Measures

   C.  **Focus on New Major Issues** (see II.4 below.)

II.  **Review of Strategic Action Plans**

      1.  Review of Those Past-Due
      2.  Review of Those Due Current Month
      3.  Review of Those Upcoming Next Month
      4.  Generate New Strategic Action Plans as Necessary.

III.  **Set Specific Time and Place for Next Month's MER Meeting.**

---

You may wonder how a review of operations has crept into the strategic review system. There are two major reasons, both very important. First, most companies (or divisions or functions of an enterprise as the case may be) already hold monthly operating performance reviews. Slotting a review of the Strategic Action Plans into the agenda at the end of that existing monthly meeting is a natural fit. (If you are not reviewing operations monthly, I strongly suggest that you do!) The second reason for covering operations and strategic reviews together on a monthly basis is that both philosophically and practically, strategic planning should have its fulfillment in operations. From a philosophical standpoint, the entire thesis of my Strategic Planning Technology is that long-range plans should only be devised with the view that they will get done! From a practical standpoint, combining the two aspects in one meeting is a great way to capture major new strategic opportunities that are identified during the operating review portion of the meeting, by making and adding new strategic action plans to be tracked in the strategic review portion of the meeting. The specific elements of the MER are discussed in the next section.

## Understanding the Monthly Executive Review Agenda

The first part of the MER Agenda is the *Review of Monthly Operational Performance.* Of course, every company that holds a monthly meeting to review operations has its own agenda. I have divided this first section into two classical sections: "Operations" and "Financials." The third section will be covered later.

### *Operations*

The Operations section first covers, for more than symbolic reasons, how the enterprise is doing in "Customer and Employee Satisfaction." The traditional concept of organizations has been woefully myopic, stuck in an internal, financially oriented rut. The focus should be balanced with how the external people (the customers) feel the company is doing, how they regard its products and/or services, and how the internal people (the employees) feel the company is doing in every regard. Again, if your enterprise is not quantitatively and perpetually measuring the feelings of its customers and employees, and does not review them monthly, I would challenge you not only to begin doing so, but to examine your corporate culture to determine what has kept you from doing so.

The second part of the Operations review is "Functional Performance Highlights." This typically can be done in one of two ways:

1. Each executive prepares a one-page sheet with bullets ("•"), summarizing the highlights of each functional area for the prior month. Highlights may include major achievements, concerns, opportunities, and a status on ongoing projects.

2. The second way is more informal: seated at the conference table, each person in turn gives a quick, two-to-five-minute oral summary of his or her function's monthly highlights.

Either way, the key is always to practice the 80/20 Rule. All participants should ask of themselves and each other: *"What 20% of the items of this past month represent 80% of the importance?"* In other words, what minimum of vital information brings a maximum of value? Keep the pace fast and discussion netted out and to the point. To save time, take any peripheral or subset items off-line, to be pursued between the appropriate parties after the meeting. If one item that is brought up is a major, complex point, move it to the very end of your meeting after everything else has been addressed and completed.

### Financials

The second part of the Monthly Operational Performance section is the long-running traditional favorite of the monthly company review: the Financials. My orientation is the year-to-date and current-month status of the income (profit and loss) statement, with four categories:

1. *Sales,* to whatever degree of specificity is helpful (by division, product, service, totals, etc.).

2. *Expenses,* including cost of goods/services, selling expenses, general and administrative expenses, and any other expenses you wish to track closely. At IBM, we focused regularly on "discretionary expenses," which included travel, subscriptions, special meetings, professional services/dues, and so forth.

3. *Profits,* which is the obvious third category and an important target for being in business in itself. Cash flow analysis is a related measure to net profits that is very important for ensuring that the ongoing, financial requirements of running the business are met.

4. *Other financial measurements* that you may have in addition to these, such as detailed cost analysis by product or service, inventory,

scrap, rework, capital, research and development, and other special financial categories.

## Focus on New Major Issues

The third and last Monthly Operation Review item is the bridge between Operations and Strategy: the "Focus on New Major Issues." Why is this so? Because for your strategic plan to be a *living document,* two things must be done:

1. The *original,* or latest, strategic plan, especially its batch of developed action plans, must be *reviewed regularly.*

2. *New* action plans must be *formally identified, written down,* and *folded into the existing strategic action-plan list on a monthly basis.* This leads us to the second major part of the MER: reviewing strategic action plans.

## Review of Strategic Action Plans

As you will see later on in this chapter, the review of all "open" (uncompleted) strategic action plans in chronological order on a monthly basis is the practical, systematic manner in which the strategic plan is implemented month by month.

## How to Review Strategic Action Plans

The logical way to review action plans is to look at them in the order of their due-date. Accordingly, the sequence shown for reviewing all action plans is as follows:

1. Review all action plans that are *"Past-Due,"* or late, whose due-dates have already come and gone. These actions need to be completed and closed out. The only exception is that at times developments will occur that necessitate delaying an action plan "to the right," or much later in time. If that is the case, then simply move that action plan down your chronologically ordered list in the order of its new due-date.

2. The next set of action plans to review are those *due in the current month.*

3. The third review is a quick reminder of those action plans with *due-dates upcoming* by next month's meeting.

4. The last step ties in with our prior discussion on the final step of the Operations section—*the identification of new strategic action plans.* Here, make sure that all of these major new action plans are documented, clearly assigned, and have appropriate due-dates. You need to determine which emergent operating issues are of such significance that they earn the right to be added to the strategic action portfolio.

Done month to month, you will be amazed how much your team gets done, how current your strategic plan stays, and how fast you achieve the goals that have the greatest significance to your organization.

## Next Month's MER Meeting

Having an automatic, pre-set time for holding your Monthly Executive Review is the best way to handle the scheduling challenge. Until you are in an automatic mode, be sure *to set a specific time and place* for next month's MER meeting. Remember to have everyone check their calendars for potential travel, meeting, and vacation conflicts.

## The Chronological Action-Plan Summary

The Action-Plan Summary (Figure 18.3) is a very simple and straightforward method of reviewing all of your strategic action plans. Five pages are provided in the complete summary, covering up to fifty strategic action-plan items, which is why the worksheet shown here is labelled "Page 1 of 5." The complete set of these five summary sheets, please turn to Addendum E at the back of the book. The worksheet is logical, and the column headings should be very familiar to you by now. The following list contains a brief explanation of each column, working from left to right.

- **Strategic Action-Plan Item:** Items should be listed beginning with the earliest due action plan, because at this point in the process they should have all been placed in chronological order by due-date. For example, the action plan due 6/15/94 would come first, the 6/22/94 action plan would be second, the 7/15/94 action plan would be third, the 7/31/94 action plan would be fourth, etc.

## Figure 18.3—Chronological Strategic Action-Plan Summary, Page 1

| Chronological Strategic Action-Plan Summary | | | | | |
|---|---|---|---|---|---|
| **Page 1 of 5**<br>Date of Origination: ___/___/___     Last Update: ___/___/___ | | | | | |
| **Strategic Action-Plan Item** | **Strategic Category Number*** | **Strategic Plan Item Number** | **Due-Date** | **Actual Date** | **Person(s) Responsible** |
| 1. | | | _/_/_ | _/_/_ | |
| 2. | | | _/_/_ | _/_/_ | |
| 3. | | | _/_/_ | _/_/_ | |
| 4. | | | _/_/_ | _/_/_ | |
| 5. | | | _/_/_ | _/_/_ | |
| 6. | | | _/_/_ | _/_/_ | |
| 7. | | | _/_/_ | _/_/_ | |
| 8. | | | _/_/_ | _/_/_ | |
| 9. | | | _/_/_ | _/_/_ | |
| 10. | | | _/_/_ | _/_/_ | |

\* If in original plan and not added later.
   Note:  Make additional pages and numbers as needed for items beyond
            page 5, #50.

- **Strategic Category Number:** This will be a number from #1 to #16, reflecting the sixteen strategies categories.

- **Strategic Plan Item Number:** This is from the original Major Strategic Goals Summarization Sheets you filled out for Venue Two (Figure 15.2).

- **Due-Date:** In this column, you fill in the segmented blanks, with "__/__/__" standing for "MM/DD/YY," or the Month/Day/Year that the action plan is due to be completed.

- **Actual Date:** This column remains blank until the action plan is completed and you have an actual completion date, at which point that date can be filled in the space provided.

- **Person(s) Responsible:** This space is to record the name(s) of the person(s) who is (are) responsibility for implementing the action plan.

I recommend that once you have generated your action plan list from the strategic session, you input the list in chronological order on the spreadsheet (Lotus/Excel, etc.) or word-processing software (WordPerfect, MS Word, etc.) of your choice. All have the capability of sorting a list on a given column. Once this list is initialized on-line, it is very easy to update and re-sort on the due-date column after each month's meeting, including the "add's" and "changes." One other reminder regarding the addition of new action plans: You can use the *same* strategic action-plan forms to document *new* individual action plans using the Year-One Strategic Action-Plan Form from Venue Four (Chapter Seventeen, Figure 17.1), also found in Addendum D at the back of this book.

## Systematic Follow-Ups and Updates

The "systematic follow-ups" are the Monthly Executive Reviews we have just covered in some detail. The "updates" are less frequently held but equally powerful. I suggest the following schedule of updates:

|  | **Time Frame Example** |  |
|---|---|---|
| 1. If strategic planning is held in: | January, | 1994 |
| 2. Hold the first plan review update in: | July, | 1994 |

3. Hold the second major update one year later:    July,    1995
4. Hold the third major update one year later:    July,    1996

Why do you hold the first major update within six months? Because *early check-up and reinforcement is necessary the first time you use the Strategic Planning Technology* to make sure you are staying on track, and to make any necessary early-course corrections based upon your first six months of implementational experience.

Please remember this experience-proved verity: *The success of your plan* (that contains the hope and way of business progress and profit acceleration) *hinges on strong, steady discipline to hold the monthly and periodic review meetings.*

## Implementation

The simple Strategic Planning Technology Implementation Checklist in Figure 18.4 is to ensure your strategic plan makes the all-critical transition from executive-generation to execution of the plan by the larger enterprise team. This checklist is self-explanatory. The key is that it be completed as the last part of your planning session. Why? You want to place a down-payment on your success by setting the key implementational steps in motion.

## Conclusion

If you believe that this Strategic Planning Technology will be a significant help for you or your company, I encourage you to write up your own action plans utilizing the forms in Addendum D. And as W. Clement Stone has long reminded us: "Do it now!" I will not repeat the plethora of long- and short-term benefits that come from making strategic planning work for you, but would only remind you of the many we have covered in this book. Like one hospital advertisement suggests: Even if you do not use this Strategic Planning Technology, help yourself in any way you can by, in one way or another, developing the habit of "planning your work and working your plan." Those who pull this huge lever, in their businesses and in their lives, will reap rewards far greater than they could without doing so. If hundreds and thousands of companies make a long-term commitment to planning and implementation, they should not only survive but prosper into the next millennium, and in so doing, bring great satisfaction and success to their stakeholders and to the smaller and larger communities in which they operate.

## Figure 18.4—Strategic Planning Technology Implementation Checklist

| Strategic Planning Technology Implementation Checklist | | | |
|---|---|---|---|
| | "Check" If Done | Due-Date | Actual Date |
| 1. Assign one individual responsible as Strategic Implementation Coordinator Name:_____ | ☐ | __/__/__ | __/__/__ |
| 2. Receive Facilitator's Final Strategic Session Summary Report. | ☐ | __/__/__ | __/__/__ |
| 3. Generate Summarized Strategic Action-Plan List in Chronological Order. | ☐ | __/__/__ | __/__/__ |
| 4. Schedule and Announce the First Monthly Executive Review to be held **one month** after Strategic Session (**Minimum agenda**: Review of Strategic Action Plans). | ☐ | __/__/__ | __/__/__ |
| 5. Hold first MER. | ☐ | __/__/__ | __/__/__ |
| 6. Schedule second MER. | ☐ | __/__/__ | __/__/__ |
| 7. Continue this cycle on a monthly basis. | ☐ | __/__/__ | __/__/__ |

Finally, with whatever plans you develop for business and for life, *don't ever let them hit the bookshelf.* You will delight in all that you can accomplish, not only by achieving better results sooner, but by making the journey so very significant and satisfying every step along the way!

# Chapter Nineteen

# Total Quality Management: Strategy for Success Through Continuous Improvement

*by Ellen Domb, Ph.D.*

Organizations engaged in the transition from conventional management to total quality management will find that this Strategic Planning Technology can readily become their local, culturally customized version of the vertical integration element of Total Quality Management policy deployment (sometimes called by its Japanese name, *hoshin kanri,* literally "direction pointing system").

Organizations looking for a practical model and a philosophical basis for becoming the environments where Strategic Planning Technology can work will find Total Quality Management to be a good match. Edwin Artzt, Chairman of Procter & Gamble, has said that excellent strategy is vital and can start in any organization, but excellent execution and improvement of strategy comes only through policy deployment within the Total Quality Management environment.

## What is Total Quality Management?

The definition of Total Quality Management (TQM) flows from the 1990s definition of quality:

> *Quality is defined by the customer. Quality is the ability to meet customer needs, then exceed customer expectations while maintaining a cost-competitive market position.*

Total Quality Management flows naturally out of the front end of the Strategic Planning process. Total Quality Management is a structured system for creating organization-wide participation in planning and implementing a continuous improvement process to meet and exceed customer needs. TQM is characterized by customer focus, total organizational involvement, continuous improvement of processes, and fact-based decision making. As a list, this may not sound dramatic; as a philosophy turned into action, the Total Quality transformation of organizations has shaken the economic structure of the world. The changes in market and market share distribution in the automotive, electronics, machine tool, and financial businesses in the last 30 years have been revolutionary, not evolutionary.

## How do the characteristics of TQM create change?

*Customer focus:* Everyone in the organization determines who the customer is. At the strategic level, the executive group develops the concepts for the businesses that the organization will pursue. The analysis of "core competence" or strategic differentiation that is in the vision, SWOT, and variables part of Venue Two is an essential phase of selecting the customers that can be served. But customer focus goes on at all levels of the organization: The customer could be the person at the next work station, another department, a distributor. Frequently, even a supplier is a customer! Or, the customer could be the recipient of services from a social service agency, a client of a professional services organization, or a retail buyer of goods.

For any person or any part of the organization, the customer is the recipient of the output of a process. The easiest example is the purchaser of goods, the classical "customer" who receives the goods and ancillary services. When the organization learns to identify other cases easily, it is ready to move to the disciplines required to meet customer needs and to exceed customer expectations. Examples of "customer" relationships: In a hospital, the patient is the obvious customer, since he or she is the direct recipient of services. The insurance company is a customer, since it receives information. If the information is correct, accurate, timely, appropriate (meets the needs of the customer), then the hospital will get paid sooner than if the typical three cycles of clarification are performed for each bill!

The purchasing department sends a purchase order to a supplier. The supplier is the customer, since he receives a document. If the document meets his needs (clear, complete, appropriate—requests something he can do), he can then do a "quality" job of delivering the product or service requested, doing it right the first time. In this case, the simple concept of customer identification leads immediately to the need for collaboration between supplier, producer, and customer. If you treat the supplier like a customer, you'll get better service, which will in turn benefit the customer of your services.

In product development, engineers are starting to learn that their customers are manufacturing and purchasing groups. And marketing is starting to learn that its customers are development and engineering. Each group needs information from the other before starting work, and each needs constant feedback from its customer in order to do work that satisfies customer needs. When designers start treating customer service personnel like customers, the purchaser benefits from products and services that are easier to understand, to use, and to maintain. (Does the customer really care what kind of music you play on "hold" when she calls for help? Or would she rather have a product she could use without help?)

*Total Involvement:* Everyone works to satisfy the customer through continuous improvement of processes. Making all managers and workers part of the improvement process increases the acceptance of change and secures measurable financial and morale benefits for the organization more quickly than either simple "bottom-up" (quality circles, suggestion plans) or simple "top-down" (traditional authoritarian management) methods.

Why should we abandon the "Managers plan, workers work" paradigm? Because the weight of evidence is that the people closest to the work know most about how to improve it. They are in the best position to see the impact of their actions on customers, and in the best position to measure the results of changes. Managers are in the best position to evaluate impact on the other parts of the organization. The new paradigm then becomes "Managers orchestrate, everybody works and everybody improves the work."

Not everyone will be involved instantaneously in the quality transformation. A frequent, expensive mistake is trying to introduce the quality philosophy by mass training, an approach sometimes called "spray and pray"—spray some training on everyone and pray that it does some good. A pilot project approach, in which the management group selects improvement projects that are important (from the customer's point of view) but finite (so that lessons can be learned from them in a limited period of time) succeeds far more often. The pilot projects should be characteristic of the organization. Some should involve front-line workers, some managers or supervisors, some mixed levels and mixed departments, depending on the projects. During the pilot project period, the organization will learn how to manage the improvement process, how to customize training in teamwork and problem solving, how to create a continuous improvement culture, and how to transform "culture" into action plans. Typically, 25% of small companies and 10% of large ones are involved in pilot projects in the first 1–2 years. As the organization learns from its own pilot projects as well as from other organizations (customers, suppliers, world leaders, even competitors—the process now being popularized as "benchmarking"), it becomes ready to plan for total involvement.

*Continuous improvement of processes:* Large improvements are occasionally the result of single breakthrough innovations, but are much more reliably the result of accumulating many small improvements. Streamlining processes—reducing the time to complete any part of a process—reduces the time to perform the whole process as the improvements accumulate. For example, in manufacturing, faster cycle-time creates direct financial benefit through reduced work in process, reduced inventory, and reduced working capital requirements. How do we get reduced cycle time? By improving the quality of all parts of the process!

If a process is restructured so that it is always done right the first time, there is no rework and no waste. When processes are designed to be done right, the work force morale increases, less supervision is needed, less inspection is needed, and warranty costs and legal costs are reduced.

When a medical laboratory sends 8,000 bills a month with "only" a 3% error rate, and each error requires typically 74 minutes of telephone and computer time to correct, it becomes clear very quickly that improving the process so that only correct bills are sent is a bottom-line benefit. There is no single cause for bad bills. The solution: Teach a team of clinical and billing people the art and science of process improvement so that they can analyze the process, apply their knowledge of the process, and improve it one step at a time. They improve the profitability of the lab and reduce the overall cost of health care, creating both a business benefit and a social benefit.

When a chip fabricator (electronic chips, not chocolate chips) has over 400 improvement projects that together improve yield of good chips from 2% to 99.98%, the bottom-line impact should be obvious. But, the competitors are improving, too, so the prices are falling almost as fast as yield is improving, and in this case, the result of those 400 improvements is staying in business, not yet becoming more profitable. This will result in revisiting the strategic issues of which businesses the company should be in, and how it can be both improving and profitable.

Similar payoffs are seen in engineering, in health care, in service and information businesses. Improving the quality, "meeting or exceeding the customers and expectations" at all points in the process, results in savings in many areas.

*Fact-based decision making:* TQM had its origins in statistical control and evaluation of production processes. The emphasis on measurement of customer needs and expectations and the measurement of the capability of meeting those needs forms the basis of TQM. Many organizations can build on strong histories of financial and service measurements to develop fact-based continuous process improvement. Venue 3 of SPT addresses the major business and financial assumptions and targets through the out-year period.

The emphasis on measurements keeps TQM focused: How can you say our business is getting better if you aren't measuring it?

# What kind of organizations can benefit from TQM?

- Manufacturing businesses
- Service businesses
- "Middlemen"—distributors, transporters, financiers, arrangers
- Government agencies—federal, state, and local
- Nonprofit institutions—universities and colleges, hospitals, and churches

Any organization which brings people and resources together to create products or services can benefit from improved planning; increased productivity; reduced waste of time, materials, labor; reduced turnover; and improved morale of managers and workers.

# Why do organizations commit to Total Quality Management?

- Meet competitive challenges
- Reduced cost of doing business
- Improve productivity
- Improve profitability
- Qualify as a supplier with companies committed to continuous improvement
- Do more with less—less capital, less equipment, less space
- Get new products to market faster—get new services to recipients faster
- Improve employee and manager morale, reduce absenteeism, reduce turnover
- Manage change—cope with the continuously changing environment
- Provide a management philosophy to integrate many kinds of organizational change
- Meet regulatory requirements with a positive view

Organizations commit to TQM for many of the same reasons that compel them to develop viable, implementable strategic plans—with the same bias toward sustainable, measurable progress after the initial planning effort.

Figure 19.1 presents the Total Quality Management organization as a wheel rolling *up* a ramp. The steepness of the ramp represents the continuously increasing complexity and severity of the environment in which the organization must thrive. The wheel represents the three organizational phases of TQM: (1) daily control, which optimizes the work of the individual and work unit; (2) cross-functional management, which optimizes horizontal integration among functions; and (3) policy deployment, which aligns the organization vertically to achieve customer-focused strategic objectives.

But wheels roll down ramps, not up! The steeper the ramp gets, the faster the wheel rolls down. In recent years, many of our organizations have proven only too well that the usual response to increased competition, to increased customer requirements, and to complex political and economic situations is to roll downhill faster and faster. Total quality leadership provides the force that pushes the wheel up the ramp, mobilizing the creativity and energy of the entire organization.

The payoff from the continuous process improvement or daily control element of TQM is widely known. Classic examples abound and many were used as illustrations earlier in this section. Some of our favorite stories are big, some small:

- In a pilot project at a major aerospace supplier, streamlining reporting processes saved $280,000/year and reduced the time each supervisor spent on paperwork by 16 hours per month.

- A team of secretaries reevaluated their company's document flow, and saved $2500/month in FAX and overnight delivery costs alone.

- A major electronics company reduced hardware field failures by a factor of ten. Consider what this did to the cost of service, warranty, and support! In the eight years that it took, they changed their organizational structure, their strategic planning technology, their way of organizing R&D, and literally thousands of processes. Their new goal sounds even more ambitious: to reduce software failures by a factor of ten.

- A metals casting company eliminated rework. "The yield got so good, every time I went past rework I saw people reading the paper. So we stopped doing rework and the yield got even better. That may not be a fancy cost-of-quality system, but it worked!"

- Time to order parts for plant maintenance at one company was reduced from 46 days to 21 days to 3 days by a team of maintenance

## Figure 19.1—The Wheel and the Ramp

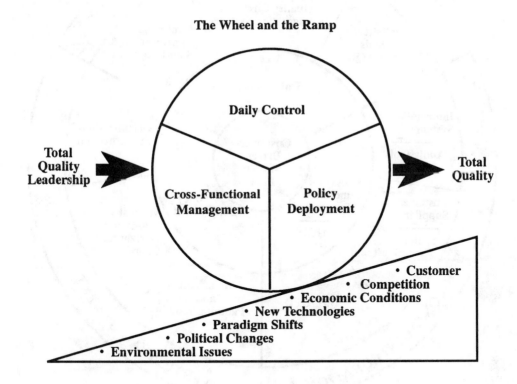

The Wheel and the Ramp

Copyright © 1991 GOAL/QPC. Used by permission.

## Figure 19.2—The Details of the Wheel

**The Details of the Wheel**

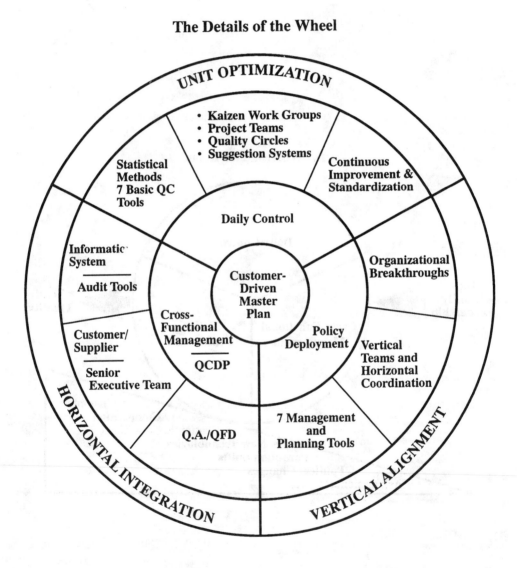

workers, buyers, and accounts, working together for the common customer.

- A hospital reduced its need for new computers to such an extent that it eliminated the need to purchase any for a year and a half. How? People learned to ask, "Who is the customer for this information?" before storing anything in the computer.

- A computer company built a factory in 1982 to produce $200 million/ year in products with 220 workers. It now produces $2 billion/year with 240 workers in half the space, with cycle time reduced from 118 days to 3.5 days for major components.

- A bank gave employees authority to spend up to $1,000 to correct errors for customers on the spot. Average spent: $7! The employees learned to prevent the errors, not spend money fixing them.

- A joint-team of U.S. Air Force personnel and contractors streamlined the proposal process to require 80% less paper and 50% less time.

- An insurance company eliminated half the "collections" department, then three-quarters of the half that was left. They found that most collection problems were due to errors in the bills, not to customers avoiding payment. Once they fixed the reasons for creating errors, they didn't need the massive collection effort.

- The registration process is the most frequent target for improvement teams at colleges and universities. Many have converted to mail-in or phone-in registration. Others have simplified the process by eliminating all activities that are not value-added to the direct customer, the student. At one large state university, lines at the cashier's office were so bad that the fire marshal threatened to close the building. By analyzing the work and developing systems based on doing right things instead of fixing wrong things, in one semester lines were gone.

Benefits of cross-functional management are less well known, since the companies that achieve them frequently treat both the results and the techniques as proprietary trade secrets. Major cases include:

- In the automotive, aircraft, and electronic industries, concurrent engineering (or simultaneous product and process development), using quality function deployment coupled with supplier-customer partnership processes frequently results in new products reaching the market 25% faster the first time the company employs cross-functional management, and 40% faster the subsequent times.

- The logistics triumph of Desert Storm was in large part the culmination of four years of learning customer-focused cross-functional management.

- Integration of suppliers' delivery systems with customers' stocking systems have created strategic advantages for both. Procter & Gamble's relationship with Wal-Mart, resupplying on a daily basis from local depots, may be best known. Both Levi Strauss and Benneton have systems that reach from the retail store to the distribution center to the manufacturer to the designer so that fashion products can be created in response to demand.

Benefits of vertical integration have been the theme of this entire work on Strategic Planning Technology. Policy Deployment, the vertical integration element of TQM, is described by Figure 19.3.

The major features of policy deployment are easily identified with the Venues of SPT. The "vision" and "3-5 year plan" and "one-year objective" elements are virtually identical to the contents of Venues One, Two, and Three. The primary differences are in the techniques used, rather than the types of conclusions reached.

The "catch-ball" process (which is exactly what it suggests!) is typically used at the one-year objective stage and at the deployment of objectives and development of functional unity plans stage. The organizational communications are analogous to the game of catch, in which the executive committee throws the ball (of strategy definition), the members of the organization catch the ball, consider the impact on their organizations and the contributions that they can make, and toss the ball back. The game is "catch," i.e., back and forth, not "throw," i.e., one way. Dialog at each interface in the organization is essential to the successful implementation of the strategic plan.

Policy deployment employs visual tools for stimulating creativity and generating consensus, principally the affinity diagram, tree diagram, and matrix diagram. The target-means matrix is used extensively to check that all the objectives within various parts of the organization are complementary. Conflicts are identified early, not built into the plans of the units to the detriment of the whole. Figure 19.4. shows an expanded target-means matrix, with task and resource requirements tables for accomplishing the tasks.

## Figure 19.3—Policy Deployment

**Policy Deployment**

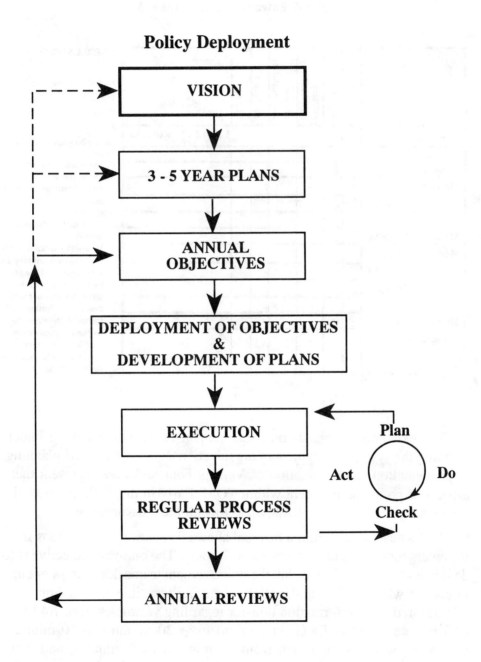

## Figure 19.4—Extended Target-Means Matrix

### Figure 4. Extended Target-Means Matrix

| | | Target 1 | Target 2 | Primary Responsibility | Support Responsibility | Resources | Measure | Schedule |
|---|---|---|---|---|---|---|---|---|
| Measure | | | | | | | | 1 2 3 4 5 6 7 8 9 10 11 12 |
| Means 1 | Tactic 1.1 | ◉ | ※ | | | | | |
| Measure | Tactic 1.2 | ◉ | | | | | | |
| | Tactic 1.3 | ○ | △ | | | | | |
| | | | | | | | | |
| Means 2 | Tactic 2.1 | ○ | ○ | | | | | |
| Measure | Tactic 2.2 | | | | | | | |
| | Tactic 2.3 | | △ | | | | | |
| | Tactic 2.4 | △ | ◉ | | | | | |
| | | | | | | | | |
| Means 3 | Tactic 3.1 | △ | ◉ | | | | | |
| Measure | | | | | | | | |

CORRELATION:

| | |
|---|---|
| Strong Positive | ◉ |
| Positive | ○ |
| Weak | △ |
| Negative | ✕ |
| Strong Negative | ※ |

Primary and Support Responsibilities:
  Organization/individual names
Resources:
  Staff, money, facilities
Measure:
  How will you know if the tactic has contributed to the means, and the means to the target: In this case, tactic 2.3 does not make much contribution, and tactic 1.1 should be re-worked to remove the conflict with target 2, even though it contributes strongly to target 1.

The extensive emphasis on measurement is used to focus on understanding the systems by which an organization does it work. The planning, implementation, and evaluation of Venues Four and Five represent these aspects of policy deployment within TQM. Early in the TQM process, the systems are not well enough known to link all the measurements.

A classic example from a hospital shows 9 causes for admissions from the emergency room taking more than 2 hours. The one-year objective is to do it in less than 15 minutes, but the improvement teams don't know enough to predict whether the combination of cutting test time from 1 hour to 5 minutes, reducing information transfer regarding vacancies from 1.4 hours to 5 minutes, cutting EKG set-up time from 20 minutes to 10 minutes, decreasing wait for physician from 35 minutes to 5 minutes, and other time-cutting measures will result in the reduced time that is necessary for customer satisfaction (and in this case, "satisfaction" can mean survival!).

Does this mean that they can't apply policy deployment? This is an area of considerable controversy in the consulting community, but of no importance at all to the organizations that are using and learning from policy deployment. They are in Venue Five and are learning by doing.

The less knowledge a group has about the relationships between their processes and the impact on the system for delivering customer satisfaction, the harder it will be to set good goals. At this stage, the TQM emphasis on measurement should be used to learn about the system. The emphasis of the monthly executive review, the monitoring vehicle for the SPT and TQM process, is as follows:

- How good was the plan? What did the organization learn to improve the plan?

- How was the plan carried out? Any conflicts that were not anticipated? How were they dealt with, so we can learn from them?

- Do any resource or priority issues need attention to achieve the plan for the next time period?

- What changes (if any) are needed in either the plan or the execution?

The tie-in between SPT and TQM is seamless throughout Venues Four and Five. The strategic plan is a strategic action plan, a living document that becomes the life of the organization. When the organization is well advanced in the Daily Management phase of TQM, vast amounts of data will be available to predict the outcome of improvement initiatives and of breakthrough concepts, and the changes to the plan will then be driven more by outside events and less by the accumulation of the organization's self-knowledge.

Implicit in the SPT is the final phase of policy deployment, the annual review, which combines elements of celebrating the year's achievements, integrating the learning that the organization has gained about itself, and evaluating the planning process to decide how to best use the process for subsequent years. These become Valuation Items 13 and 15 in Venue One.

In the same way that the Valuation Section in SPT's Venue One annually ascertains strategic health, the Malcolm Baldrige National Quality Award Criteria can be used to assess the organization's TQM process. The Malcolm Baldrige National Quality Award was created by Congress in 1987 to recognize businesses that excel in quality management and quality achievement. Award recipients are expected to share information about their quality journeys with other organizations. The criteria for the award are subject to wide debate and are improved every year.

The questions in the Baldrige Award follow a pattern:

- Are you doing this? (asked for each of 32 key areas)

- If you are doing it, do you record your results?

- If you are doing it, and you record the results, do you have a plan for doing it better in the future?

- Are you studying how others do it? Competitors? Suppliers? Customers? World-class organizations in other businesses?

An example of two of the questions is shown in Figure 19.5. (The complete guidelines are available free—see the reference section of this chapter.)

Figure 19.6 is a table for self-assessment, using the Baldrige Award criteria. Management groups new to the assessment process can prioritize their areas for action by looking for those questions where they answer "No" to "Can we answer this question?" and "Yes" to "Needed for strategic plan."

To determine your score category for any question, refer to Figure 5c., from the Guidelines for Scoring the Baldrige Award.

This can be the most revealing part of the management team's self-assessment, since they must decide if they have actually used and are getting documented benefits from the concepts, or if they have only talked about them.

Government agencies may prefer to use the guidelines for the Federal Quality Award or the George Low Award (NASA), since they are tailored specifically for them. Many federal, state, and local agencies, and many nonprofit organizations have used the Baldrige Award Criteria for self-assessment, and have gained great insight into the areas they need to prioritize for improvement.

Surveys have been widely marketed to help companies assess themselves against the Baldrige criteria. These surveys should be used with caution because they ask employees' opinions of the company's activities. Many employees may not be informed on issues outside their departments, yet may be embarrassed to answer "Don't know." There is the need to combine survey results and management internal assessment carefully to create a baseline assessment of your total quality management process.

# Figure 19.5—Example of Questions in the "Baldrige Award" Criteria

## 3.0 Strategic Quality Planning (60 pts.)

The **Strategic Quality Planning** Category examines the company's planning process and how all key quality requirements are integrated into overall business planning. Also examined are the company's short- and longer-term plans and how quality and performance requirements are deployed to all work units.

### 3.1 Strategic Quality and Company Performance Planning Process (35 pts.)

Describe the company's strategic planning process for the short-term (1–2 year) and longer term (3 years or more) for quality and customer satisfaction leadership. Include how this process integrates quality and company performance requirements and how plans are deployed.

**AREAS TO ADDRESS**

a. How the company develops plans and strategies for the short term and longer term. Describe data and analysis results used in developing business plans and priorities, and how they consider: (1) customer requirements and the expected evolution of these requirements; (2) projections of the competitive environment; (3) risks: financial, market, and societal; (4) company capabilities, including research and development to address key new requirements or technology leadership opportunity; and (5) supplier capabilities.

b. How plans are implemented. Describe: (1) the method of company uses to deploy overall plan requirements to all work units and to suppliers, and how it ensures alignment of work unit activities, and (2) how resources are committed to meet the plan requirements.

c. How the company evaluates and improves its planning process, including improvements in: (1) determining company quality and overall performance requirements; (2) deployment of requirements to work units; and (3) input from all levels of the company.

## 6.0 Quality and Operational Results (180 pts.)

### 6.1 Product and Service Quality Results (75 pts.)

Summarize trends in quality and current quality levels for key product and service features; compare the company's current quality levels with those of competitors.

**AREAS TO ADDRESS**

a. Trends and current levels for all key measures of product and service quality.

b. Current quality-level comparisons with principal competitors in the company's key markets, industry averages, industry leaders, and others as appropriate. Briefly explain bases for comparison such as: (1) independent surveys, studies, or laboratory testing; (2) benchmarks; and (3) company evaluations and testing. Describe how objectivity and validity of comparisons are assured.

### 6.2 Company Operational Results (45 pts.)

Summarize trend and levels in overall company operations performance and provide a comparison of this performance with competitors and appropriate benchmarks.

**AREAS TO ADDRESS**

a. Trends and current levels for key measures of company operational performance.

b. Comparison of performance with that of competitors, industry averages, industry leaders, and key benchmarks. Give and briefly explain basis for comparison.

## Figure 19.6—Self-Assessment Form Using the "Baldrige Award"

### Figure 5b. Self-Assessment Form Using the "Baldrige Award"

| ITEM | Points | Can we score this item? (Yes/No) | Score Category | Needed? (strategic plan, Y/N) | Priority item? ☑ |
|---|---|---|---|---|---|
| **Malcolm Baldrige National Quality Award** <br> **Self-Assessment — 1992 Criteria** ||||||
| Organization: _____  Date: _____ ||||||
| **1.0 Leadership** | 90 | | | | |
| 1.1 Senior Executive Leadership | 45 | | | | |
| 1.2 Management for Quality | 25 | | | | |
| 1.3 Public Responsibility | 20 | | | | |
| **2.0 Information and Analysis** | 80 | | | | |
| 2.1 Scope & Mgt. Quality Info. | 15 | | | | |
| 2.2 Competitive Comparisons | 25 | | | | |
| 2.3 Analysis/Use of Data | 40 | | | | |
| **3.0 Strategic Quality Planning** | 60 | | | | |
| 3.1 Strategic Planning Process | 35 | | | | |
| 3.2 Quality & Performance Plans | 25 | | | | |
| **4.0 Human Resource Utilization** | 150 | | | | |
| 4.1 Human Resource Management | 20 | | | | |
| 4.2 Employee Involvement | 40 | | | | |
| 4.3 Employee Education | 40 | | | | |
| 4.4 Recognition & Performance | 25 | | | | |
| 4.5 Well-Being & Morale | 25 | | | | |
| **5.0 Mgt. of Process Quality** | 140 | | | | |
| 5.1 Design & Intro. Qual. Prod./Svc. | 40 | | | | |
| 5.2 Process Management | 35 | | | | |
| 5.3 Business Processes | 30 | | | | |
| 5.4 Supplier Quality | 20 | | | | |
| 5.5 Quality Assessment | 15 | | | | |

## Figure 19.6—Self-Assessment Form Using the "Baldrige Award" (concluded)

Figure 5b. Self-Assessment Form Using the "Baldrige Award"

| ITEM | Points | Can we score this item? (Yes/No) | Score Category | Needed? (strategic plan, Y/N) | Priority item? ☑ |
|---|---|---|---|---|---|
| **6.0 Quality & Operational Results** | 180 | | | | |
| **6.1** Product/Service Results | 75 | | | | |
| **6.2** Company Operational Results | 45 | | | | |
| **6.3** Business/Support Results | 25 | | | | |
| **6.4** Supplier Quality Results | 35 | | | | |
| **7.0 Customer Satisfaction** | 300 | | | | |
| **7.1** Customer Relationship Mgt. | 65 | | | | |
| **7.2** Commitment to Customers | 15 | | | | |
| **7.3** Customer Satisfaction Deter. | 35 | | | | |
| **7.4** Customer Satis. Results | 75 | | | | |
| **7.5** Customer Satis. Comparison | 75 | | | | |
| **7.6** Future Req's & Expectations | 35 | | | | |

Malcolm Baldrige National Quality Award
Self-Assessment — 1992 Criteria

Organization: _____ Date: _____

The *best* way to get a baseline score is to apply for the Baldrige Award. Every applicant gets feedback from the team of examiners and judges, as well as a score. Some winning companies (e.g., Motorola, Xerox) are starting to ask all their suppliers to apply for the Baldrige Award; they claim that the process of application taught them so much, they want their suppliers to have the same learning experience.

Organizations committed to improving themselves and their relationships to all their stakeholders will be continuously learning about themselves and turning that learning into action. The policy deployment discipline and the SPT were each developed to institutionalize that learning. The organizations that will survive the volatile 1990s and lead the next generation will be those that learn to take the best of the available tools and apply them in ways that work in their culture.

SPT can be the starting point for a commitment to TQM. Policy deployment can use the consensus and planning and data-gathering disciplines of SPT and the easily accessible worksheets of SPT to improve the basis for creation of plans and stimulus for value and vision-driven creativity. "Catchball" gets alot easier when data is shared easily. Figure 19.8 shows a timeline for evolving and improving organizations, merging SPT into policy deployment as they mature in the quality transformation.

The way to find out if SPT and TQM, or your unique hybrid of the two, will work for your organization is to use it! One virtue of continuous improvement is that you can avoid "analysis paralysis": Start the process now, and improve it as you learn. Future stories of the payoffs from vertical SPT/TQM integration will come from you!

# Figure 19.7—Baldrige Award Scoring Guidelines

**Figure 5c. Baldrige Award**

**SCORING GUIDELINES**

| CATE-GORY | SCORE | APPROACH | DEPLOYMENT | RESULTS |
|---|---|---|---|---|
| 1 | 0% | • Anecdotal, no system evident | • Anecdotal | • Anecdotal |
| 2 | 10-40% | • Beginnings of systematic prevention basis | • Some to many major areas of business | • Some positive trends in the areas deployed |
| 3 | 50% | • Sound, systematic prevention basis that includes evaluation/improvement cycles<br>• Some evidence of integration | • Most major areas of business<br>• Some support areas | • Positive trends in most major areas<br>• Some evidence that results are caused by approach |
| 4 | 60-90% | • Sound, systematic prevention basis with evidence of refinement through evaluation/improvement cycles<br>• Good integration. | • Major areas of business<br>• From some to many support areas | • Good to excellent in major areas<br>• Positive trends — from some to many support areas<br>• Evidence that results are caused by approach |
| 5 | 100% | • Sound, systematic prevention basis refined through evaluation/improvement cycles.<br>• Excellent integration | • Major areas and support areas<br>• All operations | • Excellent (world-class) results in major areas<br>• Good to excellent in support areas<br>• Sustained results<br>• Results clearly caused by approach |

## Figure 19.8—Strategic Planning Timeline Integrating SPT and TQM

### Figure 6. Strategic Planning Timeline
### Integrating SPT and TQM

| TIME | ACTIVITIES |
|---|---|
| Year 1 | ❑ SPT Venues 1-5<br>❑ Organizational assessment and commitment<br>❑ Decision in Venues 1 & 2<br>   to become a TQM organization<br>❑ Action/plans & Implementation, Venues 4 & 5<br>   ● Formation of the TQM Steering Committee<br>   ● Analysis of customers (expansion of Venue 1.B.2.)<br>   ● Analysis of critical processes<br>   ● Creation of pilot projects<br>❑ Evaluation (Venue 5.A-D) |
| Year 2 | ❑ SPT Review Venue 1, update Venues 2-5, emphasizing<br>   changes<br>❑ Use the pilot project experience<br>   to expand TQM implementation<br>   ● Develop infrastructure for TQM<br>❑ Begin using elements of process and<br>   system knowledge as part of Venue 5<br>   (Merging SPT and policy deployment) |
| Year 3 | ❑ SPT with beginnings of "catch-ball" becomes<br>   possible. Vertical integration with data<br>❑ Organization-wide TQM<br>   ● Daily Management and Cross-Functional Management |

↓

**Future
Years**

# Total Quality Management/Policy Deployment— References

Akao, Y. (Ed.). (1991). Hoshin kanri: *Policy deployment for successful TQM.* Boston: Productivity Press, Inc. Translation of *Hoshin kanri katusyo no jissai.* (1988). Japanese Standards Association.

Drucker, P. F. (1992). *Managing for the future.* New York: Penguin Group.

The Ernst & Young Quality Improvement Consulting Group. (1990). *Total quality: An executive's guide for the 1990's.* Homewood, IL: Business One Irwin.

Goal/OPC Research Committee. (1989). *Hoshin planning: A planning system for implementing total quality management (TQM).* Research Rep. No. 89-10-03). Methuen, MA: Goal/QPC.

Juran, J.M. (1989). *Juran on leadership for quality: An executive handbook.* New York: Free Press.

Juran, J.M. (1992). *Juran on quality by design.* New York: Free Press.

King, B. (1989). *Hoshin planning: The developmental approach.* Methuen, MA: Goal/QPC.

Shores, A. R. (1988). *Survival of the fittest: Total quality control and management evolution.* Milwaukee, WI: ASQC Quality Press.

United States Department of Commerce, Technology Administration, NIST. (1992). *Malcolm Baldrige National Quality Award: 1992 Award Criteria.* Milwaukee, WI: ASQC Quality Press. Single copies can be ordered by phone from the NIST at 301-975-2036.

# Addendum A

# Individual Major Strategic Goals Identification Sheets

| Personal Exercise: Individual Major Strategic Goals Identification | | |
|---|---|---|

**Section I:  The Strategic Enterprise**
**Category 1:  Organization Strategy**
Includes areas such as:  structure, roles, responsibilities, reporting relationships.

| Strategic Item | Check One: Result  Goal  Means | Explanation/Notes (Why, How Measured, Etc.) |
|---|---|---|
| 1. _____ | ☐ ☐ ☐ | |
| 2. _____ | ☐ ☐ ☐ | |
| 3. _____ | ☐ ☐ ☐ | |
| 4. _____ | ☐ ☐ ☐ | |
| 5. _____ | ☐ ☐ ☐ | |

| Personal Exercise: Individual Major Strategic Goals Identification |||
|---|---|---|

**Section I: The Strategic Enterprise**

**Category 2: Cultural Strategy**

Includes areas such as: atmosphere, style, what is rewarded, what is discouraged.

| Strategic Item | Check One: Result  Goal  Means | Explanation/Notes (Why, How Measured, Etc.) |
|---|---|---|
| 1. _____ | ☐ ☐ ☐ | |
| 2. _____ | ☐ ☐ ☐ | |
| 3. _____ | ☐ ☐ ☐ | |
| 4. _____ | ☐ ☐ ☐ | |
| 5. _____ | ☐ ☐ ☐ | |

| Personal Exercise:  Individual Major Strategic Goals Identification | | |
|---|---|---|

**Section I:  The Strategic Enterprise**
**Category 3:  Leadership Strategy**
Includes areas such as:  executive development, succession, compensation, ability,
effectiveness, leadership.

| Strategic Item | Check One: Result  Goal  Means | Explanation/Notes (Why, How Measured, Etc.) |
|---|---|---|
| 1. _____ | ☐ ☐ ☐ | |
| 2. _____ | ☐ ☐ ☐ | |
| 3. _____ | ☐ ☐ ☐ | |
| 4. _____ | ☐ ☐ ☐ | |
| 5. _____ | ☐ ☐ ☐ | |

| Personal Exercise: Individual Major Strategic Goals Identification | | |
|---|---|---|

**Section I: The Strategic Enterprise**

**Category 4: Management Strategy**

Includes areas such as: management development, succession, compensation, ability, effectiveness, empowerment, autonomy.

| Strategic Item | Check One: Result  Goal  Means | Explanation/Notes (Why, How Measured, Etc.) |
|---|---|---|
| 1. _____ | ☐ ☐ ☐ | |
| 2. _____ | ☐ ☐ ☐ | |
| 3. _____ | ☐ ☐ ☐ | |
| 4. _____ | ☐ ☐ ☐ | |
| 5. _____ | ☐ ☐ ☐ | |

| Personal Exercise:  Individual Major Strategic Goals Identification |||
|---|---|---|
| **Section II:  The Strategic Resources** |||
| **Category 5:  Human Resource Strategy** |||
| Includes areas such as:  total HR headcount requirement, efficiency, effectiveness, capacity, motivation, involvement, empowerment, support, loyalty, training. |||
| **Strategic Item** | **Check One:** | **Explanation/Notes** |
|  | Result    Goal    Means | **(Why, How Measured, Etc.)** |
| 1. _____ | ☐ ☐ ☐ | |
| 2. _____ | ☐ ☐ ☐ | |
| 3. _____ | ☐ ☐ ☐ | |
| 4. _____ | ☐ ☐ ☐ | |
| 5. _____ | ☐ ☐ ☐ | |

| Personal Exercise:  Individual Major Strategic Goals Identification | | | | |
|---|---|---|---|---|
| **Section II:  The Strategic Resources** **Category 6:  Communications Strategy** Includes areas such as:  information flow up, down, out, in; communication systems, methods, effectiveness, teamwork, synergy. | | | | |
| **Strategic Item** | **Check One:** | | | **Explanation/Notes** |
|  | Result | Goal | Means | **(Why, How Measured, Etc.)** |
| 1. _____ | ☐ | ☐ | ☐ | _____ |
| 2. _____ | ☐ | ☐ | ☐ | _____ |
| 3. _____ | ☐ | ☐ | ☐ | _____ |
| 4. _____ | ☐ | ☐ | ☐ | _____ |
| 5. _____ | ☐ | ☐ | ☐ | _____ |

| Personal Exercise:  Individual Major Strategic Goals Identification | | | |
|---|---|---|---|

**Section II:  The Strategic Resources**
**Category 7:  Technology Strategy**
Includes areas such as:  understanding of, leverage of, investment in, use as exclusive differentiator.

| Strategic Item | Check One: | | Explanation/Notes |
|---|---|---|---|
| | Result | Goal | Means | (Why, How Measured, Etc.) |
| 1. _____ | ☐ | ☐ | ☐ | |
| 2. _____ | ☐ | ☐ | ☐ | |
| 3. _____ | ☐ | ☐ | ☐ | |
| 4. _____ | ☐ | ☐ | ☐ | |
| 5. _____ | ☐ | ☐ | ☐ | |

| Personal Exercise: Individual Major Strategic Goals Identification | | | | |
|---|---|---|---|---|
| **Section II: The Strategic Resources** | | | | |
| **Category 8: Cross-Functional Strategy** | | | | |
| Includes areas such as: each organizational and function's specific plans, integration, cross-pollination, coordination, synergy in unison. | | | | |
| **Strategic Item** | **Check One:** | | | **Explanation/Notes** |
| | Result | Goal | Means | (Why, How Measured, Etc.) |
| 1. _____ | ☐ | ☐ | ☐ | |
| 2. _____ | ☐ | ☐ | ☐ | |
| 3. _____ | ☐ | ☐ | ☐ | |
| 4. _____ | ☐ | ☐ | ☐ | |
| 5. _____ | ☐ | ☐ | ☐ | |

| | | | | |
|---|---|---|---|---|
| **Personal Exercise:  Individual Major Strategic Goals Identification** | | | | |

**Section III:  The Strategic Knowledge**
**Category 9:  Customer Strategy**
Includes areas such as:  commitment, focus, knowledge, support, systems, communication, problems, quality.

| Strategic Item | Check One: Result Goal Means | Explanation/Notes (Why, How Measured, Etc.) |
|---|---|---|
| 1. _____ | ☐ ☐ ☐ | _____ |
| 2. _____ | ☐ ☐ ☐ | _____ |
| 3. _____ | ☐ ☐ ☐ | _____ |
| 4. _____ | ☐ ☐ ☐ | _____ |
| 5. _____ | ☐ ☐ ☐ | _____ |

| Personal Exercise:  Individual Major Strategic Goals Identification | | |
|---|---|---|
| **Section III:  The Strategic Knowledge** **Category 10:  Competitive Strategy** Includes areas such as:  knowledge, strengths and weaknesses, opportunities and threats, major strategies, pricing, key responses. | | |
| **Strategic Item** | **Check One:** Result   Goal   Means | **Explanation/Notes** **(Why, How Measured, Etc.)** |
| 1. _____ | ☐  ☐  ☐ | |
| 2. _____ | ☐  ☐  ☐ | |
| 3. _____ | ☐  ☐  ☐ | |
| 4. _____ | ☐  ☐  ☐ | |
| 5. _____ | ☐  ☐  ☐ | |

| Personal Exercise: Individual Major Strategic Goals Identification | | | |
|---|---|---|---|
| **Section III: The Strategic Knowledge** | | | |
| **Category 11: External Relations Strategy** | | | |
| Includes areas such as: market, economy, government, social forecasts, public/ market perception, public relations, vendors, suppliers, industrial relations. | | | |
| **Strategic Item** | **Check One:** | | **Explanation/Notes** |
|  | Result | Goal   Means | (Why, How Measured, Etc.) |
| 1. _____ | ☐ | ☐   ☐ |  |
| 2. _____ | ☐ | ☐   ☐ |  |
| 3. _____ | ☐ | ☐   ☐ |  |
| 4. _____ | ☐ | ☐   ☐ |  |
| 5. _____ | ☐ | ☐   ☐ |  |

| Personal Exercise: Individual Major Strategic Goals Identification ||||
|---|---|---|---|
| **Section III: The Strategic Knowledge** ||||
| **Category 12: Financial Strategy** ||||
| Includes areas such as: financial resources, cost/expense management, budgets, targets, measurement of actuals, reviews, cash flow, financial statement goals. ||||

| Strategic Item | Check One: | | Explanation/Notes |
|---|---|---|---|
| | Result   Goal   Means | | (Why, How Measured, Etc.) |
| 1. _____ | ☐ ☐ ☐ | | |
| 2. _____ | ☐ ☐ ☐ | | |
| 3. _____ | ☐ ☐ ☐ | | |
| 4. _____ | ☐ ☐ ☐ | | |
| 5. _____ | ☐ ☐ ☐ | | |

| Personal Exercise: Individual Major Strategic Goals Identification | | | |
|---|---|---|---|
| **Section IV: The Strategic Response** | | | |
| **Category 13: Business Processes Systems Strategy** | | | |
| Includes areas such as: critical processes, identification and plans, quality, regulatory, effectiveness of processes, continuous improvement of systems, infrastructural systems. | | | |
| **Strategic Item** | **Check One:** | | **Explanation/Notes** |
| | Result  Goal  Means | | (Why, How Measured, Etc.) |
| 1. _____ | ☐ ☐ ☐ | | |
| 2. _____ | ☐ ☐ ☐ | | |
| 3. _____ | ☐ ☐ ☐ | | |
| 4. _____ | ☐ ☐ ☐ | | |
| 5. _____ | ☐ ☐ ☐ | | |

| Personal Exercise: Individual Major Strategic Goals Identification | | | | |
|---|---|---|---|---|
| **Section IV: The Strategic Response** | | | | |
| **Category 14: Market (Products & Services) Strategy** | | | | |
| Includes areas such as: products, services, markets, plans, performance, development, mix, differentiation. | | | | |

| Strategic Item | Check One: | | | Explanation/Notes (Why, How Measured, Etc.) |
|---|---|---|---|---|
| | Result | Goal | Means | |
| 1. _____ | ☐ | ☐ | ☐ | |
| 2. _____ | ☐ | ☐ | ☐ | |
| 3. _____ | ☐ | ☐ | ☐ | |
| 4. _____ | ☐ | ☐ | ☐ | |
| 5. _____ | ☐ | ☐ | ☐ | |

| Personal Exercise: Individual Major Strategic Goals Identification | | |
|---|---|---|

**Section IV: The Strategic Response**
**Category 15: Long-Range Strategy**
Includes areas such as: address uncertainty, risk, conflicts, agendas, needs,
critical success factors, investments, resources.

| Strategic Item | Check One: Result  Goal  Means | Explanation/Notes (Why, How Measured, Etc.) |
|---|---|---|
| 1. _____ | ☐ ☐ ☐ | |
| 2. _____ | ☐ ☐ ☐ | |
| 3. _____ | ☐ ☐ ☐ | |
| 4. _____ | ☐ ☐ ☐ | |
| 5. _____ | ☐ ☐ ☐ | |

| Personal Exercise: Individual Major Strategic Goals Identification |||
|---|---|---|

**Section IV: The Strategic Response**

**Category 16: Implementation Strategy**

Includes areas such as: plan, implement, quantify/qualify goals, tracking, action plans, completion, adjustment, flexibility, updates, new iterations.

| Strategic Item | Check One:<br>Result  Goal  Means | Explanation/Notes<br>(Why, How Measured, Etc.) |
|---|---|---|
| 1. _____ | ☐ ☐ ☐ | _____ |
| 2. _____ | ☐ ☐ ☐ | _____ |
| 3. _____ | ☐ ☐ ☐ | _____ |
| 4. _____ | ☐ ☐ ☐ | _____ |
| 5. _____ | ☐ ☐ ☐ | _____ |

| Personal Exercise: Individual Major Strategic Goals Identification | | |
|---|---|---|

**Section ___ :** _____

**Category ___ :** _____

Includes areas such as: _____

| Strategic Item | Check One: | | | Explanation/Notes |
|---|---|---|---|---|
| | Result | Goal | Means | (Why, How Measured, Etc.) |
| 1. _____ | ☐ | ☐ | ☐ | _____ |
| 2. _____ | ☐ | ☐ | ☐ | _____ |
| 3. _____ | ☐ | ☐ | ☐ | _____ |
| 4. _____ | ☐ | ☐ | ☐ | _____ |
| 5. _____ | ☐ | ☐ | ☐ | _____ |

| Personal Exercise: Individual Major Strategic Goals Identification | | |
|---|---|---|

**Section __ :** _____

**Category __ :** _____

Includes areas such as: _____

| Strategic Item | Check One: | | | Explanation/Notes (Why, How Measured, Etc.) |
|---|---|---|---|---|
| | Result | Goal | Means | |
| 1. _____ | ☐ | ☐ | ☐ | _____ _____ _____ |
| 2. _____ | ☐ | ☐ | ☐ | _____ _____ _____ _____ |
| 3. _____ | ☐ | ☐ | ☐ | _____ _____ _____ |
| 4. _____ | ☐ | ☐ | ☐ | _____ _____ _____ |
| 5. _____ | ☐ | ☐ | ☐ | _____ _____ _____ _____ _____ |

# Addendum B

# Major Strategic Goals Summarization Sheets

## Group Exercise:  Major Strategic Goals Summarization

**Section I:  The Strategic Enterprise**

**Category 1:  Organization Strategy**

Includes areas such as:  structure, roles, responsibilities, reporting relationships.

| | | | | | | Refer to Section:  D | | | E |
|---|---|---|---|---|---|---|---|---|---|
| **Strategic Item** | **Check One:** | | | **Individual Prioritization Votes** | **Vote Totals** | **Category Priority** | **Total Plan Priority** | **Year-One Action Plan** |
| | **Result** | **Goal** | **Means** | | | | | |
| 1. | ☐ | ☐ | ☐ | ☐ ☐ ☐ ☐ | ☐ | ☐ | ☐ | ☐ |
| 2. | ☐ | ☐ | ☐ | ☐ ☐ ☐ ☐ | ☐ | ☐ | ☐ | ☐ |
| 3. | ☐ | ☐ | ☐ | ☐ ☐ ☐ ☐ | ☐ | ☐ | ☐ | ☐ |
| 4. | ☐ | ☐ | ☐ | ☐ ☐ ☐ ☐ | ☐ | ☐ | ☐ | ☐ |
| 5. | ☐ | ☐ | ☐ | ☐ ☐ ☐ ☐ | ☐ | ☐ | ☐ | ☐ |
| 6. | ☐ | ☐ | ☐ | ☐ ☐ ☐ ☐ | ☐ | ☐ | ☐ | ☐ |
| 7. | ☐ | ☐ | ☐ | ☐ ☐ ☐ ☐ | ☐ | ☐ | ☐ | ☐ |
| 8. | ☐ | ☐ | ☐ | ☐ ☐ ☐ ☐ | ☐ | ☐ | ☐ | ☐ |
| 9. | ☐ | ☐ | ☐ | ☐ ☐ ☐ ☐ | ☐ | ☐ | ☐ | ☐ |
| 10. | ☐ | ☐ | ☐ | ☐ ☐ ☐ ☐ | ☐ | ☐ | ☐ | ☐ |
| 11. | ☐ | ☐ | ☐ | ☐ ☐ ☐ ☐ | ☐ | ☐ | ☐ | ☐ |
| 12. | ☐ | ☐ | ☐ | ☐ ☐ ☐ ☐ | ☐ | ☐ | ☐ | ☐ |
| 13. | ☐ | ☐ | ☐ | ☐ ☐ ☐ ☐ | ☐ | ☐ | ☐ | ☐ |
| 14. | ☐ | ☐ | ☐ | ☐ ☐ ☐ ☐ | ☐ | ☐ | ☐ | ☐ |
| 15. | ☐ | ☐ | ☐ | ☐ ☐ ☐ ☐ | ☐ | ☐ | ☐ | ☐ |

| Group Exercise: Major Strategic Goals Summarization | | | | | | | | | |
|---|---|---|---|---|---|---|---|---|---|
| **Section I: The Strategic Enterprise**<br>**Category 2: Cultural Strategy**<br>Includes areas such as: atmosphere, style, what is rewarded, what is discouraged. | | | | | | | | | |
| | | | | Refer to Section: D | | | | | E |
| Strategic Item | Check One: | | | Individual Prioritization Votes | Vote Totals | Category Priority | Total Plan Priority | | Year-One Action Plan |
| | Result | Goal | Means | | | | | | |
| 1. | | | | | | | | | |
| 2. | | | | | | | | | |
| 3. | | | | | | | | | |
| 4. | | | | | | | | | |
| 5. | | | | | | | | | |
| 6. | | | | | | | | | |
| 7. | | | | | | | | | |
| 8. | | | | | | | | | |
| 9. | | | | | | | | | |
| 10. | | | | | | | | | |
| 11. | | | | | | | | | |
| 12. | | | | | | | | | |
| 13. | | | | | | | | | |
| 14. | | | | | | | | | |
| 15. | | | | | | | | | |

## Group Exercise:  Major Strategic Goals Summarization

**Section I:  The Strategic Enterprise**
**Category 3:  Leadership Strategy**
Includes areas such as:  executive development, succession, compensation, ability,
    effectiveness, leadership.

| | | | | | | Refer to Section: D | | | E |
|---|---|---|---|---|---|---|---|---|---|
| **Strategic Item** | **Check One:** | | | **Individual Prioritization Votes** | | **Vote Totals** | **Category Priority** | **Total Plan Priority** | **Year-One Action Plan** |
| | Result | Goal | Means | | | | | | |
| 1. | | | | | | | | | |
| 2. | | | | | | | | | |
| 3. | | | | | | | | | |
| 4. | | | | | | | | | |
| 5. | | | | | | | | | |
| 6. | | | | | | | | | |
| 7. | | | | | | | | | |
| 8. | | | | | | | | | |
| 9. | | | | | | | | | |
| 10. | | | | | | | | | |
| 11. | | | | | | | | | |
| 12. | | | | | | | | | |
| 13. | | | | | | | | | |
| 14. | | | | | | | | | |
| 15. | | | | | | | | | |

| Group Exercise:  Major Strategic Goals Summarization | | | | | | | | |
|---|---|---|---|---|---|---|---|---|

**Section I:  The Strategic Enterprise**

**Category 4:  Management Strategy**

Includes areas such as:  management development, succession, compensation, ability, effectiveness, empowerment, autonomy.

| Strategic Item | Check One: | | | Individual Prioritization Votes | Vote Totals | Category Priority | Total Plan Priority | Year-One Action Plan |
|---|---|---|---|---|---|---|---|---|
| | Result | Goal | Means | | | Refer to Section: D | | E |
| 1. | ☐ | ☐ | ☐ | ☐ ☐ ☐ ☐ | ☐ | ☐ | ☐ | ☐ |
| 2. | ☐ | ☐ | ☐ | ☐ ☐ ☐ ☐ | ☐ | ☐ | ☐ | ☐ |
| 3. | ☐ | ☐ | ☐ | ☐ ☐ ☐ ☐ | ☐ | ☐ | ☐ | ☐ |
| 4. | ☐ | ☐ | ☐ | ☐ ☐ ☐ ☐ | ☐ | ☐ | ☐ | ☐ |
| 5. | ☐ | ☐ | ☐ | ☐ ☐ ☐ ☐ | ☐ | ☐ | ☐ | ☐ |
| 6. | ☐ | ☐ | ☐ | ☐ ☐ ☐ ☐ | ☐ | ☐ | ☐ | ☐ |
| 7. | ☐ | ☐ | ☐ | ☐ ☐ ☐ ☐ | ☐ | ☐ | ☐ | ☐ |
| 8. | ☐ | ☐ | ☐ | ☐ ☐ ☐ ☐ | ☐ | ☐ | ☐ | ☐ |
| 9. | ☐ | ☐ | ☐ | ☐ ☐ ☐ ☐ | ☐ | ☐ | ☐ | ☐ |
| 10. | ☐ | ☐ | ☐ | ☐ ☐ ☐ ☐ | ☐ | ☐ | ☐ | ☐ |
| 11. | ☐ | ☐ | ☐ | ☐ ☐ ☐ ☐ | ☐ | ☐ | ☐ | ☐ |
| 12. | ☐ | ☐ | ☐ | ☐ ☐ ☐ ☐ | ☐ | ☐ | ☐ | ☐ |
| 13. | ☐ | ☐ | ☐ | ☐ ☐ ☐ ☐ | ☐ | ☐ | ☐ | ☐ |
| 14. | ☐ | ☐ | ☐ | ☐ ☐ ☐ ☐ | ☐ | ☐ | ☐ | ☐ |
| 15. | ☐ | ☐ | ☐ | ☐ ☐ ☐ ☐ | ☐ | ☐ | ☐ | ☐ |

## Group Exercise:  Major Strategic Goals Summarization

**Section II:  The Strategic Resources**

**Category 5:  Human Resource  Strategy**

Includes areas such as:  total HR headcount requirement, efficiency, effectiveness, capacity, motivation, involvement, empowerment, support, loyalty.

| Strategic Item | Check One: | | | Individual Prioritization Votes | Vote Totals | Category Priority | Total Plan Priority | Year-One Action Plan |
|---|---|---|---|---|---|---|---|---|
| | Result | Goal | Means | | | Refer to Section: D | | E |
| 1. | | | | | | | | |
| 2. | | | | | | | | |
| 3. | | | | | | | | |
| 4. | | | | | | | | |
| 5. | | | | | | | | |
| 6. | | | | | | | | |
| 7. | | | | | | | | |
| 8. | | | | | | | | |
| 9. | | | | | | | | |
| 10. | | | | | | | | |
| 11. | | | | | | | | |
| 12. | | | | | | | | |
| 13. | | | | | | | | |
| 14. | | | | | | | | |
| 15. | | | | | | | | |

| Group Exercise: Major Strategic Goals Summarization | | | | | | | | | |
|---|---|---|---|---|---|---|---|---|---|

**Section II: The Strategic Resources**

**Category 6: Communications Strategy**

Includes areas such as: information flow up, down, out, in; communication systems, methods, effectiveness, teamwork, synergy.

| | | | | Refer to Section: D | | | | | E |
|---|---|---|---|---|---|---|---|---|---|---|
| **Strategic Item** | **Check One:** | | | **Individual Prioritization Votes** | | **Vote Totals** | **Category Priority** | **Total Plan Priority** | **Year-One Action Plan** |
| | **Result** | **Goal** | **Means** | | | | | | |
| 1. | ☐ | ☐ | ☐ | ☐☐☐☐ | | ☐ | ☐ | ☐ | ☐ |
| 2. | ☐ | ☐ | ☐ | ☐☐☐☐ | | ☐ | ☐ | ☐ | ☐ |
| 3. | ☐ | ☐ | ☐ | ☐☐☐☐ | | ☐ | ☐ | ☐ | ☐ |
| 4. | ☐ | ☐ | ☐ | ☐☐☐☐ | | ☐ | ☐ | ☐ | ☐ |
| 5. | ☐ | ☐ | ☐ | ☐☐☐☐ | | ☐ | ☐ | ☐ | ☐ |
| 6. | ☐ | ☐ | ☐ | ☐☐☐☐ | | ☐ | ☐ | ☐ | ☐ |
| 7. | ☐ | ☐ | ☐ | ☐☐☐☐ | | ☐ | ☐ | ☐ | ☐ |
| 8. | ☐ | ☐ | ☐ | ☐☐☐☐ | | ☐ | ☐ | ☐ | ☐ |
| 9. | ☐ | ☐ | ☐ | ☐☐☐☐ | | ☐ | ☐ | ☐ | ☐ |
| 10. | ☐ | ☐ | ☐ | ☐☐☐☐ | | ☐ | ☐ | ☐ | ☐ |
| 11. | ☐ | ☐ | ☐ | ☐☐☐☐ | | ☐ | ☐ | ☐ | ☐ |
| 12. | ☐ | ☐ | ☐ | ☐☐☐☐ | | ☐ | ☐ | ☐ | ☐ |
| 13. | ☐ | ☐ | ☐ | ☐☐☐☐ | | ☐ | ☐ | ☐ | ☐ |
| 14. | ☐ | ☐ | ☐ | ☐☐☐☐ | | ☐ | ☐ | ☐ | ☐ |
| 15. | ☐ | ☐ | ☐ | ☐☐☐☐ | | ☐ | ☐ | ☐ | ☐ |

| Group Exercise: Major Strategic Goals Summarization |||||||||
|---|---|---|---|---|---|---|---|---|

**Section II: The Strategic Resources**

**Category 7: Technology Strategy**

Includes areas such as: understanding of, leverage of, investment in, use as
exclusive differentiator.

| Strategic Item | Check One: | | | Individual Prioritization Votes | Vote Totals | Category Priority | Total Plan Priority | Year-One Action Plan |
|---|---|---|---|---|---|---|---|---|
| | **Result** | **Goal** | **Means** | | | | | |
| 1. | ☐ | ☐ | ☐ | ☐ ☐ ☐ ☐ | ☐ | ☐ | ☐ | ☐ |
| 2. | ☐ | ☐ | ☐ | ☐ ☐ ☐ ☐ | ☐ | ☐ | ☐ | ☐ |
| 3. | ☐ | ☐ | ☐ | ☐ ☐ ☐ ☐ | ☐ | ☐ | ☐ | ☐ |
| 4. | ☐ | ☐ | ☐ | ☐ ☐ ☐ ☐ | ☐ | ☐ | ☐ | ☐ |
| 5. | ☐ | ☐ | ☐ | ☐ ☐ ☐ ☐ | ☐ | ☐ | ☐ | ☐ |
| 6. | ☐ | ☐ | ☐ | ☐ ☐ ☐ ☐ | ☐ | ☐ | ☐ | ☐ |
| 7. | ☐ | ☐ | ☐ | ☐ ☐ ☐ ☐ | ☐ | ☐ | ☐ | ☐ |
| 8. | ☐ | ☐ | ☐ | ☐ ☐ ☐ ☐ | ☐ | ☐ | ☐ | ☐ |
| 9. | ☐ | ☐ | ☐ | ☐ ☐ ☐ ☐ | ☐ | ☐ | ☐ | ☐ |
| 10. | ☐ | ☐ | ☐ | ☐ ☐ ☐ ☐ | ☐ | ☐ | ☐ | ☐ |
| 11. | ☐ | ☐ | ☐ | ☐ ☐ ☐ ☐ | ☐ | ☐ | ☐ | ☐ |
| 12. | ☐ | ☐ | ☐ | ☐ ☐ ☐ ☐ | ☐ | ☐ | ☐ | ☐ |
| 13. | ☐ | ☐ | ☐ | ☐ ☐ ☐ ☐ | ☐ | ☐ | ☐ | ☐ |
| 14. | ☐ | ☐ | ☐ | ☐ ☐ ☐ ☐ | ☐ | ☐ | ☐ | ☐ |
| 15. | ☐ | ☐ | ☐ | ☐ ☐ ☐ ☐ | ☐ | ☐ | ☐ | ☐ |

Refer to Section: **D** ... **E**

| Group Exercise: Major Strategic Goals Summarization | | | | | | | | |
|---|---|---|---|---|---|---|---|---|

**Section II: The Strategic Resources**

**Category 8: Cross-Functional Strategy**

Includes areas such as: each organizational and function's specific plans, integration, cross-pollination, coordination, synergy in unison.

| | | | | | Refer to Section: D | | | E |
|---|---|---|---|---|---|---|---|---|
| **Strategic Item** | **Check One:** | | | **Individual Prioritization Votes** | Vote Totals | Category Priority | Total Plan Priority | Year-One Action Plan |
| | Result | Goal | Means | | | | | |
| 1. | ☐ | ☐ | ☐ | ☐ ☐ ☐ ☐ | ☐ | ☐ | ☐ | ☐ |
| 2. | ☐ | ☐ | ☐ | ☐ ☐ ☐ ☐ | ☐ | ☐ | ☐ | ☐ |
| 3. | ☐ | ☐ | ☐ | ☐ ☐ ☐ ☐ | ☐ | ☐ | ☐ | ☐ |
| 4. | ☐ | ☐ | ☐ | ☐ ☐ ☐ ☐ | ☐ | ☐ | ☐ | ☐ |
| 5. | ☐ | ☐ | ☐ | ☐ ☐ ☐ ☐ | ☐ | ☐ | ☐ | ☐ |
| 6. | ☐ | ☐ | ☐ | ☐ ☐ ☐ ☐ | ☐ | ☐ | ☐ | ☐ |
| 7. | ☐ | ☐ | ☐ | ☐ ☐ ☐ ☐ | ☐ | ☐ | ☐ | ☐ |
| 8. | ☐ | ☐ | ☐ | ☐ ☐ ☐ ☐ | ☐ | ☐ | ☐ | ☐ |
| 9. | ☐ | ☐ | ☐ | ☐ ☐ ☐ ☐ | ☐ | ☐ | ☐ | ☐ |
| 10. | ☐ | ☐ | ☐ | ☐ ☐ ☐ ☐ | ☐ | ☐ | ☐ | ☐ |
| 11. | ☐ | ☐ | ☐ | ☐ ☐ ☐ ☐ | ☐ | ☐ | ☐ | ☐ |
| 12. | ☐ | ☐ | ☐ | ☐ ☐ ☐ ☐ | ☐ | ☐ | ☐ | ☐ |
| 13. | ☐ | ☐ | ☐ | ☐ ☐ ☐ ☐ | ☐ | ☐ | ☐ | ☐ |
| 14. | ☐ | ☐ | ☐ | ☐ ☐ ☐ ☐ | ☐ | ☐ | ☐ | ☐ |
| 15. | ☐ | ☐ | ☐ | ☐ ☐ ☐ ☐ | ☐ | ☐ | ☐ | ☐ |

| Group Exercise: Major Strategic Goals Summarization |
|---|

**Section III: The Strategic Knowledge**

**Category 9: Customer Strategy**

Includes areas such as: commitment, focus, knowledge, support, systems, communication, problems, quality.

| | | | | Refer to Section: D | | | | E |
|---|---|---|---|---|---|---|---|---|
| **Strategic Item** | **Check One:** | | | **Individual Prioritization Votes** | Vote Totals | Category Priority | Total Plan Priority | Year-One Action Plan |
| | Result | Goal | Means | | | | | |
| 1. | ☐ | ☐ | ☐ | ☐ ☐ ☐ ☐ | ☐ | ☐ | ☐ | ☐ |
| 2. | ☐ | ☐ | ☐ | ☐ ☐ ☐ ☐ | ☐ | ☐ | ☐ | ☐ |
| 3. | ☐ | ☐ | ☐ | ☐ ☐ ☐ ☐ | ☐ | ☐ | ☐ | ☐ |
| 4. | ☐ | ☐ | ☐ | ☐ ☐ ☐ ☐ | ☐ | ☐ | ☐ | ☐ |
| 5. | ☐ | ☐ | ☐ | ☐ ☐ ☐ ☐ | ☐ | ☐ | ☐ | ☐ |
| 6. | ☐ | ☐ | ☐ | ☐ ☐ ☐ ☐ | ☐ | ☐ | ☐ | ☐ |
| 7. | ☐ | ☐ | ☐ | ☐ ☐ ☐ ☐ | ☐ | ☐ | ☐ | ☐ |
| 8. | ☐ | ☐ | ☐ | ☐ ☐ ☐ ☐ | ☐ | ☐ | ☐ | ☐ |
| 9. | ☐ | ☐ | ☐ | ☐ ☐ ☐ ☐ | ☐ | ☐ | ☐ | ☐ |
| 10. | ☐ | ☐ | ☐ | ☐ ☐ ☐ ☐ | ☐ | ☐ | ☐ | ☐ |
| 11. | ☐ | ☐ | ☐ | ☐ ☐ ☐ ☐ | ☐ | ☐ | ☐ | ☐ |
| 12. | ☐ | ☐ | ☐ | ☐ ☐ ☐ ☐ | ☐ | ☐ | ☐ | ☐ |
| 13. | ☐ | ☐ | ☐ | ☐ ☐ ☐ ☐ | ☐ | ☐ | ☐ | ☐ |
| 14. | ☐ | ☐ | ☐ | ☐ ☐ ☐ ☐ | ☐ | ☐ | ☐ | ☐ |
| 15. | ☐ | ☐ | ☐ | ☐ ☐ ☐ ☐ | ☐ | ☐ | ☐ | ☐ |

| Group Exercise: Major Strategic Goals Summarization | | | | | | | |
|---|---|---|---|---|---|---|---|

**Section III: The Strategic Knowledge**
**Category 10: Competitive Strategy**
Includes areas such as: knowledge, strengths and weaknesses, opportunities and threats, major strategies, pricing, key responses.

Refer to Section: D / E

| Strategic Item | Check One: Result Goal Means | Individual Prioritization Votes | Vote Totals | Category Priority | Total Plan Priority | Year-One Action Plan |
|---|---|---|---|---|---|---|
| 1. | □ □ □ | □□ □□ | □ | □ | □ | □ |
| 2. | □ □ □ | □□ □□ | □ | □ | □ | □ |
| 3. | □ □ □ | □□ □□ | □ | □ | □ | □ |
| 4. | □ □ □ | □□ □□ | □ | □ | □ | □ |
| 5. | □ □ □ | □□ □□ | □ | □ | □ | □ |
| 6. | □ □ □ | □□ □□ | □ | □ | □ | □ |
| 7. | □ □ □ | □□ □□ | □ | □ | □ | □ |
| 8. | □ □ □ | □□ □□ | □ | □ | □ | □ |
| 9. | □ □ □ | □□ □□ | □ | □ | □ | □ |
| 10. | □ □ □ | □□ □□ | □ | □ | □ | □ |
| 11. | □ □ □ | □□ □□ | □ | □ | □ | □ |
| 12. | □ □ □ | □□ □□ | □ | □ | □ | □ |
| 13. | □ □ □ | □□ □□ | □ | □ | □ | □ |
| 14. | □ □ □ | □□ □□ | □ | □ | □ | □ |
| 15. | □ □ □ | □□ □□ | □ | □ | □ | □ |

## Group Exercise: Major Strategic Goals Summarization

**Section III: The Strategic Knowledge**

**Category 11: External Relations Strategy**

Includes areas such as: market, economy, government, social forecasts, public/
market perception, public relations, vendors,
suppliers, industrial relations.

| | | | | | | | | | | | Refer to Section: D | | | | E |
|---|---|---|---|---|---|---|---|---|---|---|---|---|---|---|---|
| **Strategic Item** | **Check One:** | | | **Individual Prioritization Votes** | | | | | **Vote Totals** | **Category Priority** | **Total Plan Priority** | **Year-One Action Plan** |
| | Result | Goal | Means | | | | | | | | | |
| 1. | ☐ | ☐ | ☐ | ☐ | ☐ | ☐ | ☐ | | ☐ | ☐ | ☐ | ☐ |
| 2. | ☐ | ☐ | ☐ | ☐ | ☐ | ☐ | ☐ | | ☐ | ☐ | ☐ | ☐ |
| 3. | ☐ | ☐ | ☐ | ☐ | ☐ | ☐ | ☐ | | ☐ | ☐ | ☐ | ☐ |
| 4. | ☐ | ☐ | ☐ | ☐ | ☐ | ☐ | ☐ | | ☐ | ☐ | ☐ | ☐ |
| 5. | ☐ | ☐ | ☐ | ☐ | ☐ | ☐ | ☐ | | ☐ | ☐ | ☐ | ☐ |
| 6. | ☐ | ☐ | ☐ | ☐ | ☐ | ☐ | ☐ | | ☐ | ☐ | ☐ | ☐ |
| 7. | ☐ | ☐ | ☐ | ☐ | ☐ | ☐ | ☐ | | ☐ | ☐ | ☐ | ☐ |
| 8. | ☐ | ☐ | ☐ | ☐ | ☐ | ☐ | ☐ | | ☐ | ☐ | ☐ | ☐ |
| 9. | ☐ | ☐ | ☐ | ☐ | ☐ | ☐ | ☐ | | ☐ | ☐ | ☐ | ☐ |
| 10. | ☐ | ☐ | ☐ | ☐ | ☐ | ☐ | ☐ | | ☐ | ☐ | ☐ | ☐ |
| 11. | ☐ | ☐ | ☐ | ☐ | ☐ | ☐ | ☐ | | ☐ | ☐ | ☐ | ☐ |
| 12. | ☐ | ☐ | ☐ | ☐ | ☐ | ☐ | ☐ | | ☐ | ☐ | ☐ | ☐ |
| 13. | ☐ | ☐ | ☐ | ☐ | ☐ | ☐ | ☐ | | ☐ | ☐ | ☐ | ☐ |
| 14. | ☐ | ☐ | ☐ | ☐ | ☐ | ☐ | ☐ | | ☐ | ☐ | ☐ | ☐ |
| 15. | ☐ | ☐ | ☐ | ☐ | ☐ | ☐ | ☐ | | ☐ | ☐ | ☐ | ☐ |

| Group Exercise: Major Strategic Goals Summarization | | | | | | | | | |
|---|---|---|---|---|---|---|---|---|---|

**Section III: The Strategic Knowledge**

**Category 12: Financial Strategy**

Includes areas such as: financial resources, cost/expense management, budgets, targets, measurement of actuals, reviews, cash flow, financial statement goals.

**Refer to Section: D**      **E**

| Strategic Item | Check One: Result Goal Means | Individual Prioritization Votes | Vote Totals | Category Priority | Total Plan Priority | Year-One Action Plan |
|---|---|---|---|---|---|---|
| 1. | ☐ ☐ ☐ | ☐ ☐ ☐ ☐ | ☐ | ☐ | ☐ | ☐ |
| 2. | ☐ ☐ ☐ | ☐ ☐ ☐ ☐ | ☐ | ☐ | ☐ | ☐ |
| 3. | ☐ ☐ ☐ | ☐ ☐ ☐ ☐ | ☐ | ☐ | ☐ | ☐ |
| 4. | ☐ ☐ ☐ | ☐ ☐ ☐ ☐ | ☐ | ☐ | ☐ | ☐ |
| 5. | ☐ ☐ ☐ | ☐ ☐ ☐ ☐ | ☐ | ☐ | ☐ | ☐ |
| 6. | ☐ ☐ ☐ | ☐ ☐ ☐ ☐ | ☐ | ☐ | ☐ | ☐ |
| 7. | ☐ ☐ ☐ | ☐ ☐ ☐ ☐ | ☐ | ☐ | ☐ | ☐ |
| 8. | ☐ ☐ ☐ | ☐ ☐ ☐ ☐ | ☐ | ☐ | ☐ | ☐ |
| 9. | ☐ ☐ ☐ | ☐ ☐ ☐ ☐ | ☐ | ☐ | ☐ | ☐ |
| 10. | ☐ ☐ ☐ | ☐ ☐ ☐ ☐ | ☐ | ☐ | ☐ | ☐ |
| 11. | ☐ ☐ ☐ | ☐ ☐ ☐ ☐ | ☐ | ☐ | ☐ | ☐ |
| 12. | ☐ ☐ ☐ | ☐ ☐ ☐ ☐ | ☐ | ☐ | ☐ | ☐ |
| 13. | ☐ ☐ ☐ | ☐ ☐ ☐ ☐ | ☐ | ☐ | ☐ | ☐ |
| 14. | ☐ ☐ ☐ | ☐ ☐ ☐ ☐ | ☐ | ☐ | ☐ | ☐ |
| 15. | ☐ ☐ ☐ | ☐ ☐ ☐ ☐ | ☐ | ☐ | ☐ | ☐ |

## Group Exercise:  Major Strategic Goals Summarization

**Section IV:  The Strategic Response**

**Category 13:  Business Processes Systems Strategy**

Includes areas such as:  critical processes, identification and plans, quality, regulatory, effectiveness of processes, continuous improvement of systems, infrastructure systems.

| Strategic Item | Check One: | | | Individual Prioritization Votes | Vote Totals | Category Priority | Total Plan Priority | Year-One Action Plan |
|---|---|---|---|---|---|---|---|---|
| | **Result** | **Goal** | **Means** | Refer to Section: D | | | | E |
| 1. | ☐ | ☐ | ☐ | ☐ ☐ ☐ ☐ | ☐ | ☐ | ☐ | ☐ |
| 2. | ☐ | ☐ | ☐ | ☐ ☐ ☐ ☐ | ☐ | ☐ | ☐ | ☐ |
| 3. | ☐ | ☐ | ☐ | ☐ ☐ ☐ ☐ | ☐ | ☐ | ☐ | ☐ |
| 4. | ☐ | ☐ | ☐ | ☐ ☐ ☐ ☐ | ☐ | ☐ | ☐ | ☐ |
| 5. | ☐ | ☐ | ☐ | ☐ ☐ ☐ ☐ | ☐ | ☐ | ☐ | ☐ |
| 6. | ☐ | ☐ | ☐ | ☐ ☐ ☐ ☐ | ☐ | ☐ | ☐ | ☐ |
| 7. | ☐ | ☐ | ☐ | ☐ ☐ ☐ ☐ | ☐ | ☐ | ☐ | ☐ |
| 8. | ☐ | ☐ | ☐ | ☐ ☐ ☐ ☐ | ☐ | ☐ | ☐ | ☐ |
| 9. | ☐ | ☐ | ☐ | ☐ ☐ ☐ ☐ | ☐ | ☐ | ☐ | ☐ |
| 10. | ☐ | ☐ | ☐ | ☐ ☐ ☐ ☐ | ☐ | ☐ | ☐ | ☐ |
| 11. | ☐ | ☐ | ☐ | ☐ ☐ ☐ ☐ | ☐ | ☐ | ☐ | ☐ |
| 12. | ☐ | ☐ | ☐ | ☐ ☐ ☐ ☐ | ☐ | ☐ | ☐ | ☐ |
| 13. | ☐ | ☐ | ☐ | ☐ ☐ ☐ ☐ | ☐ | ☐ | ☐ | ☐ |
| 14. | ☐ | ☐ | ☐ | ☐ ☐ ☐ ☐ | ☐ | ☐ | ☐ | ☐ |
| 15. | ☐ | ☐ | ☐ | ☐ ☐ ☐ ☐ | ☐ | ☐ | ☐ | ☐ |

<table>
<tr><td colspan="9" align="center">**Group Exercise: Major Strategic Goals Summarization**</td></tr>
<tr><td colspan="9">

**Section IV: The Strategic Response**

**Category 14: Market (Product & Services) Strategy**

Includes areas such as: products, services, markets, plans, performance, development, mix, differentiation.

</td></tr>
</table>

| | | | | | Refer to Section: D | | | E |
|---|---|---|---|---|---|---|---|---|
| **Strategic Item** | **Check One:** | | | Individual Prioritization Votes | Vote Totals | Category Priority | Total Plan Priority | Year-One Action Plan |
| | Result | Goal | Means | | | | | |
| 1. | ☐ | ☐ | ☐ | | ☐ | ☐ | ☐ | ☐ |
| 2. | ☐ | ☐ | ☐ | | ☐ | ☐ | ☐ | ☐ |
| 3. | ☐ | ☐ | ☐ | | ☐ | ☐ | ☐ | ☐ |
| 4. | ☐ | ☐ | ☐ | | ☐ | ☐ | ☐ | ☐ |
| 5. | ☐ | ☐ | ☐ | | ☐ | ☐ | ☐ | ☐ |
| 6. | ☐ | ☐ | ☐ | | ☐ | ☐ | ☐ | ☐ |
| 7. | ☐ | ☐ | ☐ | | ☐ | ☐ | ☐ | ☐ |
| 8. | ☐ | ☐ | ☐ | | ☐ | ☐ | ☐ | ☐ |
| 9. | ☐ | ☐ | ☐ | | ☐ | ☐ | ☐ | ☐ |
| 10. | ☐ | ☐ | ☐ | | ☐ | ☐ | ☐ | ☐ |
| 11. | ☐ | ☐ | ☐ | | ☐ | ☐ | ☐ | ☐ |
| 12. | ☐ | ☐ | ☐ | | ☐ | ☐ | ☐ | ☐ |
| 13. | ☐ | ☐ | ☐ | | ☐ | ☐ | ☐ | ☐ |
| 14. | ☐ | ☐ | ☐ | | ☐ | ☐ | ☐ | ☐ |
| 15. | ☐ | ☐ | ☐ | | ☐ | ☐ | ☐ | ☐ |

| Group Exercise: Major Strategic Goals Summarization | | | | | | | | |
|---|---|---|---|---|---|---|---|---|

**Section IV: The Strategic Response**

**Category 15: Long-Range Strategy**

Includes areas such as: address uncertainty, risk, conflicts, agendas, needs, critical success factors, investment, resources.

| | | Refer to Section: D | | | | E |
|---|---|---|---|---|---|---|
| **Strategic Item** | **Check One:** | **Individual Prioritization Votes** | Vote Totals | Category Priority | Total Plan Priority | Year-One Action Plan |
| | Result Goal Means | | | | | |
| 1. | ☐ ☐ ☐ | ☐ ☐ ☐ ☐ | ☐ | ☐ | ☐ | ☐ |
| 2. | ☐ ☐ ☐ | ☐ ☐ ☐ ☐ | ☐ | ☐ | ☐ | ☐ |
| 3. | ☐ ☐ ☐ | ☐ ☐ ☐ ☐ | ☐ | ☐ | ☐ | ☐ |
| 4. | ☐ ☐ ☐ | ☐ ☐ ☐ ☐ | ☐ | ☐ | ☐ | ☐ |
| 5. | ☐ ☐ ☐ | ☐ ☐ ☐ ☐ | ☐ | ☐ | ☐ | ☐ |
| 6. | ☐ ☐ ☐ | ☐ ☐ ☐ ☐ | ☐ | ☐ | ☐ | ☐ |
| 7. | ☐ ☐ ☐ | ☐ ☐ ☐ ☐ | ☐ | ☐ | ☐ | ☐ |
| 8. | ☐ ☐ ☐ | ☐ ☐ ☐ ☐ | ☐ | ☐ | ☐ | ☐ |
| 9. | ☐ ☐ ☐ | ☐ ☐ ☐ ☐ | ☐ | ☐ | ☐ | ☐ |
| 10. | ☐ ☐ ☐ | ☐ ☐ ☐ ☐ | ☐ | ☐ | ☐ | ☐ |
| 11. | ☐ ☐ ☐ | ☐ ☐ ☐ ☐ | ☐ | ☐ | ☐ | ☐ |
| 12. | ☐ ☐ ☐ | ☐ ☐ ☐ ☐ | ☐ | ☐ | ☐ | ☐ |
| 13. | ☐ ☐ ☐ | ☐ ☐ ☐ ☐ | ☐ | ☐ | ☐ | ☐ |
| 14. | ☐ ☐ ☐ | ☐ ☐ ☐ ☐ | ☐ | ☐ | ☐ | ☐ |
| 15. | ☐ ☐ ☐ | ☐ ☐ ☐ ☐ | ☐ | ☐ | ☐ | ☐ |

| Group Exercise: Major Strategic Goals Summarization | | | | | | | | | |
|---|---|---|---|---|---|---|---|---|---|

**Section IV: The Strategic Response**

**Category 16: Implementation Strategy**

Includes areas such as: plan, implement, quantify/qualify goals, tracking, action plans, completion, adjustment, flexibility, updates, new iterations.

**Refer to Section: D**    **E**

| Strategic Item | Check One: | | | Individual Prioritization Votes | Vote Totals | Category Priority | Total Plan Priority | Year-One Action Plan |
|---|---|---|---|---|---|---|---|---|
| | Result | Goal | Means | | | | | |
| 1. | ☐ | ☐ | ☐ | ☐☐☐☐ | ☐ | ☐ | ☐ | ☐ |
| 2. | ☐ | ☐ | ☐ | ☐☐☐☐ | ☐ | ☐ | ☐ | ☐ |
| 3. | ☐ | ☐ | ☐ | ☐☐☐☐ | ☐ | ☐ | ☐ | ☐ |
| 4. | ☐ | ☐ | ☐ | ☐☐☐☐ | ☐ | ☐ | ☐ | ☐ |
| 5. | ☐ | ☐ | ☐ | ☐☐☐☐ | ☐ | ☐ | ☐ | ☐ |
| 6. | ☐ | ☐ | ☐ | ☐☐☐☐ | ☐ | ☐ | ☐ | ☐ |
| 7. | ☐ | ☐ | ☐ | ☐☐☐☐ | ☐ | ☐ | ☐ | ☐ |
| 8. | ☐ | ☐ | ☐ | ☐☐☐☐ | ☐ | ☐ | ☐ | ☐ |
| 9. | ☐ | ☐ | ☐ | ☐☐☐☐ | ☐ | ☐ | ☐ | ☐ |
| 10. | ☐ | ☐ | ☐ | ☐☐☐☐ | ☐ | ☐ | ☐ | ☐ |
| 11. | ☐ | ☐ | ☐ | ☐☐☐☐ | ☐ | ☐ | ☐ | ☐ |
| 12. | ☐ | ☐ | ☐ | ☐☐☐☐ | ☐ | ☐ | ☐ | ☐ |
| 13. | ☐ | ☐ | ☐ | ☐☐☐☐ | ☐ | ☐ | ☐ | ☐ |
| 14. | ☐ | ☐ | ☐ | ☐☐☐☐ | ☐ | ☐ | ☐ | ☐ |
| 15. | ☐ | ☐ | ☐ | ☐☐☐☐ | ☐ | ☐ | ☐ | ☐ |

## Group Exercise:  Major Strategic Goals Summarization

Section _____: _____

Category _____: _____

Includes areas such as: _____

| | | | | | Refer to Section:  D | | | E |
|---|---|---|---|---|---|---|---|---|
| **Strategic Item** | **Check One:** | | | **Individual Prioritization Votes** | **Vote Totals** | **Category Priority** | **Total Plan Priority** | **Year-One Action Plan** |
| | **Result** | **Goal** | **Means** | | | | | |
| 1. | ☐ | ☐ | ☐ | ☐ ☐ ☐ ☐ | ☐ | ☐ | ☐ | ☐ |
| 2. | ☐ | ☐ | ☐ | ☐ ☐ ☐ ☐ | ☐ | ☐ | ☐ | ☐ |
| 3. | ☐ | ☐ | ☐ | ☐ ☐ ☐ ☐ | ☐ | ☐ | ☐ | ☐ |
| 4. | ☐ | ☐ | ☐ | ☐ ☐ ☐ ☐ | ☐ | ☐ | ☐ | ☐ |
| 5. | ☐ | ☐ | ☐ | ☐ ☐ ☐ ☐ | ☐ | ☐ | ☐ | ☐ |
| 6. | ☐ | ☐ | ☐ | ☐ ☐ ☐ ☐ | ☐ | ☐ | ☐ | ☐ |
| 7. | ☐ | ☐ | ☐ | ☐ ☐ ☐ ☐ | ☐ | ☐ | ☐ | ☐ |
| 8. | ☐ | ☐ | ☐ | ☐ ☐ ☐ ☐ | ☐ | ☐ | ☐ | ☐ |
| 9. | ☐ | ☐ | ☐ | ☐ ☐ ☐ ☐ | ☐ | ☐ | ☐ | ☐ |
| 10. | ☐ | ☐ | ☐ | ☐ ☐ ☐ ☐ | ☐ | ☐ | ☐ | ☐ |
| 11. | ☐ | ☐ | ☐ | ☐ ☐ ☐ ☐ | ☐ | ☐ | ☐ | ☐ |
| 12. | ☐ | ☐ | ☐ | ☐ ☐ ☐ ☐ | ☐ | ☐ | ☐ | ☐ |
| 13. | ☐ | ☐ | ☐ | ☐ ☐ ☐ ☐ | ☐ | ☐ | ☐ | ☐ |
| 14. | ☐ | ☐ | ☐ | ☐ ☐ ☐ ☐ | ☐ | ☐ | ☐ | ☐ |
| 15. | ☐ | ☐ | ☐ | ☐ ☐ ☐ ☐ | ☐ | ☐ | ☐ | ☐ |

## Group Exercise: Major Strategic Goals Summarization

**Section** _____ : _____

**Category** _____ : _____

Includes areas such as: _____

| Strategic Item | Check One: | | | Individual Prioritization Votes (Refer to Section: D) | Vote Totals | Category Priority | Total Plan Priority | Year-One Action Plan (E) |
|---|---|---|---|---|---|---|---|---|
| | Result | Goal | Means | | | | | |
| 1. | ☐ | ☐ | ☐ | ☐☐ ☐ ☐☐ ☐ | ☐ | ☐ | ☐ | ☐ |
| 2. | ☐ | ☐ | ☐ | ☐☐ ☐ ☐☐ ☐ | ☐ | ☐ | ☐ | ☐ |
| 3. | ☐ | ☐ | ☐ | ☐☐ ☐ ☐☐ ☐ | ☐ | ☐ | ☐ | ☐ |
| 4. | ☐ | ☐ | ☐ | ☐☐ ☐ ☐☐ ☐ | ☐ | ☐ | ☐ | ☐ |
| 5. | ☐ | ☐ | ☐ | ☐☐ ☐ ☐☐ ☐ | ☐ | ☐ | ☐ | ☐ |
| 6. | ☐ | ☐ | ☐ | ☐☐ ☐ ☐☐ ☐ | ☐ | ☐ | ☐ | ☐ |
| 7. | ☐ | ☐ | ☐ | ☐☐ ☐ ☐☐ ☐ | ☐ | ☐ | ☐ | ☐ |
| 8. | ☐ | ☐ | ☐ | ☐☐ ☐ ☐☐ ☐ | ☐ | ☐ | ☐ | ☐ |
| 9. | ☐ | ☐ | ☐ | ☐☐ ☐ ☐☐ ☐ | ☐ | ☐ | ☐ | ☐ |
| 10. | ☐ | ☐ | ☐ | ☐☐ ☐ ☐☐ ☐ | ☐ | ☐ | ☐ | ☐ |
| 11. | ☐ | ☐ | ☐ | ☐☐ ☐ ☐☐ ☐ | ☐ | ☐ | ☐ | ☐ |
| 12. | ☐ | ☐ | ☐ | ☐☐ ☐ ☐☐ ☐ | ☐ | ☐ | ☐ | ☐ |
| 13. | ☐ | ☐ | ☐ | ☐☐ ☐ ☐☐ ☐ | ☐ | ☐ | ☐ | ☐ |
| 14. | ☐ | ☐ | ☐ | ☐☐ ☐ ☐☐ ☐ | ☐ | ☐ | ☐ | ☐ |
| 15. | ☐ | ☐ | ☐ | ☐☐ ☐ ☐☐ ☐ | ☐ | ☐ | ☐ | ☐ |

# Addendum C

## Strategic Income Statement Detail Sheets

| Group Exercise:  Strategic Income Statement Detail | | | | | | | |
|---|---|---|---|---|---|---|---|
| **Individual Product or Service Revenue Calculation** | | | | | | | |

**Organizational Function or Division:** _____

**Product or Service # and Name:  1.** _____

(Note:  The product or service # above correlates to the row numbers on the Strategic Income Statement Summary)

(Check One: ☐ Millions ☐ Thousands)

| Assumption Variables: | Prior Year Actual: 199___ | Current Year Estimate: 199__ | Strategic Period Time Frame | | | | |
|---|---|---|---|---|---|---|---|
| | | | Year 1 199__ | Year 2 199__ | Year 3 199__ | Year 4 199__ | Year 5 199__ |
| 1.  Unit or Transaction Annual Volume: | ☐ | ☐ | ☐ | ☐ | ☐ | ☐ | ☐ |
| 2.  Price Per Unit or Transaction: | ☐ | ☐ | ☐ | ☐ | ☐ | ☐ | ☐ |
| 3.  Total Revenue by Year: | ☐ | ☐ | ☐ | ☐ | ☐ | ☐ | ☐ |
| Optional: | | | | | | | |
| 4.  Total Expenses: | ☐ | ☐ | ☐ | ☐ | ☐ | ☐ | ☐ |
| 5.  Total Profits: | ☐ | ☐ | ☐ | ☐ | ☐ | ☐ | ☐ |

Notes: _____

_____

_____

| Group Exercise: Strategic Income Statement Detail |
|:---:|

| Individual Product or Service Revenue Calculation |
|:---:|

**Organizational Function or Division:** _____

**Product or Service # and Name:  2.** _____

(Note:  The product or service # above correlates to the row
numbers on the Strategic Income Statement Summary)

(Check One:  ☐ Millions   ☐ Thousands)

| Assumption Variables: | Prior Year Actual: 199__ | Current Year Estimate: 199__ | Strategic Period Time Frame | | | | |
|---|---|---|---|---|---|---|---|
| | | | Year 1 199__ | Year 2 199__ | Year 3 199__ | Year 4 199__ | Year 5 199__ |
| 1. Unit or Transaction Annual Volume: | ☐ | ☐ | ☐ | ☐ | ☐ | ☐ | ☐ |
| 2. Price Per Unit or Transaction: | ☐ | ☐ | ☐ | ☐ | ☐ | ☐ | ☐ |
| 3. Total Revenue by Year: | ☐ | ☐ | ☐ | ☐ | ☐ | ☐ | ☐ |
| Optional: | | | | | | | |
| 4. Total Expenses: | ☐ | ☐ | ☐ | ☐ | ☐ | ☐ | ☐ |
| 5. Total Profits: | ☐ | ☐ | ☐ | ☐ | ☐ | ☐ | ☐ |

Notes: _____

_____

_____

| Group Exercise: Strategic Income Statement Detail |
| --- |
| **Individual Product or Service Revenue Calculation** |

**Organizational Function or Division:** _____
**Product or Service # and Name:  3.** _____
(Note:  The product or service # above correlates to the row
numbers on the Strategic Income Statement Summary)
(Check One:  ☐ Millions    ☐ Thousands)

| Assumption Variables: | Prior Year Actual: 199__ | Current Year Estimate: 199__ | Year 1 199__ | Year 2 199__ | Year 3 199__ | Year 4 199__ | Year 5 199__ |
| --- | --- | --- | --- | --- | --- | --- | --- |
| 1. Unit or Transaction Annual Volume: | | | | | | | |
| 2. Price Per Unit or Transaction: | | | | | | | |
| 3. Total Revenue by Year: | | | | | | | |
| Optional: | | | | | | | |
| 4. Total Expenses: | | | | | | | |
| 5. Total Profits: | | | | | | | |

Notes: _____
_____
_____

| Group Exercise: Strategic Income Statement Detail | | | | | | | |
|---|---|---|---|---|---|---|---|
| **Individual Product or Service Revenue Calculation** | | | | | | | |

**Organizational Function or Division:** _____
**Product or Service # and Name:  4.** _____
(Note:  The product or service # above correlates to the row
numbers on the Strategic Income Statement Summary)
**(Check One:**  ☐ **Millions**   ☐ **Thousands)**

| Assumption Variables: | Prior Year Actual: 199__ | Current Year Estimate: 199__ | Strategic Period Time Frame | | | | |
|---|---|---|---|---|---|---|---|
| | | | Year 1 199__ | Year 2 199__ | Year 3 199__ | Year 4 199__ | Year 5 199__ |
| 1.  Unit or Transaction Annual Volume: | ☐ | ☐ | ☐ | ☐ | ☐ | ☐ | ☐ |
| 2.  Price Per Unit or Transaction: | ☐ | ☐ | ☐ | ☐ | ☐ | ☐ | ☐ |
| 3.  Total Revenue by Year: | ☐ | ☐ | ☐ | ☐ | ☐ | ☐ | ☐ |
| Optional: | | | | | | | |
| 4.  Total Expenses: | ☐ | ☐ | ☐ | ☐ | ☐ | ☐ | ☐ |
| 5.  Total Profits: | ☐ | ☐ | ☐ | ☐ | ☐ | ☐ | ☐ |

Notes: _____
_____
_____

## Group Exercise:  Strategic Income Statement Detail

### Individual Product or Service Revenue Calculation

**Organizational Function or Division:** _____
**Product or Service # and Name:  5.** _____
(Note:  The product or service # above correlates to the row
numbers on the Strategic Income Statement Summary)
**(Check One:  ☐ Millions   ☐ Thousands)**

| Assumption Variables: | Prior Year Actual: 199__ | Current Year Estimate: 199__ | Strategic Period Time Frame | | | | |
|---|---|---|---|---|---|---|---|
| | | | Year 1 199__ | Year 2 199__ | Year 3 199__ | Year 4 199__ | Year 5 199__ |
| 1.  Unit or Transaction Annual Volume: | ☐ | ☐ | ☐ | ☐ | ☐ | ☐ | ☐ |
| 2.  Price Per Unit or Transaction: | ☐ | ☐ | ☐ | ☐ | ☐ | ☐ | ☐ |
| 3.  Total Revenue by Year: | ☐ | ☐ | ☐ | ☐ | ☐ | ☐ | ☐ |
| Optional: | | | | | | | |
| 4.  Total Expenses: | ☐ | ☐ | ☐ | ☐ | ☐ | ☐ | ☐ |
| 5.  Total Profits: | ☐ | ☐ | ☐ | ☐ | ☐ | ☐ | ☐ |

Notes: _____
_____
_____

| Group Exercise:  Strategic Income Statement Detail | | | | | | | |
|---|---|---|---|---|---|---|---|
| **Individual Product or Service Revenue Calculation** | | | | | | | |

**Organizational Function or Division:** _____

**Product or Service # and Name: 6.** _____

(Note:  The product or service # above correlates to the row numbers on the Strategic Income Statement Summary)

(Check One:  ☐Millions    ☐Thousands)

| | Prior | Current | Strategic Period Time Frame | | | | |
|---|---|---|---|---|---|---|---|
| **Assumption Variables:** | **Year Actual: 199__** | **Year Estimate: 199__** | **Year 1 199__** | **Year 2 199__** | **Year 3 199__** | **Year 4 199__** | **Year 5 199__** |
| 1.  Unit or Transaction Annual Volume: | ☐ | ☐ | ☐ | ☐ | ☐ | ☐ | ☐ |
| 2.  Price Per Unit or Transaction: | ☐ | ☐ | ☐ | ☐ | ☐ | ☐ | ☐ |
| 3.  Total Revenue by Year: | ☐ | ☐ | ☐ | ☐ | ☐ | ☐ | ☐ |
| Optional: | | | | | | | |
| 4.  Total Expenses: | ☐ | ☐ | ☐ | ☐ | ☐ | ☐ | ☐ |
| 5.  Total Profits: | ☐ | ☐ | ☐ | ☐ | ☐ | ☐ | ☐ |

Notes:  _____

_____

_____

| Group Exercise: Strategic Income Statement Detail |
|---|

**Individual Product or Service Revenue Calculation**

**Organizational Function or Division:** _____

**Product or Service # and Name: 7.** _____

(Note: The product or service # above correlates to the row
numbers on the Strategic Income Statement Summary)

(Check One: ☐ Millions ☐ Thousands)

| Assumption Variables: | Prior Year Actual: 199__ | Current Year Estimate: 199__ | Year 1 199__ | Year 2 199__ | Year 3 199__ | Year 4 199__ | Year 5 199__ |
|---|---|---|---|---|---|---|---|
| | | | **Strategic Period Time Frame** | | | | |
| 1. Unit or Transaction Annual Volume: | | | | | | | |
| 2. Price Per Unit or Transaction: | | | | | | | |
| 3. Total Revenue by Year: | | | | | | | |
| Optional: | | | | | | | |
| 4. Total Expenses: | | | | | | | |
| 5. Total Profits: | | | | | | | |

Notes: _____
_____
_____

| | | | Group Exercise: Strategic Income Statement Detail | | | | |
|---|---|---|---|---|---|---|---|

**Group Exercise:  Strategic Income Statement Detail**

**Individual Product or Service Revenue Calculation**

**Organizational Function or Division:** _____
**Product or Service # and Name:  8.** _____
(Note:  The product or service # above correlates to the row
numbers on the Strategic Income Statement Summary)
**(Check One:** ☐ **Millions** ☐ **Thousands)**

| Assumption Variables: | Prior Year Actual: 199__ | Current Year Estimate: 199__ | Strategic Period Time Frame | | | | |
|---|---|---|---|---|---|---|---|
| | | | Year 1 199__ | Year 2 199__ | Year 3 199__ | Year 4 199__ | Year 5 199__ |
| 1. Unit or Transaction Annual Volume: | ☐ | ☐ | ☐ | ☐ | ☐ | ☐ | ☐ |
| 2. Price Per Unit or Transaction: | ☐ | ☐ | ☐ | ☐ | ☐ | ☐ | ☐ |
| 3. Total Revenue by Year: | ☐ | ☐ | ☐ | ☐ | ☐ | ☐ | ☐ |
| Optional: | | | | | | | |
| 4. Total Expenses: | ☐ | ☐ | ☐ | ☐ | ☐ | ☐ | ☐ |
| 5. Total Profits: | ☐ | ☐ | ☐ | ☐ | ☐ | ☐ | ☐ |

Notes: _____
_____
_____

| Group Exercise: Strategic Income Statement Detail | | | | | | | |
|---|---|---|---|---|---|---|---|
| **Individual Product or Service Revenue Calculation** | | | | | | | |

**Organizational Function or Division:** _____

**Product or Service # and Name: 9.** _____

(Note: The product or service # above correlates to the row numbers on the Strategic Income Statement Summary)

(Check One: ☐ Millions ☐ Thousands)

| Assumption Variables: | Prior Year Actual: 199__ | Current Year Estimate: 199__ | Strategic Period Time Frame | | | | |
|---|---|---|---|---|---|---|---|
| | | | Year 1 199__ | Year 2 199__ | Year 3 199__ | Year 4 199__ | Year 5 199__ |
| 1. Unit or Transaction Annual Volume: | ☐ | ☐ | ☐ | ☐ | ☐ | ☐ | ☐ |
| 2. Price Per Unit or Transaction: | ☐ | ☐ | ☐ | ☐ | ☐ | ☐ | ☐ |
| 3. Total Revenue by Year: | ☐ | ☐ | ☐ | ☐ | ☐ | ☐ | ☐ |
| Optional: | | | | | | | |
| 4. Total Expenses: | ☐ | ☐ | ☐ | ☐ | ☐ | ☐ | ☐ |
| 5. Total Profits: | ☐ | ☐ | ☐ | ☐ | ☐ | ☐ | ☐ |

Notes: _____
_____
_____

| | | | | | | | |
|---|---|---|---|---|---|---|---|
| **Group Exercise:  Strategic Income Statement Detail** | | | | | | | |
| **Individual Product or Service Revenue Calculation** | | | | | | | |

**Organizational Function or Division:** _____
**Product or Service # and Name: 10.** _____
(Note:  The product or service # above correlates to the row
numbers on the Strategic Income Statement Summary)
**(Check One:** ☐ **Millions** ☐ **Thousands)**

| Assumption Variables: | Prior Year Actual: 199__ | Current Year Estimate: 199__ | Strategic Period Time Frame | | | | |
|---|---|---|---|---|---|---|---|
| | | | Year 1 199__ | Year 2 199__ | Year 3 199__ | Year 4 199__ | Year 5 199__ |
| 1. Unit or Transaction Annual Volume: | ☐ | ☐ | ☐ | ☐ | ☐ | ☐ | ☐ |
| 2. Price Per Unit or Transaction: | ☐ | ☐ | ☐ | ☐ | ☐ | ☐ | ☐ |
| 3. Total Revenue by Year: | ☐ | ☐ | ☐ | ☐ | ☐ | ☐ | ☐ |
| Optional: | | | | | | | |
| 4. Total Expenses: | ☐ | ☐ | ☐ | ☐ | ☐ | ☐ | ☐ |
| 5. Total Profits: | ☐ | ☐ | ☐ | ☐ | ☐ | ☐ | ☐ |

Notes: _____
_____
_____

# Addendum D

# Year-One Strategic Action-Plan Forms

## Year-One Strategic Action Plan

Category #: _____    Category Title: _____

Strategic Item #: _____    Item Description: _____

Implementational Action: _____

Person(s) Responsible:

Due-Date: _____/_____/_____    Actual Date: _____/_____/_____

How Measured/Notes: _____

## Year-One Strategic Action Plan

Category #: _____    Category Title: _____

Strategic Item #: _____    Item Description: _____

Implementational Action: _____

Person(s) Responsible:

Due-Date: _____/_____/_____    Actual Date: _____/_____/_____

How Measured/Notes: _____

## Year-One Strategic Action Plan

Category #: _____     Category Title: _____

Strategic Item #: _____     Item Description: _____

Implementational Action: _____

Person(s) Responsible:

Due-Date: _____/_____/_____          Actual Date: _____/_____/_____

How Measured/Notes: _____

## Year-One Strategic Action Plan

Category #: _____     Category Title: _____

Strategic Item #: _____     Item Description: _____

Implementational Action: _____

Person(s) Responsible:

Due-Date: _____/_____/_____          Actual Date: _____/_____/_____

How Measured/Notes: _____

## Year-One Strategic Action Plan

Category #: _____    Category Title: _____

Strategic Item #: _____    Item Description: _____

Implementational Action: _____

Person(s) Responsible:

Due-Date: _____/_____/_____         Actual Date: _____/_____/_____

How Measured/Notes: _____

---

## Year-One Strategic Action Plan

Category #: _____    Category Title: _____

Strategic Item #: _____    Item Description: _____

Implementational Action: _____

Person(s) Responsible:

Due-Date: _____/_____/_____         Actual Date: _____/_____/_____

How Measured/Notes: _____

---

### Year-One Strategic Action Plan

Category #: _____    Category Title: _____

Strategic Item #: _____    Item Description: _____

Implementational Action: _____

Person(s) Responsible:

Due-Date: _____/_____/_____    Actual Date: _____/_____/_____

How Measured/Notes: _____

---

### Year-One Strategic Action Plan

Category #: _____    Category Title: _____

Strategic Item #: _____    Item Description: _____

Implementational Action: _____

Person(s) Responsible:

Due-Date: _____/_____/_____    Actual Date: _____/_____/_____

How Measured/Notes: _____

## Year-One Strategic Action Plan

Category #: _____ Category Title: _____

Strategic Item #: _____ Item Description: _____

Implementational Action: _____

Person(s) Responsible:

Due-Date: _____/_____/_____     Actual Date: _____/_____/_____

How Measured/Notes: _____

## Year-One Strategic Action Plan

Category #: _____ Category Title: _____

Strategic Item #: _____ Item Description: _____

Implementational Action: _____

Person(s) Responsible:

Due-Date: _____/_____/_____     Actual Date: _____/_____/_____

How Measured/Notes: _____

## Year-One Strategic Action Plan

Category #: _____     Category Title: _____

Strategic Item #: _____     Item Description: _____

Implementational Action: _____

Person(s) Responsible:

Due-Date: _____/_____/_____     Actual Date: _____/_____/_____

How Measured/Notes: _____

## Year-One Strategic Action Plan

Category #: _____     Category Title: _____

Strategic Item #: _____     Item Description: _____

Implementational Action: _____

Person(s) Responsible:

Due-Date: _____/_____/_____     Actual Date: _____/_____/_____

How Measured/Notes: _____

# Addendum E

# Chronological Strategic Action-Plan Summary Forms

| Chronological Strategic Action-Plan Summary | | | | | |
|---|---|---|---|---|---|
| Page 1 of 5<br>Date of Origination: ____/____/____    Last Update: ____/____/____ | | | | | |
| **Strategic Action-Plan Item** | **Strategic Category Number\*** | **Strategic Plan Item Number** | **Due-Date** | **Actual Date** | **Person(s) Responsible** |
| 1. | | | __/__/__ | __/__/__ | |
| 2. | | | __/__/__ | __/__/__ | |
| 3. | | | __/__/__ | __/__/__ | |
| 4. | | | __/__/__ | __/__/__ | |
| 5. | | | __/__/__ | __/__/__ | |
| 6. | | | __/__/__ | __/__/__ | |
| 7. | | | __/__/__ | __/__/__ | |
| 8. | | | __/__/__ | __/__/__ | |
| 9. | | | __/__/__ | __/__/__ | |
| 10. | | | __/__/__ | __/__/__ | |

\* If in original plan and not added later.
Note: Make additional pages and numbers as needed for items beyond page 5, #50.

| Chronological Strategic Action-Plan Summary | | | | | |
|---|---|---|---|---|---|
| **Page 2 of 5**<br>Date of Origination: \_\_\_\_/\_\_\_\_/\_\_\_\_    Last Update:  \_\_\_\_/\_\_\_\_/\_\_\_\_ | | | | | |
| **Strategic<br>Action-Plan Item** | **Strategic<br>Category<br>Number\*** | **Strategic<br>Plan Item<br>Number** | **Due-<br>Date** | **Actual<br>Date** | **Person(s)<br>Responsible** |
| 11. | | | \_\_/\_\_/\_\_ | \_\_/\_\_/\_\_ | |
| 12. | | | \_\_/\_\_/\_\_ | \_\_/\_\_/\_\_ | |
| 13. | | | \_\_/\_\_/\_\_ | \_\_/\_\_/\_\_ | |
| 14. | | | \_\_/\_\_/\_\_ | \_\_/\_\_/\_\_ | |
| 15. | | | \_\_/\_\_/\_\_ | \_\_/\_\_/\_\_ | |
| 16. | | | \_\_/\_\_/\_\_ | \_\_/\_\_/\_\_ | |
| 17. | | | \_\_/\_\_/\_\_ | \_\_/\_\_/\_\_ | |
| 18. | | | \_\_/\_\_/\_\_ | \_\_/\_\_/\_\_ | |
| 19. | | | \_\_/\_\_/\_\_ | \_\_/\_\_/\_\_ | |
| 20. | | | \_\_/\_\_/\_\_ | \_\_/\_\_/\_\_ | |

\* If in original plan and not added later.
 Note: Make additional pages and numbers as needed for items beyond page 5, #50.

| Chronological Strategic Action-Plan Summary | | | | | |
|---|---|---|---|---|---|
| Page 3 of 5<br>Date of Origination: ____/____/____ Last Update: ____/____/____ | | | | | |
| Strategic<br>Action-Plan Item | Strategic<br>Category<br>Number | Strategic<br>Plan Item<br>Number* | Due-<br>Date | Actual<br>Date | Person(s)<br>Responsible |
| 21. | | | __/__/__ | __/__/__ | |
| 22. | | | __/__/__ | __/__/__ | |
| 23. | | | __/__/__ | __/__/__ | |
| 24. | | | __/__/__ | __/__/__ | |
| 25. | | | __/__/__ | __/__/__ | |
| 26. | | | __/__/__ | __/__/__ | |
| 27. | | | __/__/__ | __/__/__ | |
| 28. | | | __/__/__ | __/__/__ | |
| 29. | | | __/__/__ | __/__/__ | |
| 30. | | | __/__/__ | __/__/__ | |
| * If in original plan and not added later.<br> Note: Make additional pages and numbers as needed for items beyond page 5, #50. | | | | | |

| Chronological Strategic Action-Plan Summary | | | | | |
|---|---|---|---|---|---|
| Page 4 of 5<br>Date of Origination: ___/___/___    Last Update: ___/___/___ | | | | | |
| Strategic<br>Action-Plan Item | Strategic<br>Category<br>Number | Strategic<br>Plan Item<br>Number* | Due-<br>Date | Actual<br>Date | Person(s)<br>Responsible |
| 31. | | | __/__/__ | __/__/__ | |
| 32. | | | __/__/__ | __/__/__ | |
| 33. | | | __/__/__ | __/__/__ | |
| 34. | | | __/__/__ | __/__/__ | |
| 35. | | | __/__/__ | __/__/__ | |
| 36. | | | __/__/__ | __/__/__ | |
| 37. | | | __/__/__ | __/__/__ | |
| 38. | | | __/__/__ | __/__/__ | |
| 39. | | | __/__/__ | __/__/__ | |
| 40. | | | __/__/__ | __/__/__ | |

* If in original plan and not added later.
  Note: Make additional pages and numbers as needed for items beyond page 5, #50.

| Chronological Strategic Action-Plan Summary | | | | | |
|---|---|---|---|---|---|
| **Page 5 of 5**<br>Date of Origination: ____/____/____ Last Update: ____/____/____ | | | | | |
| **Strategic<br>Action-Plan Item** | **Strategic<br>Category<br>Number** | **Strategic<br>Plan Item<br>Number*** | **Due-<br>Date** | **Actual<br>Date** | **Person(s)<br>Responsible** |
| 41. | | | __/__/__ | __/__/__ | |
| 42. | | | __/__/__ | __/__/__ | |
| 43. | | | __/__/__ | __/__/__ | |
| 44. | | | __/__/__ | __/__/__ | |
| 45. | | | __/__/__ | __/__/__ | |
| 46. | | | __/__/__ | __/__/__ | |
| 47. | | | __/__/__ | __/__/__ | |
| 48. | | | __/__/__ | __/__/__ | |
| 49. | | | __/__/__ | __/__/__ | |
| 50. | | | __/__/__ | __/__/__ | |

\* If in original plan and not added later.
  <u>Note</u>: Make additional pages and numbers as needed for items beyond page 5, #50.

# About the Author

William C. Bean is a pioneer of a fledgling industry: corporate performance optimization. The sphere of this discipline extends beyond product and process management approaches to set holistic, flexible, leveraged strategic and business plans, grooved from their conception for solid, direct, and immediate implementation, ratcheting results to higher levels than can be achieved otherwise.

Bill's rich blend of business experience began at Harvard University in financial administration, then at IBM, where he had twelve assignments in eleven levels of the corporation over ten years. Bill was in charge of IBM's corporate education strategic and business plans and controls, when IBM invested approximately 2 billion dollars per year for the maximization of its people and organization.

Bill began his United States consulting and training practice in 1988. His several dozen clients range from *Fortune* 500 to *Inc.* 500 to smaller high-growth companies spanning over twenty industries. Bill became the CEO and President of Productivity and Profit Improvement Associates, affiliated with Brian Tracy Learning Systems, to guide its growth in offices, curriculum, and tools to help companies and professionals grow.

In 1992, he began the William C. Bean Group, affiliated with VIA, an international consulting company, to spearhead the new consulting industry practice area of corporate and individual performance optimization, resuscitating strategic and business planning into effective, meaningful efforts, and flowing them into total quality management (TQM) and continuous improvement modes as a permanent part of healthy corporate development.

Dr. Ellen Domb, who wrote Chapter 19 of this book concerning the linkage of strategic planning with total quality management, is the president of the Upland, California based PQR Group. She teaches and consults on TQM in many industries world-wide, and can be reached for further questions regarding her work at the PQR Group at (909) 949-0857.

Besides *Strategic Planning That Makes Things Happen,* Bill is the author of *Strategic Planning Technology,* an intensely practical workbook and video program that guides leaders step-by-step through holistic planning and implementation in order to optimize business results.

Bill resides in the San Diego area with his wife, Vicki, and three children, Rebecca, Suzanna, and Billy. Bill is an extremely impactful keynote speaker, edits non-fiction works, has written over 200 poems, gives conferences to young people across the United States, and is active in church work. He is co-authoring a breakthrough book on personal goal setting that will be published by early 1994.

For more information about Bill's written and video programs, contact Human Resource Development Press at (800) 822-2801.

Bill can be contacted regarding his corporate performance optimization at the William C. Bean Group, 1315 Crest Drive, Encinitas, California, 92024, (619) 943-0300.